Popular
Quotations
A – Z

Editor Brian O'Kill

Longman

Preface

WHEN THE ALARM CLOCK murdered my sleep this morning, I reached out an idle hand to turn on the radio. It was giving out a dreary report on a debate in the House of Commons, but one phrase spoken by an MP jerked me awake: 'We have seen the future — and it is frightening'. It sounded familiar, although I could not quite place it (see **S40.1**).

I hauled myself out of bed and went downstairs for the newspapers. A once-prominent politician had died the previous day, and the personal frailties which had been so sardonically reported during his lifetime were now submerged in Shakespearean tributes to his good qualities. 'Now cracks a noble heart' (see **S15.74**), wrote one obituarist; 'He was a man, take him for all in all' (**S15.36**), said another. As I leafed through other pages, the headlines seemed to be full of familiar phrases: 'Keep Your Powder Dry' (**C52.6**), 'Insurers find winter a time of discontent' (**S15.237**), 'Always Verify' (**R20.1**).

Later, I strolled round my garden and caught sight of a neighbour complacently admiring a small plaque which he had just fixed to a wall of his shed. 'A garden is a lovesome thing', it proclaimed (**B45.1**). I chatted to him for a few minutes, until the rain began to fall. 'The English winter . . .' he commented; perhaps he was going on to quote Byron (**B62.25**), but I left him to it and hastened down the road for a cheering and inebriating cup.

In the Axe and Compasses, two men at the bar were complaining about the problems of buying timber in metres rather than feet. 'Do you know what Napoleon said about the metric system?' I asked, hoping to console them. They didn't; nor, unfortunately, did I — at least, although I could remember the gist of what he said, the exact wording had gone from my mind (**N2.1**). Feeling rather foolish, I retreated to a table and set down my drink on a beermat advertising a well-known brand of Scotch: *The stuff that drams are made of* (**S15.275**). Sitting in taverns while the tempest hurled, I thought (**H39.12**) — but these gloomy meditations were interrupted by a shout of greeting from a cricketing colleague. A wicketkeeper, he is distinguished by the nickname of 'the Ancient Mariner' — not because he is elderly or has ever been to sea, but because, although not quite in the sense Coleridge intended, 'he stoppeth one of three' (**C32.10**). As for the runs he scores, they are like the lands where the Jumblies live (**L12.4**). . .

This story could go on for ever, but its point is surely made: our daily speech and writing are shot through with quotations, with other people's words which we repeat, adapt, or refer to. Some of these have become so familiar that we may no longer realize that they are quotations from specific sources; like proverbs and idioms, they have become assimilated into our everyday vocabulary. Such is the case with 'a thorn in the flesh' (**B23.24**), 'fools rush in' (**P20.15**), and 'all hell broke loose' (**M34.28**). Their source forgotten, in several instances they have passed into common use in a misquoted or adapted form — 'fresh fields and pastures new' (**M34.14**), 'An Englishman's home is his castle' (**C31.1**) — or even with their original sense perverted — 'all but leather or prunella' (**P20.21**), 'the monstrous regiment of women' (**K14.1**). Others, while being used and recognized as quotations, are — mainly for humorous effect — deliberately altered, punned upon, or used in a context quite different from that of their original use. There was, for instance, the fish sauce which was said to 'cover the multitude of fins' (**B23.260**), the Marxist's exhortation to 'read Marx, learn and inwardly digest' (**P26.7**), and the railway traveller who complained of 'change and delay in all around' (**L40.2**). A further touchstone for the familiar quotation is its use in conversation as a kind of 'phatic' language, intended primarily to create a sociable atmosphere by establishing a common ground of cultural reference. I know of two people who talk to each other, without any pretentiousness, almost entirely in Shakespearean tags. To them, the weather is never merely rain, frost, ice, or sun; it is 'the furious winter's rages' (**S15.28**), 'a frost, a killing frost' (**S15.97**), 'when blood is nipp'd' (**S15.145**), and 'the beauteous eye of heaven' (**S15.120**).

In compiling this book, for the most part I have selected passages which are widely known and used, which are genuinely *quotations* rather than merely *quotables*. It is not chiefly intended to be an anthology of epigrams and aphorisms, of great thoughts about life, of wonderful witticisms, or of the highlights of the world's literature. Many of the quotations included here have, indeed, become popular because of their intrinsic merit; they seem to give definitive expression to a common thought or feeling: 'What oft was thought, but ne'er so well exprest' (**P20.11**). The popularity of some others probably owes less to the wit or wisdom of their wording than to the memorable circumstances in which they were uttered — for example, 'Let not poor Nelly starve' (**C18.2**) or 'I have not yet begun to fight' (**J12.1**). As for the rest, one can say only that something distinctive about them has caught the imagination, and stuck in the memory, of many people; it may be a touch of grandeur, of cleverness, or even of absurdity.

Because of limitations of space, it has been necessary to exclude all common quotations of unknown or collective authorship, such as most proverbs, advertisements, graffiti, nursery rhymes, folk songs, and catchphrases. The only exceptions are the Bible and the Book of Common Prayer, many of whose phrases are so ingrained in our thought and language that it is impossible to omit them. On the other hand, I have seasoned this selection of well-known quotations with a sprinkling of unfamiliar passages which perhaps deserve to be known and used more widely; see, for instance, the topical comments of Sir Thomas Elyot (**E11.1**) and Philip Stubbes (**S47.1**) on the violence associated with football, or the backhanded justification of marriage (**M28.1**) proposed by Quintus Caecilius Metellus Macedonicus (and that's a name to drop!). I hope that this book, assembling 2500 quotations from almost 600 writers of many eras and nationalities, will offer the reader a variety of rewards. Apart from the pleasure of browsing through it, it will serve to identify quotations whose author and source one does not know, to give the full and correct text of those that are half-remembered, and to suggest relevant quotations, with which speech and writing may be enlivened, on hundreds of subjects.

Brian O'Kill
Editor

How to use the dictionary

The Text

Quotations are arranged here under their authors' names, in alphabetical order. For ease of reference, each author has been assigned an alphanumeric symbol (eg **B35**), and his/her dates, nationality, and main occupation have been shown for further information.

The quotations for each author are all separately numbered and appear in alphabetical order of the titles of their sources, which are shown in square brackets after every quotation. Quotations from the Bible follow the canonical order of the books. Spoken quotations usually follow written ones, except in the case of a few people (eg Sir Winston Churchill) who are famed more for their speeches than for their writings. When there is more than one quotation from a single source, they simply follow the order in which they appear in that source. For printed works, sufficiently specific references have been given to enable the passage to be found readily: act and scene have usually been shown for plays, chapter for prose works, part or canto for long poems, and chapter and verse for biblical quotations. The abbreviation '*do.*' (=ditto) has been used to show that the source is the same as the last one specified, while 'attr.' indicates a quotation commonly attributed to an author but not definitely proved to have been spoken or written by him/her.

Quotations originating in languages other than English have been given in their original form when that is well known or seems to lose its effect in translation, but an English version is always provided. In the case of speeches from plays, novels, and poems, the speaker's name is shown only when it is of particular significance or when more than one speaker is involved in the quotation. Explanatory material (eg clarifying the subject of a quotation) always appears in square brackets; it may precede or follow the quotation, or occur within it. To save space, quotations in verse have been run on, with the line breaks indicated by oblique strokes.

The Index

The index serves two important purposes: it enables you to trace a quotation whose authorship you do not know or cannot remember, and it provides a guide to the subjects of the quotations. The key words — usually the nouns — in each quotation form the headings of the index, where they are shown in their immediate context. Thus Abraham Lincoln's 'The ballot is stronger than the bullet' appears in the index under both **Ballot** and **Bullet.** A swung dash (~) is used to represent the key word in its context, so that the entry at **Bullet** shows

ballot is stronger than the ~ **L25.2.**

Each index entry gives a precise reference to the appropriate quotation: the first part (before the full stop) refers to the letter and number given to each author, the second part to the numbered quotations shown under an author's name. Plurals of nouns and inflections of verbs are listed separately from their base form, but possessive forms (eg poet's) are listed at the base form.

A1 **Acheson, Dean** (1893–1971) US lawyer
1 Great Britain has lost an empire and has not yet
found a role. [speech at West Point military academy,
1962]

A2 **Acton, Lord** (1834–1902) English historian
1 Power tends to corrupt, and absolute power
corrupts absolutely. Great men are almost always bad
men. [letter to Bishop Mandell Creighton, 5 April
1887]

A3 **Adams, Sarah F.** (1805–48)
English poet and hymn-writer
1 Nearer, my God, to thee, / Nearer to thee! [*Nearer
My God to Thee*]

A4 **Addison, Joseph** (1672–1719)
English essayist and poet
1 The woman that deliberates is lost. [*Cato*, IV. 1]
2 What pity is it / That we can die but once to serve
our country! [*do.*, IV. 4]
3 Music, the greatest good that mortals know, / And
all of heaven we have below. [*A song for St.
Cecilia's Day*]
4 If we may believe our logicians, man is
distinguished from all other creatures by the faculty
of laughter. [*The Spectator*, 494]
5 'We are always doing', says he, 'something for
posterity, but I would fain see posterity do something
for us.' [*do.*, 583]
6 See in what peace a Christian can die. [last words]

A5 **Ady, Thomas** (fl. 1655) English poet
1 Matthew, Mark, Luke and John, / The bed be
blest that I lie on. [*A Candle in the Dark*]

A6 **Aesop** (*ab* 620– *ab* 560 BC) Greek fabulist
1 Beware that you do not lose the substance by
grasping at the shadow.[*Fables*, 'The Dog and the
Shadow']
2 The gods help them that help themselves. [*do.*,
'Hercules and the Waggoner']
3 Don't count your chickens before they are hatched.
[*do.*, 'The Milkmaid and her Pail']

A7   **Albee, Edward** (1928–) US dramatist
1 Who's afraid of Virginia Woolf? [title of play]

A8   **Alcuin** (735–804) English theologian and scholar
1 *Nec audiendi qui solent dicere, Vox populi, vox Dei,*
quum tumultuositas vulgi semper insaniae proxima sit.
Nor should we listen to those who say 'The voice of
the people is the voice of God', since the turbulence
of the mob is always close to madness. [letter to
Charlemagne, 800]

A9   **Aldrich, Henry** (1647–1710)
English divine and scholar
1 If all be true that I do think, / There are five
reasons we should drink; / Good wine – a friend – or
being dry – / Or lest we should be by and
by – / Or any other reason why. [*Reasons for
Drinking*]

A10   **Alexander, Cecil Frances** (1818–95)
English poet and hymn-writer
1 All things bright and beautiful, / All creatures
great and small, / All things wise and wonderful, /
The Lord God made them all. [*All Things Bright and
Beautiful*]
2 The rich man in his castle, / The poor man at his
gate, / God made them, high or lowly, / And
order'd their estate. [*do.*]

A11   **Ali, Muhammad** (*né* **Cassius Clay**) (1942–)
US boxer
1 I am the greatest. [repeated remark]
2 Float like a butterfly, sting like a bee. [*do.*]

A12   **Allainval, Abbé Lénor d'** (1700–53)
French dramatist
1 *L'embarras des richesses.* A confusing abundance.
[title of play]

A13   **Allen, Woody** (1937–) US comedian and film-maker
1 Life is divided into the horrible and the miserable.
[*Annie Hall* (film)]
2 My brain: it's my second favourite organ.
[*Sleeper* (film)]
3 It's not that I'm afraid to die. I just don't want to
be there when it happens. [*Without Feathers*]

A14   **Ambrose, Saint** (340?–397) Bishop of Milan
1 When you are in Rome, live as the Romans do;

when you are elsewhere, live as they live elsewhere.
[cited by Jeremy Taylor, *Ductor Dubitantium*]

A15   **Andrewes, Lancelot** (1555–1626)
English prelate and scholar
1 A cold coming they had of it, at this time of the
year; just the worst time of the year, to take a
journey, and specially a long journey, in. The ways
deep, the weather sharp, the days short . . . the very
dead of Winter. [*Sermon 15, Of the Nativity*]

A16   **Appleton, Thomas** (1812–84)
1 Good Americans, when they die, go to Paris.
[remark]

A17   **Archilochus** (7th c BC) Greek poet
1 The fox knows many things, but the hedgehog
knows one great thing. [*Fragment* 103]

A18   **Archimedes** (287?–212 BC) Greek scientist
1 *Eureka!* I have found it! [remark on discovering a
method for determining the purity of gold]
2 Give me a firm place to stand, and I will move the
earth. [remark on the lever]

A19   **Ariosto, Lodovico** (1474–1533) Italian poet
1 *Natura il fece, e poi roppe la stampa.* Nature made
him, and then broke the mould. [*Orlando Furioso*, X]

A20   **Aristotle** (384–322 BC) Greek philosopher
1 Man is by nature a political animal. [*Politics*, I]
2 Plato is dear to me, but dearer still is truth. [attr.]

A21   **Armstrong, Neil** (1930–) US astronaut
1 That's one small step for a man, one giant leap for
mankind. [remark on setting foot on the moon, 21
July 1969]

A22   **Arnold, Matthew** (1822–88) English poet and critic
1 Our society distributes itself into Barbarians,
Philistines, and Populace. [*Culture and Anarchy*]
2 The pursuit of perfection, then, is the pursuit of
sweetness and light. [*do.*]
3 Ah, love, let us be true / To one another! for the
world, which seems / To lie before us like a land of
dreams, / So various, so beautiful, so new, / Hath
really neither joy, nor love, nor light, / Nor
certitude, nor peace, nor help for pain; / And we are
here as on a darkling plain / Swept with confused

alarms of struggle and flight, / Where ignorant armies clash by night. [*Dover Beach*]

4 [On Oxford] Home of lost causes, and forsaken beliefs, and unpopular names, and impossible loyalties! [*Essays in Criticism (First Series)*, 'Preface']

5 [On P. B. Shelley] A beautiful and ineffectual angel, beating in the void his luminous wings in vain. [*do. (Second Series)*, 'Shelley']

6 Culture, the acquainting ourselves with the best that has been known and said in the world, and thus with the history of the human spirit. [*Literature and Dogma*, 'Preface']

7 Go, for they call you, Shepherd, from the hill. [*The Scholar-Gipsy*]

8 All the live murmur of a summer's day. [*do.*]

9 Before this strange disease of modern life, / With its sick hurry, its divided aims, / Its heads o'ertaxed, its palsied hearts, was rife. [*do.*]

10 Others abide our question. Thou art free. / We ask and ask: thou smilest and art still, / Out-topping knowledge. [*Shakespeare*]

11 And that sweet city with her dreaming spires, / She needs not June for beauty's heightening. [*Thyrsis*]

12 [On Sophocles] Who saw life steadily, and saw it whole: / The mellow glory of the Attic stage. [*To a Friend*]

13 The unplumb'd, salt, estranging sea. [*To Marguerite: Isolation*]

A23 **Asaf, George** (1880–1951)
1 What's the use of worrying? / It never was worthwhile, / So pack up your troubles in your old kit-bag, / And smile, smile, smile. [*Pack Up Your Troubles in Your Old Kit-Bag*]

A24 **Ascham, Roger** (1515–68) English scholar
1 Learning teacheth more in one year than experience in twenty; and learning teacheth safety, when experience maketh more miserable than wise. [*The Schoolmaster*]

A25 **Asquith, Herbert Henry** (1852–1928) English statesman
1 Wait and see. [phrase used in several speeches in 1910]

A26 **Auden, W. H.** (1907–73) English poet

1 The desires of the heart are as crooked as corkscrews, / Not to be born is the best for man; / The second-best is a formal order, / The dance's pattern; dance while you can. [*The Dead Echo*]

2 The true men of action in our time, those who transform the world, are not the politicians and statesmen, but the scientists. [*The Dyer's Hand*]

3 To us he is no more a person / Now but a whole climate of opinion. [*In Memory of Sigmund Freud*]

4 In the nightmare of the dark / All the dogs of Europe bark, / And the living nations wait, / Each sequestered in its hate. [*In Memory of W. B. Yeats*]

5 Intellectual disgrace / Stares from every human face, / And the seas of pity lie / Locked and frozen in each eye. [*do.*]

6 Lay your sleeping head, my love, / Human on my faithless arm. [*Lullaby*]

7 About suffering they were never wrong, / The Old Masters. [*Musée des Beaux Arts*]

8 This is the Night Mail crossing the Border / Bringing the cheque and the postal order. / Letters for the rich, letters for the poor, / The shop at the corner, the girl next door. [*Night Mail*]

9 Look, stranger, on this island now / The leaping light for your delight discovers. [*Seascape*]

10 Send to us power and light, a sovereign touch / Curing the intolerable neural itch, / The exhaustion of weaning, the liar's quinsy, / And the distortions of ingrown virginity. [*Sir, No Man's Enemy*]

11 History to the defeated / May say alas but cannot help or pardon. [*Spain*]

A27 **Augustine, Saint** (354–430) Bishop of Hippo
1 Give me chastity and continency, but not yet. [*Confessions*, bk 8, ch. 7]

A28 **Augustus** (63 BC–AD 14) Roman emperor
1 He so improved the city [i.e. Rome] that he justly boasted that he found it brick and left it marble. [Suetonius, *The Lives of the Caesars*]

A29 **Austen, Jane** (1775–1817) English novelist
1 One half of the world cannot understand the pleasures of the other. [*Emma*, ch. 9]
2 Let other pens dwell on guilt and misery.

[*Mansfield Park*, ch.48]

3 A woman especially, if she have the misfortune of knowing any thing, should conceal it as well as she can. [*Northanger Abbey*, ch. 14]

4 It is a truth universally acknowledged, that a single man in possession of a good fortune, must be in want of a wife. [*Pride and Prejudice*, ch. 1]

5 Happiness in marriage is entirely a matter of chance. [*do.*, ch. 6]

A30 **Austin, Alfred** (1835–1913) English poet

1 Across the wires the electric message came: / 'He is no better, he is much the same'. [*On the Illness of the Prince of Wales*; attr. to Austin, but probably not by him]

B1 **Bacon, Francis** (1561–1626)

English philosopher and statesman

1 If a man will begin with certainties, he shall end in doubts; but if he will be content to begin with doubts, he shall end in certainties. [*The Advancement of Learning*, I]

2 What is truth? said jesting Pilate; and would not stay for an answer. [*Essays*, 1, 'Of Truth']

3 Men fear death as children fear to go in the dark; and as that natural fear in children is increased with tales, so is the other. [*do.*, 2, 'Of Death']

4 It is as natural to die as to be born; and to a little infant, perhaps, the one is as painful as the other. [*do.*]

5 Wives are young men's mistresses; companions for middle age; and old men's nurses. [*do.*, 8, 'Of Marriage and Single Life']

6 He was reputed one of the wise men, that made answer to the question, when a man should marry? 'A young man not yet, an elder man not at all'. [*do.*]

7 If the hill will not come to Mahomet, Mahomet will go to the hill. [*do.*, 12, 'Of Boldness']

8 If a man be gracious and courteous to strangers, it shews he is a citizen of the world. [*do.*, 13, 'Of Goodness, and Goodness of Nature']

9 It is a miserable state of mind to have few things to desire, and many things to fear. [*do.*, 19, 'Of Empire']

10 Be so true to thyself, as thou be not false to others. [*do.*, 23, 'Of Wisdom for a Man's Self']

11 Whosoever is delighted in solitude is either a wild beast, or a god. [*do.*, 27, 'Of Friendship']

12 There is no excellent beauty that hath not some strangeness in the proportion. [*do.*, 43, 'Of Beauty']

13 Houses are built to live in, and not to look on. [*do.*, 45, 'Of Building']

14 God Almighty first planted a garden; and, indeed, it is the purest of human pleasures; it is the greatest refreshment to the spirits of man. [*do.*, 46, 'Of Gardens']

15 Some books are to be tasted, others to be swallowed, and some few to be chewed and digested. [*do.*, 50, 'Of Studies']

16 Reading maketh a full man; conference a ready man; and writing an exact man. [*do.*]

17 I have taken all knowledge to be my province. [letter to Lord Burleigh, 1592]

B2 **Bagehot, Walter** (1826–77) English economist

1 Royalty is a government in which the attention of the nation is concentrated on one person doing interesting actions. A Republic is a government in which that attention is divided between many, who are all doing uninteresting actions. Accordingly, so long as the human heart is strong and the human reason weak, Royalty will be strong because it appeals to diffused feeling, and Republics weak because they appeal to the understanding. [*The English Constitution*]

2 Poverty is an anomaly to rich people. It is very difficult to make out why people who want dinner do not ring the bell. [*Literary Studies*]

B3 **Bairnsfather, Bruce** (1888–1959) English cartoonist

1 Well, if you knows of a better 'ole, go to it. [*Fragments from France*, 1]

B4 **Ball, John** (d. 1381)
English priest and social agitator

1 When Adam delved and Eve span, / Who was then the gentleman? [text for sermon]

B5 **Barnum, Phineas** (1810–91) US showman

1 There's a sucker born every minute. [attr.]

B6   **Barrie, J. M.** (1860–1937)
Scottish novelist and dramatist
1 When the first baby laughed for the first time, the
laugh broke into a thousand pieces and they all went
skipping about, and that was the beginning of fairies.
[*Peter Pan*, I]
2 Every time a child says 'I don't believe in fairies'
there is a little fairy somewhere that falls down dead.
[*do.*]
3 There are few more impressive sights in the world
than a Scotsman on the make. [*What Every Woman
Knows*, II]

B7   **Baruch, Bernard** (1870–1965)
US businessman and statesman
1 Let us not be deceived – we are today in the midst
of a cold war. [speech, 16 Apr. 1947]

B8   **Baudelaire, Charles** (1821–67) French poet
1 *Là, tout n'est qu'ordre et beauté, / Luxe, calme et
volupté.* There, everything is simply order and beauty,
luxury, peace, and pleasure. [*L'Invitation au Voyage*]

B9   **Beatty, Earl** (1871–1936) British admiral
1 There's something wrong with our bloody ships
today, Chatfield. [remark during the Battle of Jutland,
1916]

B10   **Beaumarchais, Pierre-Augustin Caron de**
(1732–99) French dramatist
1 *Je me presse de rire de tout, de peur d'être obligé d'en
pleurer.* I force myself to laugh at everything, for fear
of being compelled to weep at it. [*Le Barbier de
Séville (The Barber of Seville)*, I. 2]
2 *Boire sans soif et faire l'amour en tout temps,
madame; il n'y a que ça qui nous distingue des autres
bêtes.* Drinking when we're not thirsty and making
love in all seasons, madam, it's only that which
distinguishes us from other animals. [*Le Mariage de
Figaro (The Marriage of Figaro)*, II, 21]

B11   **Beckett, Samuel** (1906–) Irish author
1 Then I went back into the house and wrote, It is
midnight. The rain is beating on the windows. It was
not midnight. It was not raining. [*Molloy*, closing
lines]

2 ESTRAGON. . . . . Let's go.
VLADIMIR. We can't.
ESTRAGON. Why not?
VLADIMIR. We're waiting for Godot. [*Waiting for Godot*, I and *passim*]
3 VLADIMIR. That passed the time.
ESTRAGON. It would have passed in any case.
VLADIMIR. Yes, but not so rapidly. [*do.*, I]

B12   **Beecham, Sir Thomas** (1879–1961)
English conductor
1 A musicologist is a man who can read music but can't hear it. [attr.]
2 At a rehearsal I let the orchestra play as they like. At the concert I make them play as *I* like. [attr.]

B13   **Beerbohm, Max** (1872–1956)
English critic and caricaturist
1 Most women are not so young as they are painted. [*A Defence of Cosmetics*]
2 To give an accurate and exhaustive account of that period would need a far less brilliant pen than mine. [*1880*]
3 The dullard's envy of brilliant men is always assuaged by the suspicion that they will come to a bad end. [*Zuleika Dobson*, ch. 4]
4 'I don't', she added, 'know anything about music, really. But I know what I like.' [*do.*, ch. 16]

B14   **Beethoven, Ludwig van** (1770–1827)
German composer
1 *Muss es sein? Es muss sein.* Must it be? It must be. [Captions to last movement of String Quartet in F, op. 135]

B15   **Belloc, Hilaire** (1870–1953) British author
1 The Chief Defect of Henry King / Was chewing little bits of string. [*Cautionary Tales*, 'Henry King']
2 And always keep a hold of Nurse / For fear of finding something worse. [*do.*, 'Jim']
3 We had intended you to be / The next Prime Minister but three: / The stocks were sold; the Press was squared; / The Middle Class was quite prepared. / But as it is! . . .My language fails! / Go out and govern New South Wales! [*do.*, 'Lord Lundy']
4 Matilda told such dreadful lies, / It made one gasp

and stretch one's eyes. [*do.*, 'Matilda']

5 For every time she shouted 'Fire!' / They only answered 'Little Liar!' [*do.*]

6 When I am dead, I hope it may be said: / 'His sins were scarlet, but his books were read.' [*Epigrams*, 'On His Books']

7 The Devil, having nothing else to do, / Went off to tempt my Lady Poltagrue. / My Lady, tempted by a private whim, / To his extreme annoyance, tempted him. [*do.*, 'On Lady Poltagrue, a Public Peril']

8 Remote and ineffectual Don / That dared attack my Chesterton. [*Lines to a Don*]

9 Whatever happens, we have got / The Maxim Gun, and they have not. [*The Modern Traveller*]

10 Do you remember an Inn, / Miranda? / Do you remember an Inn? / And the tedding and the spreading / Of the straw for a bedding, / And the fleas that tease in the High Pyrenees, / And the wine that tasted of the tar? [*Tarantella*]

11 Change your hearts or you will lose your Inns and you will deserve to have lost them. But when you have lost your Inns drown your empty selves, for you will have lost the last of England. [*This and That*, 'On Inns']

B16   **Benda, Julien** (1868–1956)
French philosopher and critic
1 *La trahison des clercs.* The treason of the intellectuals. [title of book]

B17   **Benson, A. C.** (1862–1925) English author
1 Land of Hope and Glory, Mother of the Free, / How shall we extol thee, who are born of thee? / Wider still and wider shall thy bounds be set; / God who made thee mighty, make thee mightier yet. [*Land of Hope and Glory*]

B18   **Bentham, Jeremy** (1748–1832)
English jurist and philosopher
1 The greatest happiness of the greatest number is the foundation of morals and legislation. [*The Commonplace Book*]

B19   **Bentley, Edmund Clerihew** (1875–1956)
English author
1 What I like about Clive / Is that he is no longer alive. / There is a great deal to be said / For being

dead [*Biography for Beginners*]

2 John Stuart Mill / By a mighty effort of will / Overcame his natural bonhomie / And wrote 'Principles of Political Economy'. [*do.*]

3 Sir Christopher Wren / Said, 'I am going to dine with some men. / If anybody calls / Say I am designing St. Paul's.' [*do.*]

B20   **Berlin, Irving** (1888–) US (Russian-born) composer

1 The song is ended / But the melody lingers on. [*The Song is Ended*]

2 There's No Business Like Show Business. [title of song]

3 I'm dreaming of a white Christmas, / Just like the ones I used to know. [*White Christmas*]

B21   **Betjeman, Sir John** (1906–84) English poet

1 Phone for the fish-knives, Norman, / As Cook is a little unnerved; / You kiddies have crumpled the serviettes / And I must have things daintily served. [*How to Get On in Society*]

2 Think of what our Nation stands for, / Books from Boots and country lanes, / Free speech, free passes, class distinction, / Democracy and proper drains. [*In Westminster Abbey*]

3 And now, dear Lord, I cannot wait / Because I have a luncheon date. [*do.*]

4 Come friendly bombs, and fall on Slough / It isn't fit for humans now, / There isn't grass to graze a cow / Swarm over, Death! [*Slough*]

5 Miss J. Hunter Dunn, Miss J. Hunter Dunn, / Furnish'd and burnish'd by Aldershot sun. [*A Subaltern's Love Song*]

B22   **Bevin, Ernest** (1881–1951) English politician

1 I didn't ought never to have done it. [remark on his having given official recognition to Communist China]

B23   **The Bible** (Authorized Version)

1 In the beginning God created the heaven and the earth. And the earth was without form, and void; and darkness was upon the face of the deep. [*Genesis* 1:1–2]

2 And God said, Let there be light: and there was light. [*do.* 1:3]

3 And God said, Let us make man in our image, after

our likeness: and let them have dominion over the fish of the sea, and over the fowl of the air, and over the cattle, and over all the earth, and over every creeping thing that creepeth upon the earth. [*do.* 1:26]

4 So God created man in his own image, in the image of God created he him; male and female created he them. [*do.* 1:27]

5 Be fruitful, and multiply, and replenish the earth, and subdue it. [*do.* 1:28]

6 But of the tree of the knowledge of good and evil, thou shalt not eat of it: for in the day that thou eatest thereof thou shalt surely die. [*do.* 2:17]

7 It is not good that the man should be alone; I will make him an help meet for him. [*do.* 2:18]

8 Now the serpent was more subtil than any beast of the field. [*do.* 3:1]

9 For dust thou art, and unto dust shalt thou return. [*do.* 3:19]

10 Am I my brother's keeper? [*do.* 4:9]

11 There were giants in the earth in those days. [*do.* 6:4]

12 There went in two and two unto Noah in the Ark, the male and the female. [*do.* 7:9]

13 His [i.e. Ishmael's] hand will be against every man, and every man's hand against him. [*do.* 16:12]

14 Ye shall eat the fat of the land. [*do.* 45:18]

15 I have been a stranger in a strange land. [*Exodus* 2:22]

16 A land flowing with milk and honey. [*do.* 3:8]

17 I AM THAT I AM. [*do.* 3:14]

18 Let my people go, that they may serve me. [*do.* 8:1]

19 Thou shalt have no other gods before me. [*do.* 20:3]

20 Thou shalt not take the name of the Lord thy God in vain. [*do.* 20:7]

21 Six days shalt thou labour, and do all thy work: But the seventh day is the sabbath of the Lord thy God. [*do.* 20:9–10]

22 Honour thy father and thy mother: that thy days may be long upon the land which the Lord thy God giveth thee. [*do.* 20:12]

23 Thou shalt not kill. [*do.* 20:13]

24 Thou shalt not commit adultery. [*do.* 20:14]

25 Thou shalt not steal. [*do.* 20:15]

26 Thou shalt not bear false witness against thy neighbour. [*do.* 20:16]

27 Thou shalt not covet thy neighbour's house, thou shalt not covet thy neighbour's wife, nor his manservant, nor his maidservant, nor his ox, nor his ass, nor any thing that is thy neighbour's. [*do.* 20:17]

28 And if any mischief follow, then thou shalt give life for life, eye for eye, tooth for tooth, hand for hand, foot for foot. [*do.* 21:23–24]

29 Let him go for a scapegoat into the wilderness. [*Leviticus* 16:10]

30 Thou shalt love thy neighbour as thyself. [*do.* 19:18]

31 What hath God wrought! [*Numbers* 23:23]

32 For the Lord thy God is a jealous god among you. [*Deuteronomy* 6:15]

33 Man doth not live by bread only, but by every word that proceedeth out of the mouth of the Lord doth man live. [*do.* 8:3]

34 For the poor shall never cease out of the land. [*do.* 15:11]

35 Hewers of wood and drawers of water. [*Joshua* 9:21]

36 I am going the way of all the earth. [*do.* 23:14]

37 At her feet he bowed, he fell, he lay down: at her feet he bowed, he fell: where he bowed, there he fell down dead. [*Judges* 5:27]

38 Out of the eater came forth meat, and out of the strong came forth sweetness. [*do.* 14:14]

39 He smote them hip and thigh. [*do.* 15:8]

40 And all the people arose as one man. [*do.* 20:8]

41 Intreat me not to leave thee, or to return from following after thee: for whither thou goest, I will go; and where thou lodgest, I will lodge: thy people shall be my people, and thy God my God. [*Ruth* 1:16]

42 Quit yourselves like men. [*1 Samuel* 4:9]

43 How are the mighty fallen! [*2 Samuel* 1:19]

44 I am distressed for thee, my brother Jonathan: very pleasant hast thou been unto me: thy love to me was wonderful, passing the love of women. [*do.* 1:26]

45 He slept with his fathers. [*1 Kings* 14:20]

46 Behold, there ariseth a little cloud out of the sea, like a man's hand. [*do.* 18:44]

47 And a certain man drew a bow at a venture, and

smote the king of Israel between the joints of the harness. [*do*. 22:34]

48 Is thy servant a dog, that he should do this great thing? [*2 Kings* 8:13]

49 Naked came I out of my mother's womb, and naked shall I return thither: the Lord gave, and the Lord hath taken away; blessed be the name of the Lord. [*Job* 1:21]

50 Let the day perish wherein I was born, and the night in which it was said, There is a man child conceived. [*do*. 3:3]

51 There the wicked cease from troubling; and there the weary be at rest. [*do*. 3:17]

52 Man that is born of a woman is of few days, and full of trouble. [*do*. 14:1]

53 I am escaped with the skin of my teeth. [*do*. 19:20]

54 Oh that my words were now written! oh that they were printed in a book! [*do*. 19:23]

55 I know that my redeemer liveth, and that he shall stand at the latter day upon the earth. [*do*. 19:25]

56 Why do the heathen rage, and the people imagine a vain thing? [*Psalms* 2:1]

57 Out of the mouth of babes and sucklings hast thou ordained strength. [*do*. 8:2]

58 What is man, that thou art mindful of him? [*do*. 8:4]

59 The fool hath said in his heart, There is no God. [*do*. 14:1]

60 The heavens declare the glory of God; and the firmament sheweth his handywork. [*do*. 19:1]

61 The Lord is my shepherd; I shall not want. [*do*. 23:1]

62 He maketh me to lie down in green pastures: he leadeth me beside the still waters. [*do*. 23:2]

63 Yea, though I walk through the valley of the shadow of death, I will fear no evil: for thou art with me; thy rod and thy staff they comfort me. [*do*. 23:4]

64 The earth is the Lord's, and all that therein is: the compass of the world, and they that dwell therein. [*do*. 24:1 (Book of Common Prayer version)]

65 Into thy hands I commend my spirit. [*do*. 31:6 (Book of Common Prayer version)]

66 But the meek shall inherit the earth. [*do*. 37:11]

67 I have been young, and now am old; yet have I

not seen the righteous forsaken, nor his seed begging bread. [*do.* 37:25]

68 God is our refuge and strength, a very present help in trouble. Therefore will not we fear. [*do.* 46:1–2 (the Book of Common Prayer version has 'our hope and strength')]

69 Oh that I had wings like a dove! for then would I fly away, and be at rest. [*do.* 55:6]

70 For a thousand years in thy sight are but as yesterday: seeing that is past as a watch in the night. [*do.* 90:4 (Book of Common Prayer version)]

71 The days of our years are threescore years and ten; and if by reason of strength they be fourscore years, yet is their strength labour and sorrow; for it is soon cut off, and we fly away. [*do.* 90:10]

72 As for man, his days are as grass: as a flower of the field, so he flourisheth. [*do.* 103:15]

73 They that go down to the sea in ships, that do business in great waters; these see the works of the Lord, and his wonders in the deep. [*do.* 107:23–24]

74 The stone which the builders refused is become the head stone of the corner. [*do.* 118:22]

75 I will lift up mine eyes unto the hills, from whence cometh my help. [*do.* 121:1]

76 Out of the depths have I cried unto thee, O Lord. Lord, hear my voice. [*do.* 130:1–2]

77 By the rivers of Babylon, there we sat down, yea, we wept, when we remembered Zion. [*do.* 137:1]

78 Go to the ant, thou sluggard; consider her ways, and be wise. [*Proverbs* 6:6]

79 Can a man take fire in his bosom, and his clothes not be burned? [*do.* 6:27]

80 For wisdom is better than rubies. [*do.* 8:11]

81 Stolen waters are sweet, and bread eaten in secret is pleasant. [*do.* 9:17]

82 Hope deferred maketh the heart sick. [*do.* 13:12]

83 He that spareth his rod hateth his son: but he that loveth him chasteneth him betimes. [*do.* 13:24]

84 A soft answer turneth away wrath. [*do.* 15:1]

85 Pride goeth before destruction, and an haughty spirit before a fall. [*do.* 16:18]

86 Wine is a mocker, strong drink is raging. [*do.* 20:1]

87 A good name is rather to be chosen than great riches. [*do.* 22:1]

88 If thine enemy be hungry, give him bread to eat; and if he be thirsty, give him water to drink: For thou shalt heap coals of fire upon his head, and the Lord shall reward thee. [*do.* 25:21–22]

89 Answer not a fool according to his folly, lest thou also be like unto him. Answer a fool according to his folly, lest he be wise in his own conceit. [*do.* 26:4–5]

90 As a dog returneth to his vomit, so a fool returneth to his folly. [*do.* 26:11]

91 Where there is no vision, the people perish. [*do.* 29:18]

92 Who can find a virtuous woman? for her price is far above rubies. [*do.* 31:10]

93 Vanity of vanities, saith the Preacher, vanity of vanities; all is vanity. What profit hath a man of all his labour which he taketh under the sun? One generation passeth away, and another generation cometh: but the the earth abideth for ever. [*Ecclesiastes* 1:2–4]

94 All things are full of labour; man cannot utter it: the eye is not satisfied with seeing, nor the ear filled with hearing. The thing that hath been, it is that which shall be; and that which is done is that which shall be done: and there is no new thing under the sun. [*do.* 1:8–9]

95 All is vanity and vexation of spirit. [*do.* 1:14]

96 To every thing there is a season, and a time to every purpose under the heaven: A time to be born, and a time to die; a time to plant, and a time to pluck up that which is planted; A time to kill, and a time to heal; a time to break down, and a time to build up; A time to weep, and a time to laugh; a time to mourn, and a time to dance. [*do.* 3:1–4]

97 Be not righteous over much. [*do.* 7:16]

98 I returned, and saw under the sun, that the race is not to the swift, nor the battle to the strong, neither yet bread to the wise, nor yet riches to men of understanding, nor yet favour to men of skill; but time and chance happeneth to them all. [*do.* 9:11]

99 Cast thy bread upon the waters: for thou shalt find it after many days. [*do.* 11:1]

100 Remember now thy Creator in the days of thy youth, while the evil days come not, nor the years draw nigh, when thou shalt say, I have no pleasure in them. [*do.* 12:1]

101 Of making many books there is no end; and much study is a weariness of the flesh. [*do.* 12:12]

102 Stay me with flagons, comfort me with apples: for I am sick of love. [*Song of Solomon* 2:5]

103 The flowers appear on the earth; the time of the singing of birds is come, and the voice of the turtle is heard in our land. [*do.* 2:12]

104 Though your sins be as scarlet, they shall be as white as snow. [*Isaiah* 1:18]

105 They shall beat their swords into plowshares, and their spears into pruninghooks: nation shall not lift up sword against nation, neither shall they learn war any more. [*do.* 2:4]

106 The people that walked in darkness have seen a great light. [*do.* 9:2]

107 For unto us a child is born, unto us a son is given: and the government shall be upon his shoulder: and his name shall be called Wonderful, Counseller, The mighty God, The everlasting Father, The Prince of Peace. [*do.* 9:6]

108 The wolf also shall dwell with the lamb, and the leopard shall lie down with the kid; and the calf and the young lion and the fatling together; and a little child shall lead them. [*do.* 11:6]

109 How art thou fallen from heaven, O Lucifer, son of the morning! [*do.* 14:12]

110 Watchman, what of the night? Watchman, what of the night? The watchman said, The morning cometh, and also the night. [*do.* 21:11–12]

111 Let us eat and drink; for to-morrow we shall die. [*do.* 22:13]

112 Set thine house in order: for thou shalt die, and not live. [*do.* 38:1]

113 The voice of him that crieth in the wilderness, Prepare ye the way of the Lord, make straight in the desert a highway for our God. [*do.* 40:3]

114 All flesh is grass. [*do.* 40:6]

115 There is no peace, saith the Lord, unto the wicked. [*do.* 48:22]

116 He is brought as a lamb to the slaughter. [*do.* 53:7]

117 He was cut off out of the land of the living. [*do.* 53:8]

118 Can the Ethiopian change his skin, or the leopard his spots? [*Jeremiah* 13:23]

119 MENE, MENE, TEKEL, UPHARSIN. [*Daniel* 5:25]

120 Thou art weighed in the balances, and art found wanting. [*do.* 5:27]

121 Now, O king, establish the decree, and sign the writing, that it be not changed, according to the law of the Medes and Persians, which altereth not. [*do.* 6:8]

122 They have sown the wind, and they shall reap the whirlwind. [*Hosea* 8:7]

123 And it shall come to pass afterward, that I will pour out my spirit upon all flesh; and your sons and your daughters shall prophesy, your old men shall dream dreams, your young men shall see visions. [*Joel* 2:28]

124 Great is Truth, and mighty above all things. [*1 Esdras* (Apocrypha) 4:41]

125 Let thy speech be short, comprehending much in a few words. [*Ecclesiasticus* (Apocrypha) 32:8]

126 Let us now praise famous men, and our fathers that begat us. [*do.* 44:1]

127 Repent ye: for the kingdom of heaven is at hand. [*Matthew* 3:2]

128 The voice of one crying in the wilderness. [*do.* 3:3]

129 This is my beloved Son, in whom I am well pleased. [*do.* 3:17]

130 Man shall not live by bread alone, but by every word that proceedeth out of the mouth of God. [*do.* 4:4]

131 Follow me, and I will make you fishers of men. [*do.* 4:19]

132 Blessed are the poor in spirit: for theirs is the kingdom of heaven. Blessed are they that mourn: for they shall be comforted. Blessed are the meek: for they shall inherit the earth. Blessed are they which do hunger and thirst after righteousness: for they shall be filled. Blessed are the merciful: for they shall obtain mercy. Blessed are the pure in heart: for they shall see God. Blessed are the peacemakers: for they shall be called the children of God. [*do.* 5:3–9]

133 Ye are the salt of the earth: but if the salt have lost his savour, wherewith shall it be salted? [*do.* 5:13]

134 Think not that I am come to destroy the law, or the prophets: I am come not to destroy, but to fulfil. [*do.* 5:17]

135 Resist not evil: but whosoever shall smite thee on thy right cheek, turn to him the other also. [*do*. 5:39]

136 He maketh his sun to rise on the evil and on the good, and sendeth rain on the just and on the unjust. [*do*. 5:45]

137 When thou doest alms, let not thy left hand know what thy right hand doeth. [*do*. 6:3]

138 After this manner therefore pray ye: Our Father which art in heaven, Hallowed by thy name. Thy kingdom come. Thy will be done in earth, as it is in heaven. Give us this day our daily bread. And forgive us our debts, as we forgive our debtors. And lead us not into temptation, but deliver us from evil: For thine is the kingdom, and the power, and the glory, for ever. Amen. [*do*. 6:9–13]

139 Lay not up for yourselves treasures upon earth, where moth and rust doth corrupt, and where thieves break through and steal: But lay up for yourselves treasures in heaven. [*do*. 6:19–20]

140 No man can serve two masters...Ye cannot serve God and mammon. [*do*. 6:24]

141 Which of you by taking thought can add one cubit unto his stature? [*do*. 6:27]

142 Consider the lilies of the field, how they grow; they toil not, neither do they spin. [*do*. 6:28]

143 Sufficient unto the day is the evil thereof. [*do*. 6:34]

144 Judge not, that ye be not judged. [*do*. 7:1]

145 Why beholdest thou the mote that is in thy brother's eye, but considerest not the beam that is in thine own eye? [*do*. 7:3]

146 Neither cast ye your pearls before swine. [*do*. 7:6]

147 Ask, and it shall be given you; seek, and ye shall find; knock, and it shall be opened unto you. [*do*. 7:7]

148 Therefore all things whatsoever ye would that men should do to you, do ye even so to them: for this is the law and the prophets. [*do*. 7:12]

149 Strait is the gate, and narrow is the way, which leadeth unto life, and few there be that find it. [*do*. 7:14]

150 Beware of false prophets, which come to you in sheep's clothing, but inwardly they are ravening wolves. [*do*. 7:15]

151 By their fruits ye shall know them. [*do*. 7:20]

152 Lord, I am not worthy that thou shouldest come under my roof. [*do.* 8:8]

153 But the children of the kingdom shall be cast out into outer darkness: there shall be weeping and gnashing of teeth. [*do.* 8:12]

154 Freely ye have received, freely give. [*do.* 10:8]

155 He that is not with me is against me. [*do.* 12:30]

156 The tree is known by his fruit. [*do.* 12:33]

157 A prophet is not without honour, save in his own country, and in his own house. [*do.* 13:57]

158 If the blind lead the blind, both shall fall into the ditch. [*do.* 15:14]

159 Thou art Peter, and upon this rock I will build my church; and the gates of hell shall not prevail against it. [*do.* 16:18]

160 Get thee behind me, Satan. [*do.* 16:23]

161 Except ye be converted, and become as little children, ye shall not enter into the kingdom of heaven. [*do.* 18:3]

162 If thine eye offend thee, pluck it out. [*do.* 18:9]

163 What therefore God hath joined together, let not man put asunder. [*do.* 19:6]

164 It is easier for a camel to go through the eye of a needle, than for a rich man to enter into the kingdom of God. [*do.* 19:24]

165 With men this is impossible; but with God all things are possible. [*do.* 19:26]

166 But many that are first shall be last; and the last shall be first. [*do.* 19:30]

167 It is written, My house shall be called the house of prayer; but ye have made it a den of thieves. [*do.* 21:13]

168 For many are called, but few are chosen. [*do.* 22:14]

169 Render therefore unto Caesar the things which are Caesar's; and unto God the things that are God's. [*do.* 22:21]

170 Ye are like unto whited sepulchres, which indeed appear beautiful outward, but are within full of dead men's bones, and of all uncleanness. [*do.* 23:27]

171 For nation shall rise against nation, and kingdom against kingdom. [*do.* 24:7]

172 When ye therefore shall see the abomination of desolation, spoken of by Daniel the prophet, stand in the holy place. [*do.* 24:15]

173 Heaven and earth shall pass away, but my words shall not pass away. [*do.* 24:35]

174 Ye have the poor always with you. [*do.* 26:11]

175 This night, before the cock crow, thou shalt deny me thrice. [*do.* 26:34]

176 The spirit indeed is willing, but the flesh is weak. [*do.* 26:41]

177 All they that take the sword shall perish with the sword. [*do.* 26:52]

178 Jesus cried with a loud voice, saying, Eli, Eli, lama sabachthani? that is to say, My God, my God, why hast thou forsaken me? [*do.* 27:46]

179 And, lo, I am with you alway, even unto the end of the world. [*do.* 28:20]

180 The sabbath was made for man, and not man for the sabbath. [*Mark* 2:27]

181 If a house be divided against itself, that house cannot stand. [*do.* 3:25]

182 He that hath ears to hear, let him hear. [*do.* 4:9]

183 For what shall it profit a man, if he shall gain the whole world, and lose his own soul? [*do.* 8:36]

184 Lord, I believe; help thou mine unbelief. [*do.* 9:24]

185 Suffer the little children to come unto me, and forbid them not: for of such is the kingdom of God. [*do.* 10:14]

186 My soul doth magnify the Lord, And my spirit hath rejoiced in God my Saviour. [*Luke* 1:46–47]

187 Behold, I bring you good tidings of great joy. [*do.* 2:10]

188 Glory to God in the highest, and on earth peace, good will toward men. [*do.* 2:14]

189 Lord, now lettest thou thy servant depart in peace, according to thy word. [*do.* 2:29]

190 Wist ye not that I must be about my Father's business? [*do.* 2:49]

191 Physician, heal thyself. [*do.* 4:23]

192 Love your enemies, do good to them which hate you. [*do.* 6:27]

193 Give, and it shall be given unto you. [*do.* 6:38]

194 The labourer is worthy of his hire. [*do.* 10:7]

195 Go, and do thou likewise. [*do.* 10:37]

196 For whosoever exalteth himself shall be abased; and he that humbleth himself shall be exalted. [*do.* 14:11]

197 Joy shall be in heaven over one sinner that repenteth, more than over ninety and nine just persons, which need no repentance. [*do.* 15:7]

198 Bring hither the fatted calf, and kill it; and let us eat, and be merry. [*do.* 15:23]

199 Between us and you there is a great gulf fixed. [*do.* 16:26]

200 The kingdom of God is within you. [*do.* 17:21]

201 Father, forgive them; for they know not what they do. [*do.* 23:34]

202 Father, into thy hands I commend my spirit. [*do.* 23:46]

203 In the beginning was the Word, and the Word was with God, and the Word was God. [*John* 1:1]

204 And the light shineth in darkness; and the darkness comprehended it not. [*do.* 1:5]

205 The Word was made flesh, and dwelt among us. [*do.* 1:14]

206 Behold the Lamb of God, which taketh away the sin of the world. [*do.* 1:29]

207 Ye must be born again. [*do.* 3:7]

208 The wind bloweth where it listeth. [*do.* 3:8]

209 For God so loved the world, that he gave his only begotten Son, that whosoever believeth in him should not perish, but have everlasting life. [*do.* 3:16]

210 Except ye see signs and wonders, ye will not believe. [*do.* 4:48]

211 Rise, take up thy bed, and walk. [*do.* 5:8]

212 It is the spirit that quickeneth; the flesh profiteth nothing. [*do.* 6:63]

213 He that is without sin among you, let him first cast a stone at her. [*do.* 8:7]

214 I am the light of the world. [*do.* 8:12]

215 I am the good shepherd: the good shepherd giveth his life for the sheep. [*do.* 10:11]

216 I am the resurrection, and the life. [*do.* 11:25]

217 Jesus wept. [*do.* 11:35]

218 A new commandment I give unto you, That ye love one another. [*do.* 13:34]

219 Greater love hath no man than this, that a man lay down his life for his friends. [*do.* 15:13]

220 Pilate saith unto him, What is truth? [*do.* 18:38]

221 Silver and gold have I none; but such as I have give I thee. [*Acts of the Apostles* 3:6]

222 It is hard for thee to kick against the pricks. [*do.*

9:5]

223 God is no respecter of persons. [*do.* 10:34]

224 For in him we live, and move, and have our being. [*do.* 17:28]

225 It is more blessed to give than to receive. [*do.* 20:35]

226 These, having not the law, are a law unto themselves. [*Romans* 2:14]

227 For where no law is, there is no transgression. [*do.* 4:15]

228 The wages of sin is death. [*do.* 6:23]

229 If God be for us, who can be against us? [*do.* 8:31]

230 Vengeance is mine; I will repay, saith the Lord. [*do.* 12:19]

231 The night is far spent, the day is at hand: let us therefore cast off the works of darkness, and let us put on the armour of light. [*do.* 13:12]

232 Let every man be fully persuaded in his own mind. [*do.* 14:5]

233 Absent in body, but present in spirit. [*1 Corinthians* 5:3]

234 It is better to marry than to burn. [*do.* 7:9]

235 The fashion of this world passeth away. [*do.* 7:31]

236 I am made all things to all men. [*do.* 9:22]

237 For the earth is the Lord's, and the fulness thereof. [*do.* 10:26]

238 Though I speak with the tongues of men and of angels, and have not charity, I am become as sounding brass, or a tinkling cymbal. [*do.* 13:1]

239 When I was a child, I spake as a child, I understood as a child, I thought as a child: but when I became a man, I put away childish things. For now we see through a glass, darkly; but then face to face: now I know in part; but then shall I know even as also I am known. And now abideth faith, hope, charity, these three; but the greatest of these is charity. [*do.* 13:11–13]

240 O death, where is thy sting? O grave, where is thy victory? [*do.* 15:55]

241 The letter killeth, but the spirit giveth life. [*2 Corinthians* 3:6]

242 God loveth a cheerful giver. [*do.* 9:7]

243 For ye suffer fools gladly, seeing ye yourselves

are wise. [*do.* 11:19]

244 There was given to me a thorn in the flesh, the messenger of Satan to buffet me. [*do.* 12:7]

245 The right hands of fellowship. [*Galatians* 2:9]

246 Be not deceived; God is not mocked: for whatsoever a man soweth, that shall he also reap. [*do.* 6:7]

247 We are members one of another. [*Ephesians* 4:25]

248 Be ye angry and sin not: let not the sun go down upon your wrath. [*do.* 4:26]

249 Work out your own salvation with fear and trembling. [*Philippians* 2:12]

250 The peace of God, which passeth all understanding. [*do.* 4:7]

251 Set your affection on things above, not on things on the earth. [*Colossians* 3:2]

252 Drink no longer water, but use a little wine for thy stomach's sake and thine often infirmities. [*1 Timothy* 5:23]

253 For we brought nothing into this world, and it is certain we can carry nothing out. [*do.* 6:7]

254 The love of money is the root of all evil. [*do.* 6:10]

255 Unto the pure all things are pure. [*Titus* 1:15]

256 Faith is the substance of things hoped for, the evidence of things not seen. [*Hebrews* 11:1]

257 Let your yea be yea; and your nay, nay. [*James* 5:12]

258 All flesh is as grass. [*1 Peter* 1:24]

259 Giving honour unto the wife, as unto the weaker vessel. [*do.* 3:7]

260 Charity shall cover the multitude of sins. [*do.* 4:8]

261 He that loveth not knoweth not God; for God is love. [*1 John* 4:8]

262 There is no fear in love; but perfect love casteth out fear. [*do.* 4:18]

263 I am Alpha and Omega, the beginning and the ending, saith the Lord. [*Revelation* 1:8]

264 Be thou faithful unto death, and I will give thee a crown of life. [*do.* 2:10]

265 And I looked, and behold a pale horse: and his name that sat on him was Death, and Hell followed with him. [*do.* 6:8]

266 And when he had opened the seventh seal, there

was silence in heaven about the space of half an hour.
[*do.* 8:1]
267 It was in my mouth sweet as honey: and as soon
as I had eaten it, my belly was bitter. [*do.* 10:10]
268 Let him that hath understanding count the
number of the beast: for it is the number of a man;
and his number is six hundred threescore and six. [*do.*
13:18]
269 And I saw a new heaven and a new earth: for the
first heaven and the first earth were passed away; and
there was no more sea. [*do.* 21:1]
270 And God shall wipe away all tears from their
eyes; and there shall be no more death, neither
sorrow, nor crying, neither shall there be any more
pain: for the former things are passed away. [*do.* 21:4]

B24   **Bickerstaffe, Isaac** (*d.* 1812?) English dramatist
1 There was a jolly miller once, / Lived on the river
Dee; / He worked and sang from morn till night; /
No lark more blithe than he. [*Love in a Village*, I. 5]
2 And this the burthen of his song, / For ever us'd
to be, / I care for nobody, not I, / If no one cares
for me. [*do.*]

B25   **Bierce, Ambrose** (1842–1914?) US author
1 *Bore*, n. A person who talks when you wish him to
listen. [*The Devil's Dictionary*]
2 *Brain*, n. An apparatus with which we think that
we think. [*do.*]
3 *Cat*, n. A soft indestructible automaton provided by
nature to be kicked when things go wrong in the
domestic circle. [*do.*]
4 *Christmas*, n. A day set apart and consecrated to
gluttony, drunkenness, maudlin sentiment, gift-taking,
public dullness and domestic behaviour. [*do.*]
5 *Future*, n. That period of time in which our affairs
prosper, our friends are true and our happiness is
assured. [*do.*]
6 *Telephone*, n. An invention of the devil which
abrogates some of the advantages of making a
disagreeable person keep his distance. [*do.*]

B26   **Binyon, Laurence** (1869–1943) English poet
1 They shall grow not old, as we that are left grow
old: / Age shall not weary them, nor the years
condemn. / At the going down of the sun and in the

morning / We will remember them. [*For the Fallen (1914–1918)*]

B27   **Birkenhead, Earl of (F. E. Smith)** (1872–1930)
English jurist and statesman
1 The world continues to offer glittering prizes to those who have stout hearts and sharp swords. [address at Glasgow University, 1923]

B28   **Bishop, Thomas Brigham** (1835–1905)
US songwriter
1 John Brown's body lies a-mouldering in the grave, / His soul is marching on! [*John Brown's Body*. Also attr. to C. S. Hall]

B29   **Bismarck, Prince Otto von** (1815–98)
German statesman
1 *Die Politik ist die Lehre von Möglichen.* Politics is the art of the possible. [remark. Compare **B59.1**]

B30   **Blackstone, Sir William** (1723–80) English jurist
1 That the king can do no wrong, is a necessary and fundamental principle of the English constitution. [*Commentaries on the Laws of England*, bk 3]
2 It is better that ten guilty persons escape than one innocent suffer. [*do.*, bk 4]

B31   **Blake, William** (1757–1827) English artist and poet
1 To see a World in a grain of sand / And a Heaven in a wild flower, / Hold Infinity in the palm of your hand / And Eternity in an hour. [*Auguries of Innocence*]
2 A robin redbreast in a cage / Puts all Heaven in a rage. [*do.*]
3 Does the Eagle know what is in the pit? / Or wilt thou go ask the Mole? / Can Wisdom be put in a silver rod? / Or Love in a golden bowl? [*The Book of Thel*]
4 What was the sound of Jesus' breath? / He laid His hand on Moses' law; / The ancient Heavens, in silent awe / Writ with curses from pole to pole, / All away began to roll. [*The Everlasting Gospel*]
5 Truly, my Satan, thou art but a dunce, / And dost not know the garment from the man. / Every harlot was a virgin once, / Nor can'st thou ever change Kate into Nan. [*The Gates of Paradise*]
6 I must create a system or be enslav'd by another man's. / I will not reason and compare: my business

is to create. [*Jerusalem*]

7 Without Contraries is no progression. Attraction and Repulsion, Reason and Energy, Love and Hate, are necessary to Human existence. [*The Marriage of Heaven and Hell*]

8 The road of excess leads to the palace of Wisdom. [*do.*, 'Proverbs of Hell']

9 A fool sees not the same tree that a wise man sees [*do.*]

10 Damn braces. Bless relaxes. [*do.*]

11 If the doors of perception were cleansed everything would appear to man as it is, infinite. [*do.*, 'A Memorable Fancy']

12 And did those feet in ancient time / Walk upon England's mountains green? / And was the holy lamb of God / On England's pleasant pastures seen? [*Milton*, 'Preface']

13 And was Jerusalem builded here / Among these dark Satanic mills? [*do.*]

14 I will not cease from mental fight, / Nor shall my sword sleep in my hand / Till we have built Jerusalem / In England's green and pleasant land. [*do.*]

15 Love seeketh not itself to please, / Nor for itself hath any care, / But for another gives its ease, / And builds a Heaven in Hell's despair. [*Songs of Experience*, 'The Clod and the Pebble']

16 Love seeketh only Self to please, / To bind another to its delight, / Joys in another's loss of ease, / And builds a Hell in Heaven's despite. [*do.*]

17 O Rose, thou art sick! / The invisible worm / That flies in the night, / In the howling storm, / Has found out thy bed / Of crimson joy, / And his dark secret love / Does thy life destroy. [*do.*, 'The Sick Rose']

18 Tiger! Tiger! burning bright / In the forests of the night, / What immortal hand or eye / Could frame thy fearful symmetry? [*do.*, 'The Tiger']

19 When the stars threw down their spears, / And water'd heaven with their tears, / Did he smile his work to see? / Did he who made the Lamb make thee? [*do.*]

20 Little Lamb, who made thee? / Dost thou know who made thee? [*Songs of Innocence*, 'The Lamb']

21 Great things are done when men and mountains

meet; / This is not done by jostling in the street.
[untitled epigram]

B32   **Blunden, Edmund** (1896–1974) English poet
1 I have been young, and now am not too old; / And
I have seen the righteous forsaken, / His health, his
honour and his quality taken. / This is not what we
were formerly told. [*Report on Experience.* Compare
B23.67]

B33   **Boethius** (480?–524?) Roman philosopher
1 For in every adversity of fortune the worst sort of
misery is to have been happy. [*The Consolation of
Philosophy*, bk 2]

B34   **Bogart, Humphrey** (1899–1957) US film actor
1 Play it, Sam. Play 'As Time Goes By'. [*Casablanca*
(film). Often quoted as 'Play it again, Sam']
2 Here's looking at you, kid! [*do.*]

B35   **Borrow, George** (1803–81) English author
1 Youth will be served, every dog has his day, and
mine has been a fine one. [*Lavengro*, ch. 92]

B36   **Bosquet, Pierre** (1810–61) French marshal
1 *C'est magnifique, mais ce n'est pas la guerre.* It is
magnificent, but it is not war. [remark on the charge
of the Light Brigade at the Battle of Balaclava, 1854]

B37   **Boulay de la Meurthe, Antoine** (1761–1840)
French politician
1 *C'est pire qu'un crime, c'est une faute.* It is worse
than a crime, it is a blunder. [remark on the
execution of the Duc d'Enghien in 1804]

B38   **Bradford, John** (1510?–55)
English Protestant martyr
1 There, but for the grace of God, goes John
Bradford. [remark on seeing some criminals being
taken to execution]

B39   **Brathwaite, Richard** (1588?–1673) English poet
1 To Banbury came I, O profane one! / Where I saw
a Puritane-one / Hanging of his cat on Monday /
For killing of a mouse on Sunday. [*Barnabee's
Journal*]

B40   **Bright, John** (1811–89)
English orator and statesman
1 England is the mother of parliaments. [speech in

Birmingham, 18 Jan. 1865]

B41 **Brillat-Savarin, Anthelme** (1755–1826)
French gastronome
1 *Dis-moi ce que tu manges, je te dirai ce que tu es.* Tell
me what you eat, and I will tell you what you are.
[*Physiologie du Goût.* Compare **F3.1**]

B42 **Brontë, Emily** (1818–48) English author
1 No coward soul is mine, / No trembler in the
world's storm-troubled sphere: / I see Heaven's
glories shine, / And faith shines equal, arming me
from fear. [*Last Lines*]
2 I lingered round them, under that benign sky:
watched the moths fluttering among the heath and
hare-bells; listened to the soft wind breathing through
the grass; and wondered how any one could ever
imagine unquiet slumbers for the sleepers in that
quiet earth. [*Wuthering Heights*, closing lines]

B43 **Brooke, Rupert** (1887–1915) English poet
1 Just now the lilac is in bloom, / All before my
little room. [*The Old Vicarage, Grantchester*]
2 Oh! yet / Stands the Church clock at ten to
three? / And is there honey still for tea? [*do.*]
3 Now, God be thanked who has matched us with
His hour, / And caught our youth, and wakened us
from sleeping. [*Peace*]
4 If I should die, think only this of me: / That
there's some corner of a foreign field / That is for
ever England. [*The Soldier*]

B44 **Brown, Thomas** (1663–1704) English satirist
1 I do not love thee, Doctor Fell, / The reason why
I cannot tell; / But this alone I know full well, / I
do not love thee, Doctor Fell. [allegedly impromptu
translation of an epigram by Martial]

B45 **Brown, T. E.** (1830–97) English poet
1 A garden is a lovesome thing, God wot!
[*My Garden*]

B46 **Browne, Sir Thomas** (1605–82)
English physician and author
1 He who discommendeth others obliquely
commendeth himself. [*Christian Morals*]
2 All things are artificial; for nature is the art of God.
[*Religio Medici*, I, 16]

3 No man can justly censure or condemn another; because, indeed, no man truly knows another. [*do.*, II, 4]

4 I could be content that we might procreate like trees, without conjunction, or that there were any way to perpetuate the World without this trivial and vulgar way of coition: it is the foolishest act a wise man commits in all his life; nor is there any thing that will more deject his cooled imagination, when he shall consider what an odd and unworthy piece of folly he hath committed. [*do.*, 9]

5 For the world, I count it not an inn, but an hospital; and a place, not to live, but to die in. [*do.*, 11]

6 There is surely a piece of divinity in us; something that was before the elements, and owes no homage unto the sun. [*do.*]

7 What song the Syrens sang, or what name Achilles assumed when he hid himself among women, though puzzling questions, are not beyond all conjecture. [*Urn Burial*, ch. 5]

B47 **Browning, Elizabeth Barrett** (1806–61)
English poet
1 What was he doing, the great god Pan, / Down in the reeds by the river? [*A Musical Instrument*]
2 How do I love thee? Let me count the ways. [*Sonnets from the Portuguese*, 43]

B48 **Browning, Robert** (1812–89) English poet
1 Ah, but a man's reach should exceed his grasp, / Or what's a heaven for? [*Andrea del Sarto*]
2 One who never turned his back but marched breast forward, / Never doubted clouds would break, / Never dreamed, though right were worsted, wrong would triumph, / Held we fall to rise, are baffled to fight better, / Sleep to wake. [*Asolando*, 'Epilogue']
3 Truth that peeps / Over the glasses' edge when dinner's done, / And body gets its sop and holds its noise / And leaves soul free a little. [*Bishop Blougram's Apology*]
4 Just when we are safest, there's a sunset-touch, / A fancy from a flower-bell, some one's death, / A chorus-ending from Euripides, – / And that's enough for fifty hopes and fears / As old and new at once as Nature's self, / To rap and knock and enter in our

soul. [*do.*]

5 All we have gained then by our unbelief / Is a life of doubt diversified by faith, / For one of faith diversified by doubt: / We called the chess-board white, – we call it black. [*do.*]

6 Dauntless the slug-horn to my lips I set, / And blew. *Childe Roland to the Dark Tower came.* [*Childe Roland to the Dark Tower Came*]

7 Karshish, the picker-up of learning's crumbs, / The not-incurious in God's handiwork. [*An Epistle*]

8 That low man seeks a little thing to do, / Sees it and does it: / This high man, with a great thing to pursue, / Dies ere he knows it. / That low man goes on adding one to one, / His hundred's soon hit: / This high man, aiming at a million, / Misses an unit. [*A Grammarian's Funeral*]

9 Oh, to be in England / Now that April's there. [*Home-Thoughts, from Abroad*]

10 That's the wise thrush; he sings each song twice over, / Lest you should think he never could recapture / The first fine careless rapture! [*do.*]

11 I sprang to the stirrup, and Joris, and he; / I galloped, Dirck galloped, we galloped all three. [*How They Brought the Good News from Ghent to Aix*]

12 Just for a handful of silver he left us, / Just for a riband to stick in his coat. [*The Lost Leader*]

13 Never glad confident morning again! [*do.*]

14 Ah, did you once see Shelley plain, / And did he stop and speak to you / And did you speak to him again? / How strange it seems and new! [*Memorabilia*]

15 God be thanked, the meanest of his creatures / Boasts two soul-sides, one to face the world with, / One to show a woman when he loves her! [*One Word More*]

16 It was roses, roses, all the way. [*The Patriot*]

17 Hamelin Town's in Brunswick, / By famous Hanover city; / The river Weser, deep and wide, / Washes its wall on the southern side. [*The Pied Piper of Hamelin*]

18 Rats! / They fought the dogs and killed the cats, / And bit the babies in the cradles. [*do.*]

19 'You threaten us, fellow? Do your worst, / Blow your pipe there till you burst!' [*do.*]

20 The year's at the spring / And day's at the

morn; / Morning's at seven; / The hill-side's dew-
pearled; / The lark's on the wing; / The snail's on
the thorn: / God's in His heaven – / All's right with
the world! [*Pippa Passes*, I]
21 And all night long we have not stirred, / And yet
God has not said a word! [*Porphyria's Lover*]
22 I was ever a fighter, so – one fight more, / The
best and the last! / I would hate that death bandaged
my eyes, and forbore, / And bade me creep past.
[*Prospice*]
23 What of soul was left, I wonder, when the kissing
had to stop? [*A Toccata of Galuppi's*]
24 Only I discern – / Infinite passion, and the
pain / Of finite hearts that yearn. [*Two in the
Campagna*]
25 What's become of Waring / Since he gave us all
the slip? [*Waring*]

B49   **Buchan, John** (1875–1940) Scottish author
1 An atheist is a man who has no invisible means of
support. [attr. Also attr. to H. E. Fosdick]

B50   **Buffon, Comte Georges de** (1707–88)
French naturalist
1 *Le style est l'homme même.* Style is the man.
[*Discours sur le style*]

B51   **Buller, Arthur** (1874–1944) English botanist
1 There was a young lady named Bright, / Whose
speed was far faster than light; / She set out one
day / In a relative way, / And returned home the
previous night. [limerick]

B52   **Bulwer-Lytton, Edward, Baron Lytton** (1803–73)
English author
1 Beneath the rule of men entirely great, / The pen
is mightier than the sword. [*Richelieu*, II. 2]

B53   **Bunyan, John** (1626–88)
English preacher and author
1 As I walked through the wilderness of this world.
[*Pilgrim's Progress*, pt I]
2 The name of the slough was Despond. [*do.*]
3 The gentleman's name that met him was Mr
Worldly-Wiseman. [*do.*]
4 It beareth the name of Vanity-Fair, because the
town where 'tis kept is lighter than vanity. [*do.*]
5 A castle, called Doubting-Castle, the owner whereof

was Giant Despair. [*do.*]

6 So I awoke, and behold it was a dream. [*do.*]

7 He that is down, needs fear no fall; / He that is low, no pride. [*do.*, pt II]

B54 **Burgon, J. W.** (1813–88)

English cleric and author

1 Match me such marvel save in Eastern clime, / A rose-red city 'half as old as time'! [*Petra.* The final phrase is taken from Samuel Rogers]

B55 **Burke, Edmund** (1729–97)

British statesman and orator

1 I am convinced that we have a degree of delight, and that no small one, in the real misfortunes and pains of others. [*On the Sublime and Beautiful,* pt I]

2 But the age of chivalry is gone. That of sophisters, economists, and calculators, has succeeded; and the glory of Europe is extinguished for ever. [*Reflections on the Revolution in France*]

3 The concessions of the weak are the concessions of fear. [*Speech on Conciliation with America*]

4 The use of force alone is but *temporary*. It may subdue for a moment; but it does not remove the necessity of subduing again: and a nation is not governed, which is perpetually to be conquered. [*do.*]

5 All government, indeed every human benefit and enjoyment, every virtue, and every prudent act, is founded on compromise and barter. [*do.*]

6 The people are the masters. [*Speech on the Economical Reform*]

7 The greater the power, the more dangerous the abuse. [*Speech on the Middlesex Election*]

8 To complain of the age we live in, to murmur at the present possessors of power, to lament the past, to conceive extravagant hopes of the future, are the common dispositions of the greatest part of mankind. [*Thoughts on the Cause of the Present Discontents*]

B56 **Burns, Robert** (1759–96) Scottish poet

1 O Thou! Whatever title suit thee, / Auld Hornie, Satan, Nick, or Clootie. [*Address to the De'il*]

2 Had we never lov'd sae kindly, / Had we never lov'd sae blindly, / Never met, or never parted, / We had ne'er been broken-hearted. [*Ae Fond Kiss*]

3 Should auld acquaintance be forgot, / And never brought to min'? [*Auld Lang Syne*]

4 We'll tak a cup o' kindness yet, / For auld lang syne. [*do.*]

5 Gin a body meet a body / Coming through the rye; / Gin a body kiss a body, / Need a body cry? [*Coming through the Rye*]

6 A man's a man for a' that. [*For a' that and a' that*]

7 Green grow the rashes O, / Green grow the rashes O, / The sweetest hours that e'er I spend, / Are spent amang the lasses O! [*Green Grow the Rashes*]

8 John Anderson my jo, John, / When we were first acquent, / Your locks were like the raven, / Your bonnie brow was brent. [*John Anderson My Jo*]

9 Man's inhumanity to man / Makes countless thousands mourn! [*Man was Made to Mourn*]

10 My heart's in the Highlands, my heart is not here; / My heart's in the Highlands, a-chasing the deer; / Chasing the wild deer, and following the roe, / My heart's in the Highlands, wherever I go. [*My Heart's in the Highlands*]

11 Oh, my luve's like a red red rose / That's newly sprung in June: / Oh, my luve's like the melodie / That's sweetly play'd in tune. [*My Love Is Like A Red, Red Rose*]

12 Scots, wha hae wi' Wallace bled, / Scots, wham Bruce had aften led, / Welcome to your gory bed, / Or to victorie. [*Scots, Wha Hae*]

13 Fair fa' your honest sonsie face, / Great chieftain o' the puddin'-race! [*To a Haggis*]

14 O wad some Pow'r the giftie gie us / To see oursels as others see us! [*To a Louse*]

15 Wee, sleekit, cow'rin', tim'rous beastie, / O what a panic's in thy breastie! [*To a Mouse*]

16 The best-laid schemes o' mice an' men / Gang aft a-gley, / An' lea'e us nought but grief an' pain / For promis'd joy. [*do.*]

17 Ye banks and braes o' bonnie Doon, / How can ye bloom sae fresh and fair? / How can ye chant, ye little birds, / And I sae weary fu' o' care? [*Ye Banks and Braes*]

18 Thou minds me o' departed joys, / Departed never to return. [*do.*]

B57   **Burroughs, Edgar Rice** (1875–1950) US author
1 Me Tarzan, you Jane. [*Tarzan of the Apes*]

B58   **Burton, Robert** (1577–1640)

English clergyman and author
1 One religion is as true as another. [*The Anatomy of Melancholy*]

B59 **Butler, R. A.** (1902–82) English politician
1 Politics is the art of the possible. [epigraph to *The Art of the Possible*. But see **B29.1**]

B60 **Butler, Samuel** (1612–80) English satirical poet
1 Compound for sins, they are inclined to / By damning those they have no mind to. [*Hudibras*, I, 1]
2 He that complies against his will, / Is of his own opinion still. [*do.*, III, 3]

B61 **Butler, Samuel** (1835–1902)
English novelist and satirist
1 It has been said that the love of money is the root of all evil. The want of money is so quite as truly. [*Erewhon*, ch. 20]
2 Every man's work, whether it be literature or music or pictures or architecture or anything else, is always a portrait of himself. [*The Way of All Flesh*, ch. 14]

B62 **Byron, Lord** (1788–1824) English poet
1 In short, he was a perfect cavaliero, / And to his very valet seem'd a hero. [*Beppo*. Compare **C41.1**]
2 What is the worst of woes that wait on age? / What stamps the wrinkle deeper on the brow? / To view each loved one blotted from life's page, / And be alone on earth, as I am now. [*Childe Harold's Pilgrimage*, II, 98]
3 On with the dance! let joy be unconfined; / No sleep till morn, when Youth and Pleasure meet / To chase the glowing Hours with flying feet. [*do.*, III, 22]
4 I live not in myself, but I become / Portion of that around me; and to me / High mountains are a feeling, but the hum / Of human cities torture. [*do.*, 72]
5 I stood in Venice, on the Bridge of Sighs: / A palace and a prison on each hand. [*do.*, IV, 1]
6 Butcher'd to make a Roman holiday. [*do.*, 141]
7 While stands the Coliseum, Rome shall stand; / When falls the Coliseum, Rome shall fall; / And when Rome falls – the World. [*do.*, 145]
8 There is a pleasure in the pathless woods, / There is a rapture on the lonely shore, / There is society,

where none intrudes, / By the deep Sea, and music in its roar: / I love not Man the less, but Nature more. [*do.*, 178]

9 Roll on, thou deep and dark blue Ocean—roll! / Ten thousand fleets sweep over thee in vain; / Man marks the earth with ruin—his control / Stops with the shore. [*do.*, 179]

10 The Assyrian came down like the wolf on the fold, / And his cohorts were gleaming in purple and gold. [*The Destruction of Sennacherib*]

11 But – Oh! ye lords of ladies intellectual, / Inform us truly, have they not hen-peck'd you all? [*Don Juan*, I, 22]

12 What men call gallantry, and gods adultery, / Is much more common where the climate's sultry. [*do.*, 63]

13 A little still she strove, and much repented, / And whispering 'I will ne'er consent' – consented. [*do.*, 117]

14 Man's love is of man's life a thing apart; / 'Tis woman's whole existence. [*do.*, 194]

15 Let us have wine and women, mirth and laughter, / Sermons and soda-water the day after. [*do.*, II, 178]

16 Man, being reasonable, must get drunk; / The best of life is but intoxication. [*do.*, 179]

17 Marriage from love, like vinegar from wine – / A sad, sour, sober beverage – by time / Is sharpen'd from its high celestial flavour, / Down to a very homely household savour. [*do.*, III, 5]

18 All tragedies are finish'd by a death; / All comedies are ended by a marriage. [*do.*, 9]

19 The isles of Greece, the isles of Greece! / Where burning Sappho loved and sung. [*do.*, 86]

20 The mountains look on Marathon, / And Marathon looks on the sea: / And musing there an hour alone, / I dream'd that Greece might still be free. [*do.*]

21 A lady of a 'certain age', which means / Certainly aged. [*do.*, VI, 69]

22 And, after all, what is a lie? 'Tis but / The truth in masquerade. [*do.*, XI, 37]

23 'Tis strange the mind, that very fiery particle, / Should let itself be snuff'd out by an article. [*do.*, 60]

24 Now hatred is by far the longest pleasure: / Men

love in haste, but they detest at leisure. [*do.*, XIII, 6]

25 The English winter – ending in July, / To recommence in August. [*do.*, 42]

26 Society is now one polish'd horde, / Form'd of two mighty tribes, the *Bores* and *Bored*. [*do.*, 95]

27 Even I / Regain'd my freedom with a sigh. [*The Prisoner of Chillon*]

28 She walks in beauty, like the night / Of cloudless climes and starry skies; / And all that's best of dark and bright / Meet in her aspect and her eyes. [*She Walks in Beauty*]

29 So, we'll go no more a roving / So late into the night, / Though the heart be still as loving, / And the moon be still as bright. [*So, We'll Go No More A Roving*]

30 Though the night was made for loving, / And the day returns too soon, / Yet we'll go no more a roving / By the light of the moon. [*do.*]

31 The angels were all singing out of tune, / And hoarse with having little else to do, / Excepting to wind up the sun and moon, / Or curb a runaway young star or two. [*The Vision of Judgment*]

32 I awoke one morning and found myself famous. [remark on the success of *Childe Harold's Pilgrimage*]

C1   **Cabell, James Branch** (1879–1958) US novelist
1 The optimist proclaims that we live in the best of all possible worlds; and the pessimist fears this is true. [*The Silver Stallion*, IV, ch. 26]

C2   **Caesar, Julius** (100–44 BC)
Roman general and statesman
1 *Gallia est omnis divisa in partes tres.* The whole of Gaul is divided into three parts. [*De Bello Gallico*, I]
2 *Veni, vidi, vici.* I came, I saw, I conquered. [remark on his victory over Pharnaces in 47 BC]
3 *Iacta alea est.* The die is cast. [remark on crossing the Rubicon, precipitating civil war, in 49 BC]
4 Caesar's wife must be above suspicion. [attr.]
5 *Et tu, Brute?* You too, Brutus? [attr. last words]

C3   **Cage, John** (1912–) US composer
1 I have nothing to say and I am saying it. [*Silence*, 'Lecture on Nothing']

C4   **Cambronne, Comte Pierre** (1770–1842) French general
1 *La Garde meurt, mais ne se rend pas.* The Guards die, but do not surrender. [attr. reply when asked to surrender at Waterloo]

C5   **Camden, William** (1551–1623) English antiquarian and historian
1 Betwixt the stirrup and the ground / Mercy I asked, mercy I found. [*Epitaph for a Man Killed by Falling from his Horse*]

C6   **Campbell, Mrs Patrick** (1865–1940) English actress
1 I don't mind where people make love, so long as they don't do it in the street and frighten the horses. [attr.]

C7   **Campbell, Thomas** (1777–1844) Scottish poet
1 O leave this barren spot to me! / Spare, woodman, spare the beechen tree. [*The Beech-Tree's Petition*]
2 'Tis distance lends enchantment to the view, / And robes the mountain in its azure hue. [*Pleasures of Hope*]
3 Now Barabbas was a publisher. [attr. Also attr. to Byron]

C8   **Canning, George** (1770–1827) English statesman
1 I called the New World into existence to redress the balance of the Old. [speech, 12 Dec. 1826]

C9   **Carey, Henry** (*d.* 1743) English poet and dramatist
1 God save our Gracious King, / Long live our noble King, / God save the King. / Send him victorious, / Happy and glorious. [*God Save the King*]
2 Confound their politics, / Frustrate their knavish tricks. [*do.*]

C10 **Carlyle, Thomas** (1795–1881) Scottish historian and essayist
1 The three great elements of modern civilization, Gunpowder, Printing, and the Protestant Religion. [*Critical and Miscellaneous Essays*, 'State of German Literature']

2 History is the essence of innumerable biographies. [*do.*, 'On History']

3 Surely, of all 'rights of man', this right of the ignorant man to be guided by the wiser, to be, gently or forcibly, held in the true course by him, is the indisputablest. [*do.*, 'Chartism']

4 Genius (which means transcendent capacity of taking trouble, first of all). [*Frederick the Great*, bk 4, ch. 3]

5 A whiff of grapeshot. [*History of the French Revolution*, I, bk 5, ch. 3]

6 [On Robespierre] The seagreen Incorruptible. [*do.*, II, bk 4, ch. 4]

7 Respectable Professors of the Dismal Science [i.e. Political Economy]. [*Latter-Day Pamphlets*, 1]

8 Captains of industry. [*Past and Present*, bk 4, ch. 4]

9 Man is a tool-using animal . . . Without tools he is nothing, with tools he is all. [*Sartor Resartus*, I, ch. 5]

C11 **Carnegie, Dale** (1888–1955) US writer
1 How to Win Friends and Influence People. [title of book]

C12 **Carroll, Lewis (C. L. Dodgson)** (1832–1908) English mathematician and author
1 'What is the use of a book,' thought Alice, 'without pictures or conversations?' [*Alice's Adventures in Wonderland*, ch. 1]

2 'Curiouser and curiouser!' cried Alice. [*do.*, ch. 2]

3 'You are old, Father William,' the young man said, / 'And your hair has become very white; / And yet you incessantly stand on your head – / Do you think, at your age, it is right?' [*do.*, ch. 5]

4 'I have answered three questions, and that is enough,' / Said his father; 'don't give yourself airs! / Do you think I can listen all day to such stuff! / Be off, or I'll kick you downstairs!' [*do.*]

5 Speak roughly to your little boy, / And beat him when he sneezes; / He only does it to annoy, / Because he knows it teases. [*do.*, ch. 6]

6 This time it [i.e. the Cheshire cat] vanished quite slowly, beginning with the end of the tail, and ending with the grin which remained some time after the rest of it had gone. [*do.*]

7 Twinkle, twinkle, little bat! / How I wonder what you're at! [*do.*, ch. 7]

8 'Off with his head!' [*do.*, ch. 8]

9 Everything's got a moral, if only you can find it. [*do.*, ch. 9]

10 Take care of the sense, and the sounds will take care of themselves. [*do.*]

11 'Will you walk a little faster?' said a whiting to a snail, / 'There's a porpoise close behind us, and he's treading on my tail.' [*do.*, ch. 10]

12 Will you, won't you, will you, won't you, will you join the dance? [*do.*]

13 The Queen of Hearts, she made some tarts, / All on a summer day: / The Knave of Hearts he stole those tarts / And took them quite away! [*do.*, ch. 11]

14 No! No! Sentence first – verdict afterwards. [*do.*]

15 What I tell you three times is true. [*The Hunting of the Snark*, 1]

16 For the Snark *was* a Boojum, you see. [*do.*, 8]

17 He thought he saw an Elephant, / That practised on a fife: / He looked again, and found it was / A letter from his wife. / 'At length I realize,' he said, / 'The bitterness of life!' [*Sylvie and Bruno*, ch. 5]

18 'Twas brillig, and the slithy toves / Did gyre and gimble in the wabe; / All mimsy were the borogoves, / And the mome raths outgrabe. / 'Beware the Jabberwock, my son! / The jaws that bite, the claws that catch!' [*Through the Looking-Glass*, ch. 1]

19 'And hast thou slain the Jabberwock? / Come to my arms, my beamish boy! / O frabjous day! Callooh! Callay!' / He chortled in his joy. [*do.*]

20 Now, *here*, you see, it takes all the running *you* can do, to keep in the same place. If you want to get somewhere else, you must run at least twice as fast as that! [*do.*, ch. 2]

21 Tweedledum and Tweedledee / Agreed to have a battle; / For Tweedledum said Tweedledee / Had spoiled his nice new rattle. [*do.*, ch. 4]

22 The Walrus and the Carpenter / Were walking close at hand; / They wept like anything to see / Such quantities of sand: / 'If this were only cleared away,' / They said, 'it *would* be grand!' [*do.*]

23 'The time has come,' the Walrus said, / 'To talk of many things: / Of shoes – and ships – and sealing-wax – / Of cabbages – and kings – / And why the sea is boiling hot – / And whether pigs have wings.'

[*do.*]
24 'I'm very brave generally,' he went on in a low
voice: 'only today I happen to have a headache.' [*do.*]
25 The rule is, jam tomorrow and jam
yesterday – but never jam today. [*do.*, ch. 5]
26 Why, sometimes I've believed as many as six
impossible things before breakfast. [*do.*]
27 'They gave it me,' Humpty Dumpty continued
thoughtfully, . . . 'for an un-birthday present.' [*do.*]
28 'When *I* use a word,' Humpty Dumpty said in a
rather scornful tone, 'it means just what I choose it to
mean – neither more nor less.' [*do*]
29 It's as large as life, and twice as natural! [*do.*]

C13   **Cato the Elder** (234–149 BC) Roman statesman
1 *Delenda est Carthago.* Carthage must be destroyed.
[cited in Pliny, *Natural History*]

C14   **Catullus, Gaius Valerius** (84?–54 BC) Roman poet
1 *Vivamus, mea Lesbia, atque amemus.* Let us live,
my Lesbia, and love. [*Carmina*, 5]
2 *Sed mulier cupido quod dicit amanti, / In vento et
rapida scribere oportet aqua.* But what a woman says to
her eager lover should be written in wind and rushing
water. [*do.*, 70]
3 *Odi et amo: quare id faciam, fortasse
requiris. / Nescio, sed fieri sentio et excrucior.* I hate
and love; perhaps you will ask why I do so. I do not
know, but I feel it happen and I am in agony. [*do.*,
85]
4 *Atque in perpetuum, frater, ave atque vale.* And for
ever, brother, hail and farewell! [*do.*, 101]

C15   **Cavell, Edith** (1865–1915) English nurse
1 I realize that patriotism is not enough. I must have
no hatred or bitterness towards anyone. [remark on
the eve of her execution]

C16   **Cervantes, Miguel de** (1547–1616) Spanish author
1 There are only two families in the world, my old
grandmother used to say, The *Haves* and the *Have-
Nots*. [*Don Quixote*, pt II, ch. 20]
2 Tell me what company you keep and I will tell you
who you are. [*do.*, ch. 23]

C17   **Chamberlain, Neville** (1869–1940)
English statesman
1 In war, whichever side may call itself the victor,

there are no winners, but all are losers. [speech at Kettering, 3 July 1938]
2 I believe it is peace for our time ... peace with honour. [remark after the Munich Agreement, 30 Sept. 1938]
3 Hitler has missed the bus. [speech, 4 Apr. 1940]

C18 **Charles II** (1630–85) King of Great Britain
1 He had been, he said, a most unconscionable time dying; but he hoped that they would excuse it. [Macaulay, *History of England*, I, ch. 4]
2 Let not poor Nelly [i.e. Nell Gwyn] starve. [remark shortly before his death]

C19 **Charles, Prince of Wales** (1948–)
1 The monarchy is the oldest profession in the world. [remark]

C20 **Charles V** (1500–58) Holy Roman Emperor
1 I speak Spanish to God, Italian to women, French to men, and German to my horse. [attr.]

C21 **Chaucer, Geoffrey** (1340?–1400) English poet
1 Whan that Aprill with his shoures soote / The droghte of March hath perced to the roote. [*The Canterbury Tales*, 'Prologue']
2 He was a verray, parfit gentil knyght. [*do.*]
3 Sownynge in moral vertu was his speche, / And gladly wolde he lerne and gladly teche. [*do.*]
4 Nowher so bisy a man as he ther nas, / And yet he semed bisier than he was. [*do.*]
5 She was a worthy womman al hir lyve: / Housbondes at chirche-dore she hadde fyve, / Withouten oother compaignye in youthe. [*do.*]
6 The smylere with the knyf under the cloke. [*do.*, 'The Knight's Tale']
7 This world nis but a thurghfare ful of wo, / And we ben pilgrimes, passinge to and fro; / Deeth is an ende of every worldly sore. [*do.*]
8 Mordre wol out, that se we day by day. [*do.*, 'The Nun's Priest's Tale']

C22 **Chesterfield, 4th Earl of** (1694–1773)
English statesman and author
1 Be wiser than other people if you can, but do not tell them so. [letter to his son, 19 Nov. 1745]
2 Whatever is worth doing at all is worth doing well. [*do.*, 10 Mar. 1746]

3 Do as you would be done by is the surest method that I know of pleasing. [*do.*, 16 Oct. 1747]

4 I recommend you to take care of the minutes: for hours will take care of themselves. [*do.*, 6 Nov. 1747]

5 A chapter of accidents. [*do.*, 16 Feb. 1753]

C23 **Chesterton, G. K.** (1874–1936) English author

1 The strangest whim has seized me . . . After all / I think I will not hang myself today. [*A Ballade of Suicide*]

2 When fishes flew and forests walked / And figs grew upon thorn, / Some moment when the moon was blood / Then surely I was born. /
With monstrous head and sickening cry / And ears like errant wings, / The devil's walking parody / On all four-footed things. [*The Donkey*]

3 Fools! For I also had my hour; / One far fierce hour and sweet: / There was a shout about my ears, / And palms before my feet. [*do.*]

4 There is no such thing on earth as an uninteresting subject; the only thing that can exist is an uninterested person. [*Heretics*, ch. 1]

5 The artistic temperament is a disease that afflicts amateurs. [*do.*, ch. 17]

6 White founts falling in the courts of the sun, / And the Soldan of Byzantium is smiling as they run. [*Lepanto*]

7 Strong gongs groaning as the guns boom far, / Don John of Austria is going to the war. [*do.*]

8 The human race, to which so many of my readers belong. [*The Napoleon of Notting Hill*, ch. 1]

9 Before the Roman came to Rye or out to Severn strode, / The rolling English drunkard made the rolling English road. [*The Rolling English Road*]

10 The night we went to Birmingham by way of Beachy Head. [*do.*]

11 For there is good news yet to hear and fine things to be seen, / Before we go to Paradise by way of Kensal Green. [*do.*]

12 If a thing is worth doing it is worth doing badly. [*What's Wrong with the World*]

13 And Noah he often said to his wife when he sat down to dine, / 'I don't care where the water goes if it doesn't get into the wine.' [*Wine and Water*]

C24 **Churchill, Lord Randolph** (1849–95)

English statesman
1 Ulster will fight; Ulster will be right.
[letter, 7 May 1886]

C25   **Churchill, Sir Winston** (1874–1965)
English statesman
1 It cannot in the opinion of His Majesty's Government be classified as slavery in the extreme acceptance of the word without some risk of terminological inexactitude. [speech in House of Commons, 22 Feb. 1906]
2 The maxim of the British people is 'Business as usual'. [speech in the Guildhall, 9 Nov. 1914]
3 I cannot forecast to you the action of Russia. It is a riddle wrapped in a mystery inside an enigma. [broadcast, 1 Oct. 1939]
4 I have nothing to offer but blood, toil, tears and sweat. [speech in House of Commons, 13 May 1940]
5 Victory at all costs, victory in spite of all terror, victory however long and hard the road may be; for without victory there is no survival. [*do.*]
6 We shall not flag or fail. We shall fight in France, we shall fight on the seas and oceans, we shall fight with growing confidence and growing strength in the air, we shall defend our island, whatever the cost may be, we shall fight on the beaches, we shall fight on the landing grounds, we shall fight in the fields and in the streets, we shall fight in the hills; we shall never surrender. [*do.*, 4 June 1940]
7 Let us therefore brace ourselves to our duties and so bear ourselves that if the British Empire and its Commonwealth last for a thousand years men will still say, 'This was their finest hour'. [*do.*, 18 June 1940]
8 The battle of Britain is about to begin. [*do.*, 1 July 1940]
9 Never in the field of human conflict was so much owed by so many to so few. [*do.*, 20 Aug. 1940]
10 Give us the tools, and we will finish the job. [broadcast, 9 Feb. 1941]
11 When I warned them [i.e. the French government] that Britain would fight on alone whatever they did, their Generals told their Prime Minister and his divided Cabinet: 'In three weeks England will have her neck wrung like a chicken'. Some chicken! Some neck! [speech to the Canadian

Parliament, 30 Dec. 1941]

12 [Of the Battle of Egypt] This is not the end. It is not even the beginning of the end. But it is, perhaps, the end of the beginning. [speech at the Mansion House, 10 Nov. 1942]

13 I have not become the King's First Minister in order to preside over the liquidation of the British Empire. [*do.*]

14 There is no finer investment for any community than putting milk into babies. [broadcast, 21 Mar. 1943]

15 An iron curtain has descended across the Continent. [address at Westminster College, Fulton, USA, 5 Mar. 1946]

16 Many forms of government have been tried, and will be tried in this world of sin and woe. No one pretends that democracy is perfect or all-wise. Indeed, it has been said that democracy is the worst form of Government except all those other forms that have been tried from time to time. [speech in House of Commons, 11 Nov. 1947]

17 To jaw-jaw is better than to war-war. [speech in Washington, 26 June 1954]

18 Before Alamein we never had a victory. After Alamein we never had a defeat. [*The Hinge of Fate*, ch. 33]

19 This is the sort of English up with which I will not put. [attr. comment on pedantic avoidance of prepositions at the end of sentences]

20 And you, madam, are ugly. But I shall be sober in the morning. [attr. retort to a woman MP who accused him of being drunk]

21 [On Clement Attlee] He is a modest little man with much to be modest about. [attr.]

22 [On Viscount Montgomery] In defeat unbeatable; in victory unbearable. [attr.]

C26   **Cicero, Marcus Tullius** (106–43 BC)
Roman statesman and orator
1 *Salus populi suprema est lex.* The good of the people is the chief law. [*De Legibus*, III]
2 *Summum bonum.* The greatest good. [*De Officiis*, I]
3 *Cedant arma togae, concedant laurea laudi.* Let war give way to peace, laurels to praise. [*do.*]
4 *O tempora! O mores!* What times! What customs! [*In Catilinam*, I]

5 *Civis Romanus sum.* I am a Roman citizen.
[*In Verrem*, V]
6 *Cui bono.* To whose profit. [*Pro Milone*, XII]

C27 **Clare, John** (1793– 1864) English poet
1 He could not die when the trees were green, / For he loved the time too well. [*The Dying Child*]
2 Untroubling and untroubled where I lie / The grass below, above, the vaulted sky. [*I Am*]

C28 **Clive, Lord** (1725–74) English general
1 By God, Mr. Chairman, at this moment I stand astonished at my own moderation! [reply during Parliamentary inquiry, 1773]

C29 **Clough, Arthur Hugh** (1819–61) English poet
1 Thou shalt have one God only; who / Would be at the expense of two? [*The Latest Decalogue*]
2 Thou shalt not kill; but needst not strive / Officiously to keep alive. [*do.*]
3 Thou shalt not covet; but tradition / Approves all forms of competition. [*do.*]
4 Say not the struggle naught availeth, / The labour and the wounds are vain. [*Say Not the Struggle Naught Availeth*]
5 In front the sun climbs slow, how slowly, / But westward, look, the land is bright. [*do.*]

C30 **Cobbett, William** (1762–1835)
English political author
1 But what is to be the fate of the great wen of all [i.e. London]? [*Rural Rides*]

C31 **Coke, Sir Edward** (1552–1634) English jurist
1 A man's house is his castle. [*Institutes*, III]

C32 **Coleridge, Samuel Taylor** (1772–1834)
English poet
1 That willing suspension of disbelief for the moment, which constitutes poetic faith. [*Biographia Literaria*, ch. 14]
2 A sight to dream of, not to tell! [*Christabel*, I]
3 I see them all so excellently fair, / I see, not feel, how beautiful they are! [*Dejection*]
4 I may not hope from outward forms to win / The passion and the life, whose fountains are within. [*do.*]
5 We receive but what we give, / And in our life alone does Nature live. [*do.*]

6 At this moment he was unfortunately called out by a person on business from Porlock. [prefatory note to *Kubla Khan*]

7 In Xanadu did Kubla Khan / A stately pleasure-dome decree: / Where Alph, the sacred river, ran / Through caverns measureless to man / Down to a sunless sea. [*Kubla Khan*]

8 A damsel with a dulcimer / In a vision once I saw: / It was an Abyssinian maid, / And on her dulcimer she played, / Singing of Mount Abora. [*do.*]

9 Weave a circle round him thrice, / And close your eyes with holy dread, / For he on honey-dew hath fed, / And drunk the milk of Paradise. [*do.*]

10 It is an ancient Mariner, / And he stoppeth one of three. / 'By thy long grey beard and glittering eye, / Now wherefore stopp'st thou me?' [*The Rime of the Ancient Mariner*, I]

11 'God save thee, ancient Mariner! / From the fiends that plague thee thus! − / Why look'st thou so?' − With my cross-bow / I shot the Albatross. [*do.*]

12 We were the first that ever burst / Into that silent sea. [*do.*, II]

13 As idle as a painted ship / Upon a painted ocean. [*do.*]

14 Water, water, every where, / And all the boards did shrink; / Water, water, every where, / Nor any drop to drink. [*do.*]

15 Alone, alone, all, all alone / Alone on a wide wide sea! / And never a saint took pity on / My soul in agony. [*do.*, IV]

16 The many men, so beautiful! / And they all dead did lie: / And a thousand thousand slimy things / Lived on; and so did I. [*do.*]

17 The moving Moon went up the sky, / And no where did abide: / Softly she was going up, / And a star or two beside. [*do.*]

18 Oh sleep! it is a gentle thing / Beloved from pole to pole! [*do.*, V]

19 Like one, that on a lonesome road / Doth walk in fear and dread, / And having once turned round walks on, / And turns no more his head; / Because he knows, a frightful fiend / Doth close behind him tread. [*do.*, VI]

20 He prayeth well, who loveth well / Both man and bird and beast. [*do.*, VII]

21 He prayeth best, who loveth best / All things both great and small; / For the dear God who loveth us, / He made and loveth all. [*do.*]

22 A sadder and a wiser man, / He rose the morrow morn. [*do.*]

C33 **Colton, Charles Caleb** (1780?–1832) English author
1 Examinations are formidable even to the best prepared, for the greatest fool may ask more than the wisest man can answer. [*Lacon*, II]

C34 **Confucius (K'ung Futzu)** (*ab* 551–479 BC) Chinese philosopher
1 Men's natures are alike; it is their habits that carry them far apart. [*Analects*]
2 Learning without thought is labour lost; thought without learning is perilous. [*do.*]

C35 **Congreve, William** (1670–1729) English dramatist
1 Music has charms to soothe a savage breast. [*The Mourning Bride*, I.1]
2 Heaven has no rage like love to hatred turned, / Nor hell a fury like a woman scorned. [*do.*, III. 8]

C36 **Connell, James M.** (1852–1929) English socialist
1 Then raise the scarlet standard high! / Beneath its shade we'll live and die! / Though cowards flinch, and traitors jeer, / We'll keep the Red Flag flying here! [*The Red Flag*]

C37 **Connolly, Cyril** (1903–74) English author
1 It is closing time in the gardens of the West. [*The Condemned Playground*]
2 Literature is the art of writing something that will be read twice; journalism what will be grasped at once. [*Enemies of Promise*]
3 Whom the gods wish to destroy they first call promising. [*do.*]
4 Imprisoned in every fat man a thin one is wildly signalling to be let out. [*The Unquiet Grave*]

C38 **Conrad, Joseph** (1857–1924) British novelist
1 The conquest of the earth, which mostly means the taking it away from those who have a different complexion or slightly flatter noses than ourselves, is not a pretty thing when you look into it too much. [*The Heart of Darkness*, ch. 1]

2 Exterminate all brutes. [*do.*, ch. 2]
3 The horror! The horror! [*do.*, ch. 3]
4 Mistah Kurtz – he dead. [*do.*]

C39 Coolidge, Calvin (1872–1933) US president
1 There is no right to strike against the public safety by anybody, anywhere, any time. [remark on the Boston police strike, 14 Sept. 1919]
2 He said he was against it. [remark when asked what a clergyman had said in a sermon on sin]

C40 Cooper, James Fenimore (1789–1851) US novelist
1 The Last of the Mohicans. [title of novel]

C41 Cornuel, Madame (1605–94)
1 No man is a hero to his valet. [*Lettres de Mlle Aissé*, 13 Aug. 1728]

C42 Cory, William (1823–92)
English schoolmaster and poet
1 Jolly boating weather, / And a hay harvest breeze, / Blade on the feather, / Shade off the trees / Swing, swing together / With your body between your knees. [*The Eton Boating Song*]
2 They told me, Heraclitus, they told me you were dead, / They brought me bitter news to hear, and bitter tears to shed. / I wept as I remembered how often you and I / Had tired the sun with talking and sent him down the sky. [*Heraclitus*]

C43 Coubertin, Baron Pierre de (1863–1937)
French instigator of the Olympic Games
1 The most important thing in the Olympic Games is not winning but taking part ... The essential thing in life is not conquering but fighting well. [speech to officials of the Olympic Games, London, 24 July 1908]

C44 Coué, Émile (1857–1926) French psychotherapist
1 *Tous les jours, à tous points de vue, je vais de mieux en mieux.* Every day, in every way, I am getting better and better. [formula for cure by auto-suggestion]

C45 Cousin, Victor (1792–1867) French philosopher
1 *Il faut de la religion pour la religion, de la morale pour la morale, de l'art pour l'art.* We must have religion for religion's sake, morality for morality's sake, art for art's sake. [*Cours de philosophie*]

C46   **Coward, Noël** (1899–1973)
English dramatist and songwriter
1 Very flat, Norfolk. [*Private Lives*, I]
2 Extraordinary how potent cheap music is. [*do.*]
3 The Stately Homes of England / How beautiful
they stand, / To prove the upper classes / Have still
the upper hand. [*The Stately Homes of England*.
Compare **H18.2**]
4 Don't let's be beastly to the Germans. [title of
song]
5 Don't put your daughter on the stage, Mrs
Worthington. [title of song]
6 Mad dogs and Englishmen go out in the mid-day
sun. [title of song]
7 Poor Little Rich Girl. [title of song]

C47   **Cowley, Abraham** (1618–67) English poet
1 God the first garden made, and the first city Cain.
[*The Garden*]

C48   **Cowper, William** (1731–1800) English poet
1 God moves in a mysterious way / His wonders to
perform. [*Olney Hymns*, 35]
2 God made the country, and man made the town.
[*The Task*, I]
3 England, with all thy faults I love thee still, / My
country! [*do.*, II]
4 Variety's the very spice of life, / That gives it all
its flavour. [*do.*]
5 While the bubbling and loud-hissing urn / Throws
up a steamy column, and the cups / That cheer but
not inebriate, wait on each, / So let us welcome
peaceful evening in. [*do.*, IV]
6 I am monarch of all I survey, / My right there is
none to dispute. [*Verses Supposed to be Written by
Alexander Selkirk*]

C49   **Crane, Stephen** (1871–1900) US author
1 The Red Badge of Courage. [title of novel]

C50   **Cranmer, Thomas** (1489–1556) English prelate
1 This hand hath offended. [attr. remark at the stake,
on the hand with which he had signed a recantation]

C51   **Crashaw, Richard** (1612?–49) English poet
1 Love, thou art absolute sole Lord / Of life and
death. [*Hymn to . . . Saint Teresa*]

C52 **Cromwell, Oliver** (1599–1658)
English general and statesman
1 I beseech you, in the bowels of Christ, think it possible you may be mistaken. [letter to the General Assembly of the Church of Scotland, 3 Aug. 1650]
2 What shall we do with this bauble [i.e. the mace]? There, take it away. [remark on dismissing the Rump Parliament, 20 Apr. 1653]
3 You have sat too long here for any good you have been doing. Depart, I say, and let us have done with you. In the name of God, go! [*do.*]
4 Necessity hath no law. [speech to Parliament, 12 Sept. 1654]
5 Mr. Lely, I desire you would use all your skill to paint my picture truly like me, and not flatter me at all; but remark all these roughnesses, pimples, warts, and everything as you see me. [remark. Often quoted as '. . . warts and all']
6 Put your trust in God, and keep your powder dry. [attr. advice to his troops]

C53 **cummings, e. e.** (1894–1962) US poet
1 anyone lived in a pretty how town / (with up so floating many bells down) [*anyone lived in a pretty how town*]
2 a politician is an arse upon / which everyone has sat except a man. [*a politician*]

C54 **Curran, John Philpot** (1750–1817) Irish orator
1 The condition upon which God hath given liberty to man is eternal vigilance.
[speech in Dublin, 10 July 1790]

D1 **Dana, Charles A.** (1819–97) US newspaper editor
1 When a dog bites a man that is not news, but when a man bites a dog, that is news. [attr. Also attr. to J. B. Bogart (1845–1921)]

D2 **Dante** (1265–1321) Italian poet
1 *Nel mezzo del cammin di nostra vita / Mi ritrovai per una selva oscura.* In the middle of the road of our life I found myself in a dark wood. [*Divina*

Commedia: Inferno, I]
2 *Lasciate ogni speranza voi ch'entrate!* All hope
abandon, ye who enter here! [*do.*, III]
3 *E'n la sua volontade è nostra pace.* In His will is our
peace. [*do.: Paradiso*, III]
4 *L'amor che muove il sole e l'altre stelle.* Love that
moves the sun and the other stars. [*do.*, XXXIII]

D3 **Darwin, Charles** (1809–82) English naturalist
1 We must, however, acknowledge, as it seems to me,
that man with all his noble qualities . . . still bears in
his bodily frame the indelible stamp of his lowly
origin. [*The Descent of Man*, closing words]
2 I have called this principle, by which each slight
variation, if useful, is preserved, by the term of
Natural Selection. [*The Origin of Species*, ch. 3]
3 The expression often used by Mr Herbert Spencer
of the Survival of the Fittest is more accurate, and is
sometimes equally convenient. [*do.*]

D4 **Davies, W. H.** (1871–1940) Welsh poet
1 What is this life if, full of care, / We have no time
to stand and stare? [*Leisure*]

D5 **Day-Lewis, Cecil** (1904–72) English poet
1 It is the logic of our times, / No subject for
immortal verse – / That we who lived by honest
dreams / Defend the bad against the worse. [*Where
are the War Poets?*]

D6 **Decatur, Stephen** (1779–1820) US naval officer
1 Our country! In her intercourse with foreign
nations, may she always be in the right; but our
country, right or wrong. [toast given at Norfolk,
Virginia, Apr. 1816]

D7 **Defoe, Daniel** (1660?–1731) English author
1 If my own watch goes false, it deceives me and
none else; but if the town clock goes false, it deceives
the whole parish. [*The Poor Man's Plea*]

D8 **Dekker, Thomas** (1572?–1632?) English dramatist
1 Golden slumbers kiss your eyes, / Smiles awake
you when you rise. [*Patient Grissil*, IV. 2]

D9 **de la Mare, Walter** (1873–1956) English poet
1 Oh, no man knows / Through what wild
centuries / Roves back the rose. [*All That's Past*]
2 Look thy last on all things lovely, / Every hour.

[*Fare Well*]

3 'Is there anybody there?' said the traveller, /
Knocking on the moonlit door. [*The Listeners*]

4 'Tell them I came, and no one answered, / That I
kept my word,' he said. [*do.*]

5 Slowly, silently, now the moon / Walks the night
in her silver shoon. [*Silver*]

D10 **Dennis, John** (1657–1734)
English critic and dramatist
1 A man who could make so vile a pun would not
scruple to pick a pocket. [*The Gentleman's Magazine*,
1781]

D11 **De Quincey, Thomas** (1785–1859) English author
1 Certainly it is most absurdly said, in popular
language, of any man, that he is *disguised* in liquor;
for, on the contrary, most men are disguised by
sobriety; and it is when they are drinking . . . that
men display themselves in their true complexion of
character. [*Confessions of an English Opium-Eater*,
'The Pleasures of Opium']
2 On Murder considered as one of the Fine Arts.
[title of essay]

D12 **Descartes, René** (1596–1650)
French mathematician and philosopher
1 *Cogito, ergo sum.* I think, therefore I am.
[*Le Discours de la Méthode (Discourse on Method)*]

D13 **Dickens, Charles** (1812–70) English novelist
1 'There are strings,' said Mr Tappertit, '. . . in the
human heart that had better not be wibrated.'
[*Barnaby Rudge*, ch. 22]
2 Jarndyce and Jarndyce still drags its dreary length
before the Court, perennially hopeless. [*Bleak
House*, ch. 1]
3 This is a London particular . . . A fog, miss. [*do.*,
ch. 3]
4 It is a melancholy truth that even great men have
their poor relations. [*do.*, ch. 28]
5 'God bless us every one!' said Tiny Tim, the last of
all. [*A Christmas Carol*]
6 'I am a lone lorn creetur,' were Mrs Gummidge's
words . . . 'and everythink goes contrairy with me.'
[*David Copperfield*, ch. 3]
7 Barkis is willin'. [*do.*, ch. 5]

8 'In case anything turned up,' which was his [i.e. Mr Micawber's] favourite expression. [*do.*, ch. 11]

9 MICAWBER. Annual income twenty pounds, annual expenditure nineteen nineteen six, result happiness. Annual income twenty pounds, annual expenditure twenty pounds ought and six, result misery.
[*do.*, ch. 12]

10 URIAH HEEP. We are so very 'umble. [*do.*, ch. 17]

11 MICAWBER. Accidents will occur in the best-regulated families. [*do.*, ch. 28]

12 MR PEGGOTTY. I'm Gormed – and I can't say no fairer than that! [*do.*, ch. 63]

13 CAPTAIN CUTTLE. When found, make a note of. [*Dombey and Son*, ch. 15]

14 GRADGRIND. Now, what I want is, Facts . . . Facts alone are wanted in life. [*Hard Times*, bk I, ch. 1]

15 Whatever was required to be done, the Circumlocution Office was beforehand with all the public departments in the art of perceiving – HOW NOT TO DO IT. [*Little Dorrit*, bk I, ch. 10]

16 MR PECKSNIFF. Let us be moral. Let us contemplate existence. [*Martin Chuzzlewit*, ch. 9]

17 JONAS CHUZZLEWIT. Here's the rule for bargains: 'Do other men, for they would do you.' That's the true business precept. [*do.*, ch. 11]

18 MRS GAMP. He'd make a lovely corpse. [*do.*, ch. 25]

19 He [i.e. Mr Squeers] had but one eye, and the popular prejudice runs in favour of two. [*Nicholas Nickleby*, ch. 4]

20 GENTLEMAN IN THE SMALLCLOTHES. All is gas and gaiters. [*do.*, ch. 49]

21 DICK SWIVELLER. Fan the sinking flame of hilarity with the wing of friendship; and pass the rosy wine. [*The Old Curiosity Shop*, ch. 7]

22 MR BUMBLE. Oliver Twist has asked for more! [*Oliver Twist*, ch. 2]

23 Known by the *sobriquet* of 'The artful Dodger'. [*do.*, ch. 8]

24 'If the law supposes that,' said Mr Bumble . . . 'the law is a ass – a idiot.' [*do.*, ch. 51]

25 The question [for Mr Podsnap] about everything was, would it bring a blush into the cheek of the young person? [*Our Mutual Friend*, bk I, ch. 11]

26 MR PODSNAP. There is in the Englishman a combination of qualities, a modesty, an independence, a responsibility, a repose, combined with an absence of everything calculated to call a blush into the cheek of a young person, which one would seek in vain among the Nations of the Earth. [*do.*]

27 MR TWEMLOW. I think . . . that it [i.e. the House of Commons] is the best club in London. [*do.*, bk II, ch. 3]

28 He had used the word in its Pickwickian sense. [*Pickwick Papers*, ch. 1]

29 JINGLE. Kent, sir – everybody knows Kent – apples, cherries, hops, and women. [*do.*, ch. 2]

30 JOE, THE FAT BOY. I wants to make your flesh creep. [*do.*, ch. 8]

31 'It's always best on these occasions to do what the mob do.' 'But suppose there are two mobs?' suggested Mr Snodgrass. 'Shout with the largest,' replied Mr Pickwick. [*do.*, ch. 13]

32 SAM WELLER. Wery glad to see you indeed, and hope our acquaintance may be a long 'un, as the gen'l'm'n said to the fi' pun' note. [*do.*, ch. 25]

33 MR WELLER. Wen you're a married man, Samivel, you'll understand a good many things as you don't understand now; but vether it's worth while goin' through so much to learn so little, as the charity-boy said ven he got to the end of the alphabet, is a matter o' taste. [*do.*, ch. 27]

34 MR WELLER. Poetry's unnat'ral; no man ever talked poetry 'cept a beadle on boxin' day. [*do.*, ch. 33]

35 STIGGINS. It's my opinion, sir, that this meeting is drunk, sir! [*do.*]

36 SAM WELLER. Anythin' for a quiet life, as the man said wen he took the sitivation at the lighthouse. [*do.*, ch. 43]

37 It was the best of times, it was the worst of times, it was the age of wisdom, it was the age of foolishness, it was the epoch of belief, it was the epoch of incredulity, it was the season of Light, it was the season of Darkness, it was the spring of hope, it was the winter of despair. [*A Tale of Two Cities*, bk I, ch. 1]

38 SYDNEY CARTON. It is a far, far better thing that I do, than I have ever done; it is a far, far better rest that I go to, than I have ever known. [*do.*, bk III, ch. 15]

D14 **Dickinson, Emily** (1830–86) US poet
1 'Hope' is the thing with feathers – / That perches in the soul – / And sings the tune without the words – / And never stops – at all – ['*Hope' Is the Thing with Feathers*]
2 I heard a fly buzz – when I died. [*I Heard a Fly Buzz*]
3 With blue – uncertain stumbling buzz – / Between the light – and me – / And then the windows failed – and then / I could not see to see. [*do.*]
4 My life closed twice before its close – / It yet remains to see / If Immortality unveil / A third event to me /
So huge, so hopeless to conceive / As these that twice befell. / Parting is all we know of heaven, / And all we need of hell. [*My Life Closed Twice*]
5 Our lives are Swiss – / So still – so cool – / Till some odd afternoon / The Alps neglect their curtains / And we look farther on! [*Our Lives Are Swiss*]
6 Success is counted sweetest / By those who ne'er succeed. [*Success Is Counted Sweetest*]

D15 **Diderot, Denis** (1713–84) French author
1 *L'esprit de l'escalier.* Staircase wit (i.e. the witty remark one thinks of only when it is too late). [*Paradoxe sur le comédien*]

D16 **Diogenes** (412?–323 BC) Greek philosopher
1 Stand a little less between me and the sun. [remark when asked by Alexander whether he wanted anything. Plutarch, *Life of Alexander*]

D17 **Disraeli, Benjamin** (1804–81)
English statesman and author
1 Though I sit down now, the time will come when you will hear me. [maiden speech in House of Commons, 7 Dec. 1837]
2 A Conservative government is an organised hypocrisy. [speech in House of Commons, 17 Mar. 1845]
3 The question is this: Is man an ape or an angel? Now I am on the side of the angels. [speech, 25 Nov. 1864]
4 Lord Salisbury and myself have brought you back peace – but a peace I hope with honour. [speech in

House of Commons, 16 July 1878]

5 Youth is a blunder; Manhood a struggle; Old Age a regret. [*Coningsby*, bk III, ch. 1]

6 His Christianity was muscular. [*Endymion*, ch. 14]

7 I was told that the Privileged and the People formed Two Nations. [*Sybil*, bk IV, ch. 8]

8 There are three kinds of lies: lies, damned lies, and statistics. [attr.]

D18   **Dobson, Austin** (1840–1921) English poet

1 Time goes, you say? Ah no! / Alas, Time stays, *we* go. [*The Paradox of Time*]

D19   **Donne, John** (1572?–1631) English poet

1 And new Philosophy calls all in doubt, / The Element of fire is quite put out; / The Sun is lost, and th' earth, and no man's wit / Can well direct him where to look for it. [*An Anatomy of the World (The First Anniversary)*]

2 Come live with me, and be my love, / And we will some new pleasures prove / Of golden sands, and crystal brooks, / With silken lines, and silver hooks. [*The Bait*]

3 For God's sake hold your tongue, and let me love. [*The Canonization*]

4 But I do nothing upon myself, and yet I am mine own Executioner. [*Devotions*, 'Meditation 12']

5 No man is an *Island*, entire of it self; every man is a piece of the *Continent*, a part of the *main*; if a *clod* be washed away by the *sea*, *Europe* is the less, as well as if a *promontory* were, as well as if a *manor* of thy *friends* or of *thine own* were; any man's *death* diminishes *me*, because I am involved in *Mankind*; And therefore never send to know for whom the *bell* tolls; It tolls for *thee*. [*do.*, 'Meditation 17']

6 Licence my roving hands, and let them go, / Before, behind, between, above, below. / O my America! my new-found-land, / My kingdom, safeliest when with one man mann'd. [*Elegies*, 19, 'To His Mistress Going To Bed']

7 So, so, break off this last lamenting kiss, / Which sucks two souls, and vapours both away, / Turn thou ghost that way, and let me turn this, / And let our selves benight our happiest day. [*The Expiration*]

8 But O alas, so long, so far / Our bodies why do we forbear? / They're ours, though they're not we, we

are / The intelligences, they the sphere. [*The Extasie*]
9 So must pure lovers' souls descend / T'affections, and to faculties, / Which sense may reach and apprehend, / Else a great Prince in prison lies. [*do.*]
10 I wonder by my troth, what thou, and I / Did, till we lov'd? were we not wean'd till then? / But suck'd on country pleasures, childishly? / Or snorted we in the Seven Sleepers' den? [*The Good-Morrow*]
11 At the round earth's imagined corners, blow / Your trumpets, Angels, and arise, arise / From death, you numberless infinities / Of souls, and to your scattered bodies go. [*Holy Sonnets*, 7]
12 Death be not proud, though some have called thee / Mighty and dreadful, for, thou art not so. [*do.*, 10]
13 One short sleep past, we wake eternally, / And death shall be no more; death, thou shalt die. [*do.*]
14 Go, and catch a falling star, / Get with child a mandrake root, / Tell me, where all past years are, / Or who cleft the Devil's foot. [*Song: Go and Catch a Falling Star*]
15 Busy old fool, unruly Sun, / Why does thou thus, / Through windows and through curtains call on us? [*The Sun Rising*]

D20 **Douglas, Lord Alfred** (1870–1945) English author
1 I am the Love that dare not speak its name. [*Two Loves*]

D21 **Dowson, Ernest** (1867–1900) English poet
1 I have forgot much, Cynara! gone with the wind, / Flung roses, roses riotously with the throng. [*Non Sum Qualis Eram*]
2 I have been faithful to thee, Cynara! in my fashion. [*do.*]
3 They are not long, the days of wine and roses: / Out of a misty dream / Our path emerges for a while, then closes / Within a dream. [*Vitae Summa Brevis*]

D22 **Doyle, Sir Arthur Conan** (1859–1930)
British physician and author
1 It has long been an axiom of mine that the little things are infinitely the most important. [*The Adventures of Sherlock Holmes*, 'A Case of Identity']
2 It is my belief, Watson, founded upon my

experience, that the lowest and vilest alleys of London do not present a more dreadful record of sin than does the smiling and beautiful countryside. [*do.*, 'The Copper Beeches']

3 It is quite a three-pipe problem. [*do.*, 'The Red-Headed League']

4 You know my methods, Watson. [*The Memoirs of Sherlock Holmes*, 'The Crooked Man']

5 'Excellent!' I [Dr Watson] cried. 'Elementary,' said he [Holmes]. [*do.*]

6 He [i.e. Professor Moriarty] is the Napoleon of crime. [*do.*, 'The Final Problem']

7 'Is there any other point to which you would wish to draw my attention?' 'To the curious incident of the dog in the night-time.' 'The dog did nothing in the night-time.' 'That was the curious incident,' remarked Sherlock Holmes. [*do.*, 'Silver Blaze']

D23   **Drake, Sir Francis** (1540?–96)
English navigator and admiral

1 I have singed the Spanish king's beard. [remark on the expedition to Cadiz, 1587]

2 There is plenty of time to win this game, and to thrash the Spaniards too. [remark on the Armada being sighted while he was playing bowls, 1588]

D24   **Drayton, Michael** (1563–1631) English poet

1 Fair stood the wind for France / When we our sails advance. [*Agincourt*]

2 Since there's no help, come let us kiss and part – / Nay, I have done, you get no more of me; / And I am glad, yea glad with all my heart / That thus so cleanly I myself can free. [*Sonnets*, 61]

D25   **Dryden, John** (1631–1700)
English poet and dramatist

1 In pious times, e'r Priest-craft did begin, / Before Polygamy was made a Sin. [*Absalom and Achitophel*, I]

2 What e'r he did was done with so much ease, / In him alone, 'twas Natural to please. [*do.*]

3 Great Wits are sure to Madness near alli'd / And thin Partitions do their Bounds divide. [*do.*]

4 But far more numerous was the Herd of such, / Who think too little, and who talk too much. [*do.*]

5 A man so various, that he seem'd to be / Not one,

but all Mankind's Epitome. / Stiff in Opinions, always in the wrong; / Was Everything by starts, and Nothing long: / But, in the course of one revolving Moon, / Was Chymist, Fiddler, States-man, and Buffoon. [*do.*]
6 Nor is the Peoples Judgment always true: / The Most may err as grosly as the Few. [*do.*]
7 None but the Brave deserves the Fair. [*Alexander's Feast*]
8 All humane things are subject to decay, / And, when Fate summons, Monarchs must obey. [*Mac Flecknoe*]
9 The rest to some faint meaning make pretence, / But Shadwell never deviates into sense. [*do.*]
10 Happy the Man, and happy he alone, / He who can call to-day his own: / He who, secure within, can say, / Tomorrow do thy worst, for I have liv'd today. [translation of Horace]

D26 **Dubček, Alexander** (1921–) Czech politician
1 Communism with a human face. [attr.]

D27 **Du Deffand, Madame** (1697–1780)
French noblewoman
1 *La distance n'y fait rien; il n'y a que le premier pas qui coûte.* The distance is nothing; it's only the first step which is difficult. [on the legend that St Denis walked two leagues, carrying his head in his hands. Letter to d'Alembert, 7 July 1763]

D28 **Dumas, Alexandre** (1802–70) French author
1 All for one, and one for all. [*The Three Musketeers*]

D29 **Dunning, John, Baron Ashburton** (1731–83)
English lawyer and politician
1 The influence of the Crown has increased, is increasing, and ought to be diminished. [motion passed by the House of Commons, 1780]

D30 **Dyer, Sir Edward** (*d.* 1607)
English poet and courtier
1 My mind to me a kingdom is, / Such present joys therein I find, / That it excels all other bliss / That earth affords or grows by kind. [*My Mind to Me a Kingdom Is*]

D31 **Dylan, Bob** (1941–) US singer and songwriter
1 How many roads must a man walk down / Before

you can call him a man? [*Blowin' in the Wind*]
2 The answer, my friend, is blowin' in the
wind, / The answer is blowin' in the wind. [*do.*]
3 A Hard Rain's A-Gonna Fall. [title of song]
4 The Times They Are A-Changin'. [title of song]

E1   **Eden, Sir Anthony, Earl of Avon** (1897–1977)
English statesman
1 We are not at war with Egypt. We are in an armed
conflict. [speech in House of Commons, 4 Nov. 1956]

E2   **Edison, Thomas Alva** (1847–1931) US inventor
1 Genius is one per cent inspiration and ninety-nine
per cent perspiration. [newspaper interview]

E3   **Edward III** (1312–77) King of England
1 Let the boy win his spurs. [remark on the Black
Prince at the battle of Crécy, 1345]

E4   **Edward VIII (Duke of Windsor)** (1894–1972)
King of Great Britain
1 I have found it impossible to carry the heavy
burden of responsibility and to discharge my duties as
King as I would wish to do without the help and
support of the woman I love. [broadcast, 11 Dec.
1936]

E5   **Edwards, Oliver** (1711–91)
1 You are a philosopher, Dr Johnson. I have tried too
in my time to be a philosopher; but, I don't know
how, cheerfulness was always breaking in. [quoted in
Boswell's *Life of Johnson*, 1778]

E6   **Einstein, Albert** (1879–1955)
US (German-born) physicist
1 God does not play dice. [remark on the quantum
theory]

E7   **Eliot, George (Mary Ann Evans)** (1819–80)
English novelist
1 A woman can hardly ever choose . . . she is
dependent on what happens to her. She must take
meaner things, because only meaner things are within
her reach. [*Felix Holt*, ch. 27]

2 A woman, . . . let her be as good as she may, has got to put up with the life her husband makes for her. [*Middlemarch*, ch. 25]

3 I should like to know what is the proper function of women, if it is not to make reasons for husbands to stay at home, and still stronger reasons for bachelors to go out. [*The Mill on the Floss*, bk VI, ch. 6]

E8   **Eliot, T. S.** (1888–1965)
British (US-born) poet and critic
1 Because I do not hope to turn again / Because I do not hope / Because I do not hope to turn.
[*Ash-Wednesday*, I]
2 Hell is oneself; / Hell is alone, the other figures in it / Merely projections. There is nothing to escape from / And nothing to escape to. One is always alone. [*The Cocktail Party*, I. 3]
3 Time present and time past / Are both perhaps present in time future, / And time future contained in time past. [*Four Quartets*, 'Burnt Norton']
4 Human kind / Cannot bear very much reality. [*do.*]
5 Time and the bell have buried the day, / The black cloud carries the sun away. [*do.*]
6 In my beginning is my end. [*do.*, 'East Coker']
7 The intolerable wrestle / With words and meanings. [*do.*]
8 And what the dead had no speech for, when living, / They can tell you, being dead: the communication / Of the dead is tongued with fire beyond the language of the living. [*do.*, 'Little Gidding']
9 We shall not cease from exploration / And the end of all our exploring / Will be to arrive where we started / And know the place for the first time. [*do.*]
10 Here I am, an old man in a dry month, / Being read to by a boy, waiting for rain. [*Gerontion*]
11 The only way of expressing emotion in the form of art is by finding an 'objective correlative'; in other words, a set of objects, a situation, a chain of events which shall be the formula of that *particular* emotion; such that when the external facts, which must terminate in sensory experience, are given, the emotion is immediately evoked. [*Hamlet*]
12 We are the hollow men / We are the stuffed men / Leaning together / Headpiece filled with

straw. Alas! [*The Hollow Men*]

13 This is the way the world ends / Not with a bang but a whimper. [*do.*]

14 We returned to our places, these Kingdoms, / But no longer at ease here, in the old dispensation, / With an alien people clutching their gods. / I should be glad of another death. [*Journey of the Magi*]

15 Let us go then, you and I, / When the evening is spread out against the sky / Like a patient etherized upon a table. [*The Love Song of J. Alfred Prufrock*]

16 In the room the women come and go / Talking of Michelangelo. [*do.*]

17 I have measured out my life with coffee spoons. [*do.*]

18 I should have been a pair of ragged claws / Scuttling across the floors of silent seas. [*do.*]

19 No! I am not Prince Hamlet, not was meant to be; / Am an attendant lord, one that will do / To swell a progress, start a scene or two. [*do.*]

20 I grow old . . . I grow old . . . / I shall wear the bottoms of my trousers rolled. [*do.*]

21 Shall I part my hair behind? Do I dare to eat a peach? / I shall wear white flannel trousers, and walk upon the beach. / I have heard the mermaids singing, each to each. / I do not think that they will sing to me. [*do.*]

22 Yet we have gone on living, / Living and partly living. [*Murder in the Cathedral*]

23 The last temptation is the greatest treason: / To do the right deed for the wrong reason. [*do.*]

24 I feel like one who smiles, and turning shall remark / Suddenly, his expression in a glass. / My self-possession gutters; we are really in the dark. [*Portrait of a Lady*]

25 Birth, and copulation, and death. / That's all the facts when you come to brass tacks: / Birth, and copulation, and death. [*Sweeney Agonistes*]

26 April is the cruellest month, breeding / Lilacs out of the dead land, mixing / Memory and desire, stirring / Dull roots with spring rain. [*The Waste Land*, I]

27 And I will show you something different from either / Your shadow at morning striding behind you / Or your shadow at evening rising to meet you; / I will show you fear in a handful of dust. [*do.*]

28 Unreal City, / Under the brown fog of a winter dawn, / A crowd flowed over London Bridge, so many, / I had not thought death had undone so many. [*do.*]

29 But at my back from time to time I hear / The sound of horns and motors, which shall bring / Sweeney to Mrs Porter in the spring. / O the moon shone bright on Mrs Porter / And on her daughter / They wash their feet in soda water. [*do.*, III]

30 When lovely woman stoops to folly and / Paces about her room again, alone, / She smoothes her hair with automatic hand, / And puts a record on the gramophone. [*do.* Compare **G18.7**]

31 Phlebas the Phoenician, a fortnight dead, / Forgot the cry of gulls, and the deep sea swell / And the profit and loss. A current under sea / Picked his bones in whispers. [*do.*, IV]

32 These fragments I have shored against my ruins. [*do.*, V]

33 Webster was much possessed by death / And saw the skull beneath the skin; / And breastless creatures under ground / Leaned backward with a lipless grin. [*Whispers of Immortality*]

34 Grishkin is nice: her Russian eye / Is underlined for emphasis; / Uncorseted, her friendly bust / Gives promise of pneumatic bliss. [*do.*]

E9   **Elizabeth I** (1533–1603) Queen of England
1 I know I have the body of a weak and feeble woman, but I have the heart and stomach of a King, and of a King of England too. [speech at Tilbury when the Armada was approaching, 1588]
2 Though God hath raised me high, yet this I count the glory of my crown: that I have reigned with your loves. [The Golden Speech, 1601]
3 I will make you shorter by the head. [remark]

E10   **Elliott, Ebenezer** (1781–1849) English poet
1 What is a communist? One who hath yearnings / For equal division of unequal earnings. [*Epigram*]

E11   **Elyot, Sir Thomas** (1490?–1546)
English scholar and diplomat
1 [on football] Nothyng but beastely fury and extreme violence, whereof proceedeth hurte and consequently rancour and malice to remayne with thym that be wounded, wherefore it is to be put in

perpetual silence. [*The Boke Named the Governour*]

E12 **Emerson, Ralph Waldo** (1803–82)
US essayist and poet
1 There is properly no history; only biography.
[*Essays*, 'History']
2 All mankind love a lover. [*do.*, 'Love']
3 The reward of a thing well done is to have done it.
[*do.*, 'New England Reformers']
4 In skating over thin ice, our safety is in our speed.
[*do.*, 'Prudence']
5 What is a weed? A plant whose virtues have not yet
been discovered. [*Fortune of the Republic*]
6 Here once the embattled farmers stood, / And fired
the shot heard round the world. [*Hymn Sung at the
Completion of the Concord Monument*]
7 Things are in the saddle, / And ride mankind.
[*Ode, Inscribed to W. H. Channing*]
8 He builded better than he knew; – / The
conscious stone to beauty grew. [*The Problem*]
9 Hitch your wagon to a star. [*Society and Solitude*,
'Civilization']
10 America is a country of young men. [*do.*, 'Old
Age']
11 If a man write a better book, preach a better
sermon, or make a better mouse-trap than his
neighbour, though he build his house in the woods,
the world will make a beaten path to his door. [attr.
A similar sentence appears in Emerson's *Journal*, Feb.
1855]

E13 **Empson, William** (1906–84) English poet and critic
1 Slowly the poison the whole blood stream fills. / It
is not the effort nor the failure tires. / The waste
remains, the waste remains and kills. [*Missing Dates*]

E14 **Estienne, Henri** (1528?–98) French scholar
1 *Si jeunesse savait; si vieillesse pouvait.* If only youth
knew, if only age could. [*Les Prémices*]

E15 **Euclid** (fl. *ab* 300 BC) Greek mathematician
1 *Quod erat demonstrandum.* Which was to be proved.
[*Elements*]

E16 **Euripides** (480?–406? BC) Greek dramatist
1 Those whom God wishes to destroy, he first makes
mad. [fragment. Often quoted in a Latin version,
Quos deus vult perdere prius dementat]

F1   **Fawkes, Guy** (1570–1606) English conspirator
1 Desperate diseases require desperate remedies.
[remark on the Gunpowder Plot]

F2   **Ferdinand I** (1503–64) Holy Roman Emperor
1 *Fiat justitia et pereat mundus.* Let justice be done,
even though the world perish. [his motto. Also quoted
as . . . *et ruat caelum* or . . . *et ruant coeli* (. . . even
though the heavens fall)]

F3   **Feuerbach, Ludwig** (1804–72) German philosopher
1 *Der Mensch ist, was er isst.* Man is what he eats.
[*Blätter für Literarische Unterhaltung*, 12 Nov. 1850.
Compare **B41.1**]

F4   **Fielding, Henry** (1707–54) English novelist
1 Oh! the roast beef of England, / And old
England's roast beef. [*The Grub Street Opera*, III. 3]
2 Greatness consists in bringing all manner of
mischief on mankind, and goodness in removing it
from them. [*Jonathan Wild*, ch. 1]

F5   **Fields, W. C.** (1880–1946) US actor and scriptwriter
1 It's a funny old world – a man's lucky if he can get
out of it alive. [*You're Telling Me* (film)]
2 Never Give a Sucker an Even Break. [title of film]
3 We lived for days on nothing but food and water.
[attr.]
4 On the whole, I'd rather be in Philadelphia. [attr.
epitaph]

F6   **FitzGerald, Edward** (1809–83)
English poet and translator
1 Awake! for Morning in the Bowl of Night / Has
flung the Stone that puts the Stars to Flight: / And
Lo! the Hunter of the East has caught / The Sultan's
Turret in a Noose of Light. [*The Rubáiyát of Omar
Khayyám*, 1]
2 Here with a Loaf of Bread beneath the Bough, / A
Flask of Wine, a Book of Verse – and Thou / Beside
me singing in the Wilderness – / And Wilderness is
Paradise enow. [*do.*, 11]

3 Myself when young did eagerly frequent / Doctor and Saint, and heard great Argument / About it and about: but evermore / Came out by the same Door as in I went. [*do.*, 27]

4 I came like Water, and like Wind I go. [*do.*, 28]

5 'Tis all a Chequer-board of Nights and Days / Where Destiny with Men for Pieces plays: / Hither and thither moves, and mates, and slays, / And one by one back in the Closet lays. [*do.*, 49]

6 The Moving Finger writes; and, having writ, / Moves on: nor all they Piety nor Wit / Shall lure it back to cancel half a Line, / Nor all thy Tears wash out a Word of it. [*do.*, 51]

7 And much as Wine has play'd the Infidel, / And robb'd me of my Robe of Honour – Well, / I often wonder what the Vintners buy / One half so precious as the Goods they sell. [*do.*, 71]

8 Ah, Love! could thou and I with Fate conspire / To grasp this sorry Scheme of Things entire, / Would we not shatter it to bits – and then / Re-mould it nearer to the Heart's Desire! [*do.*, 73]

F7   **Fitzgerald, F. Scott** (1896–1940) US novelist
1 In a real dark night of the soul it is always three o'clock in the morning. [*The Crack-Up*]
2 FITZGERALD. The rich are different from us. HEMINGWAY. Yes, they have more money. [*do.*, 'Notebooks E']

F8   **Fitzsimmons, Robert** (1862–1917) English boxer
1 The bigger they come, the harder they fall. [remark]

F9   **Flecker, James Elroy** (1884–1915) English poet
1 For lust of knowing what should not be known, / We take the Golden Road to Samarkand. [*Hassan*, V. 2]

F10 **Florian, Jean-Pierre Claris de** (1755–94) French author
1 *Plaisir d'amour ne dure qu'un moment, / Chagrin d'amour dure toute la vie.* The pleasure of love lasts only a moment; the sorrow of love lasts throughout life. [*Celestine*]

F11 **Foote, Samuel** (1720–77) English actor and dramatist

1 So he died, and she very imprudently married the barber; and there were present the Picninnies, and the Joblilies, and the Garyalies, and the grand Panjandrum himself, with the little round button at top. [nonsense lines composed to test an actor's memory]

F12   **Ford, Henry** (1863–1947) US motor manufacturer
1 History is more or less bunk. It's tradition. We don't want tradition. We want to live in the present and the only history that is worth a tinker's damn is the history we make today. [*Chicago Tribune*, 25 May 1916]

F13   **Ford, John** (1586?–1639) English dramatist
1 'Tis Pity She's a Whore. [title of play]

F14   **Forgy, Howell** (1908–) US naval chaplain
1 Praise the Lord, and pass the ammunition. [attr. remark at Pearl Harbour, 1941]

F15   **Forster, E. M.** (1879–1970) English novelist
1 Yes – oh dear yes – the novel tells a story. [*Aspects of the Novel*, ch. 2]
2 Personal relations are the important thing for ever and ever, and not this outer life of telegrams and anger. [*Howards End*, ch. 19]
3 Only connect the prose and the passion, and both will be exalted, and human love will be seen at its height. [*do.*, ch. 22]

F16   **Foster, Stephen** (1826–64) US songwriter
1 Way down upon the Swanee River, / Far, far away, / That's where my heart is turning ever; / That's where the old folks stay. [*The Old Folks at Home*]
2 All the world is sad and dreary / Everywhere I roam, / Oh! darkies, how my heart grows weary, / Far from the old folks at home. [*do.*]

F17   **Francis I** (1494–1547) King of France
1 *Tout est perdu fors l'honneur.* All is lost except honour. [attr. remark after the battle of Pavia, 1525]

F18   **Franklin, Benjamin** (1706–90)
US statesman and philosopher
1 Remember that time is money. [*Advice to a Young Tradesman*]

2 There never was a good war, or a bad peace. [letter to Josiah Quincy, 11 Sept. 1783]
3 In this world nothing can be said to be certain, except death and taxes. [letter to Jean-Baptiste Le Roy, 13 Nov. 1789]
4 We must indeed all hang together, or most assuredly, we shall all hang separately. [remark on signing the Declaration of Independence, 4 July 1776]

F19   **Frederick the Great** (1712–86) King of Prussia
1 My people and I have come to an agreement which satisfies us both. They are to say what they please, and I am to do what I please. [attr.]

F20   **Freud, Sigmund** (1856–1939)
Austrian psychoanalyst
1 The psychic development of the individual is a short repetition of the course of development of the race. [*Leonardo da Vinci*]
2 Religion is an illusion and it derives its strength from the fact that it falls in with our instinctual desires. [*New Introductory Lectures on Psychoanalysis*, 35]
3 Conscience is the internal perception of the rejection of a particular wish operating within us. [*Totem and Taboo*]

F21   **Frost, Robert** (1874–1963) US poet
1 Home is the place where, when you have to go there, / They have to take you in. [*The Death of the Hired Man*]
2 Good fences make good neighbours. [*Mending Wall*]
3 The woods are lovely, dark, and deep, / But I have promises to keep, / And miles to go before I sleep, / And miles to go before I sleep. [*Stopping by Woods on a Snowy Evening*]
4 I never dared to be radical when young / For fear it would make me conservative when old. [*Ten Mills*]

F22   **Fuller, Thomas** (1608–61)
English divine and historian
1 Time, tide, and a printer's press, are three unmannerly things, that will stay for no man. [*The History of the Worthies of England*, 'Westmoreland']

G1   **Galilei, Galileo** (1564–1642)
Italian astronomer and physicist
1 *Eppur si muove.* But it [i.e. the earth] does move.
[attr. remark after being forced to recant his belief
that the earth moves round the sun]

G2   **Gandhi, Mahatma** (1869–1948) Hindu leader
1 I think it would be an excellent idea. [attr. reply to
a question on what he thought of Western
civilization]

G3   **Garbo, Greta** (1905–) Swedish film actress
1 I want to be alone. [*Grand Hotel* (film)]

G4   **Garrick, David** (1717–79) English actor
1 Heart of oak are our ships, / Heart of oak are our
men: / We always are ready; / Steady, boys,
steady; / We'll fight and we'll conquer again and
again. [*Heart of Oak*]

G5   **Gavarni (S. G. Chevalier)** (1804–66)
French illustrator
1 *Les enfants terribles.* The embarrassing young. [title
of a series of prints]

G6   **Gay, John** (1685–1732) English poet and dramatist
1 Life is a jest; and all things show it. / I thought so
once; but now I know it. [*My Own Epitaph*]

G7   **George II** (1683–1760) King of Great Britain
1 Oh! he is mad, is he? Then I wish he would bite
some other of my generals. [remark on General
Wolfe]

G8   **Gershwin, Ira** (1896–) US lyricist
1 I got rhythm, / I got music. [*I Got Music*]
2 Oh, I got plenty o' nuthin', / An' nuthin's plenty
fo' me. [*I Got Plenty o' Nuthin'*]
3 It ain't necessarily so, / It ain't necessarily
so – / De t'ings dat yo' li'ble / To read in de
Bible – / It ain't necessarily so. [*It Ain't
Necessarily So*]

G9   **Gibbon, Edward** (1737–94) English historian

1 I spent fourteen months at Magdalen College; they proved the fourteen months the most idle and unprofitable of my whole life. [*Autobiography*]

2 I sighed as a lover, I obeyed as a son. [*do.*]

3 [on London] Crowds without company, and dissipation without pleasure. [*do.*]

4 It was at Rome, on the 15th of October, 1764, as I sat musing amidst the ruins of the Capitol, while the barefoot friars were singing vespers in the Temple of Jupiter, that the idea of writing the decline and fall of the city first started to my mind. [*do.*]

5 My English text is chaste, and all licentious passages are left in the decent obscurity of a learned language. [*do.*]

6 His reign is marked by the rare advantage of furnishing very few materials for history; which is, indeed, little more than the register of the crimes, follies, and misfortunes of mankind. [on Antoninus Pius. *The Decline and Fall of the Roman Empire*, ch. 3]

7 Twenty-two acknowledged concubines, and a library of sixty-two thousand volumes attested the variety of his inclinations; and from the productions which he left behind him, it appears that both the one and the other were designed for use rather than for ostentation. [on Emperor Gordian the Younger. *do.*, ch. 7]

G10   **Gibbons, Stella** (1902–) English author
1 Something nasty in the woodshed.
[*Cold Comfort Farm*]

G11   **Gilbert, W. S.** (1836–1911)
English librettist and poet
1 He led his regiment from behind – / He found it less exciting. [*The Gondoliers*, I]

2 Of that there is no manner of doubt – / No probable, possible shadow of doubt – / No possible doubt whatever. [*do.*]

3 Take a pair of sparkling eyes, / Hidden, ever and anon, / In a merciful eclipse. [*do.*, II]

4 CAPTAIN. I'm never, never sick at sea!
ALL. What, never?
CAPTAIN. No, never!
ALL. What, *never*?
CAPTAIN. Hardly ever!

[*HMS Pinafore*, I]

5 When I was a lad I served a term / As office boy to an Attorney's firm. / I cleaned the windows and I swept the floor, / And I polished up the handle of the big front door. / I polished up that handle so carefullee / That now I am the Ruler of the Queen's Navee! [*do.*]

6 The Law is the true embodiment / Of everything that's excellent. / It has no kind of fault or flaw, / And I, my lords, embody the Law. [*Iolanthe*, I]

7 I often think it's comical / How Nature always does contrive / That every boy and every gal / That's born into the world alive / Is either a little Liberal / Or else a little Conservative! [*do.*, II]

8 The House of Peers, throughout the war, / Did nothing in particular, / And did it very well. [*do.*]

9 When you're lying awake with a dismal headache, and repose is taboo'd by anxiety, / I conceive you may use any language you choose to indulge in, without impropriety. [*do.*]

10 Pooh-Bah (Lord High Everything Else) [*The Mikado*, cast list]

11 A wandering minstrel I – / A thing of shreds and patches, / Of ballads, songs and snatches, / And dreamy lullaby! [*do.*, I]

12 As some day it may happen that a victim must be found, / I've got a little list – I've got a little list / Of society offenders who might well be underground, / And who never would be missed – who never would be missed! [*do.*]

13 Three little maids from school are we, / Pert as a schoolgirl well can be, / Filled to the brim with girlish glee. [*do.*]

14 My object all sublime / I shall achieve in time – / To let the punishment fit the crime – / The punishment fit the crime. [*do.*, II]

15 The flowers that bloom in the spring, / Tra la. [*do.*]

16 On a tree by a river a little tom-tit / Sang 'Willow, titwillow, titwillow!' [*do.*]

17 If this young man expresses himself in terms too deep for *me*, / Why, what a very singularly deep young man this deep young man must be! [*Patience*, I]

18 I'm very good at integral and differential

calculus, / I know the scientific names of beings animalculous; / In short in matters vegetable, animal, and mineral, / I am the very model of a modern Major-General. [*The Pirates of Penzance*, I]
19 When constabulary duty's to be done – / A policeman's lot is not a happy one. [*do.*, II]
20 She may very well pass for forty-three / In the dusk, with a light behind her! [*Trial by Jury*]

G12 Ginsberg, Allen (1926–) US poet
1 I saw the best minds of my generation destroyed by madness, starving hysterical naked. [*Howl*]

G13 Gladstone, W. E. (1809–98) English statesman
1 You cannot fight against the future. Time is on our side. [speech on The Reform Bill, 1866]

G14 Glasse, Hannah (fl. 1747)
English writer on domestic science
1 Take your hare when it is cased. [*The Art of Cookery*, ch. 1. Often quoted (and attr. to Mrs Beeton) as 'First catch your hare']

G15 Gloucester, Duke of (Prince William Henry) (1743–1805)
1 Another damned, thick, square book! Always scribble, scribble, scribble! Eh! Mr Gibbon? [remark to Edward Gibbon, on being presented with the second volume of *The Decline and Fall of the Roman Empire*]

G16 Goering, Hermann (1893–1946) German politician
1 Guns will make us powerful; butter will only make us fat. [broadcast, 1936]

G17 Goethe, Johann Wolfgang von (1749–1832)
German poet and dramatist
1 *Ich bin der Geist der stets verneint.* I am the spirit that always denies. [*Faust*, pt I, 'Studierzimmer']
2 *Das Ewig-Weibliche zieht uns hinan.* The Eternal Feminine draws us upward. [*do.*, pt II, closing words]
3 *Mehr Licht!* More light! [attr. last words]

G18 Goldsmith, Oliver (1728–74) English author
1 Ill fares the land, to hast'ning ills a prey, / Where wealth accumulates, and men decay. [*The Deserted Village*]
2 And still they gaz'd, and still the wonder grew, / That one small head could carry all he knew. [*do.*]

3 The man recovered of the bite, / The dog it was that died. [*Elegy on the Death of a Mad Dog*]

4 I love everything that's old: old friends, old times, old manners, old books, old wine. [*She Stoops to Conquer*, I]

5 This is Liberty-Hall, gentlemen. [*do.*, II]

6 I chose my wife, as she did her wedding gown, not for a fine glossy surface, but such qualities as would wear well. [*The Vicar of Wakefield*, ch. 1]

7 When lovely woman stoops to folly, / And finds too late that men betray, / What charm can soothe her melancholy, / What art can wash her guilt away? [*do.*, ch. 29]

G19 **Goldwyn, Samuel** (1882–1974) US film producer
1 Anybody who goes to see a psychiatrist ought to have his head examined. [attr.]
2 I'll give you a definite maybe. [attr.]
3 Include me out. [attr.]
4 In two words: im-possible. [attr.]
5 A verbal contract isn't worth the paper it's written on. [attr.]
6 Why should people go out and pay money to see bad films when they can stay at home and see bad television for nothing? [remark]

G20 **Grahame, Kenneth** (1859–1932) Scottish author
1 There is nothing – absolutely nothing – half so much worth doing as simply messing about in boats. [*The Wind in the Willows*, ch. 1]

G21 **Graves, Robert** (1895–) English author
1 There's a cool web of language winds us in, / Retreat from too much joy or too much fear. [*The Cool Web*]
2 Goodbye to All That. [title of autobiography]

G22 **Gray, Thomas** (1716–71) English poet
1 The Curfew tolls the knell of parting day, / The lowing herd wind slowly o'er the lea, / The plowman homeward plods his weary way, / And leaves the world to darkness and to me. [*Elegy written in a Country Church-Yard*]
2 Let not Ambition mock their useful toil, / Their homely joys, and destiny obscure; / Nor Grandeur hear with a disdainful smile, / The short and simple annals of the poor. [*do.*]

3 The paths of glory lead but to the grave. [*do.*]
4 Full many a gem of purest ray serene, / The dark unfathom'd caves of ocean bear: / Full many a flower is born to blush unseen, / And waste its sweetness on the desert air. [*do.*]
5 Some village-Hampden, that with dauntless breast / The little tyrant of his fields withstood; / Some mute inglorious Milton here may rest, / Some Cromwell guiltless of his country's blood. [*do.*]
6 Far from the madding crowd's ignoble strife, / Their sober wishes never learned to stray; / Along the cool sequestered vale of life / They kept the noiseless tenor of their way. [*do.*]
7 Not all that tempts your wand'ring eyes / And heedless hearts, is lawful prize; / Nor all, that glisters, gold. [*Ode on the Death of a Favourite Cat*]
8 Alas, regardless of their doom, / The little victims play! [*Ode on a Distant Prospect of Eton College*]
9 Where ignorance is bliss, / 'Tis folly to be wise. [*do.*]

G23   **Greeley, Horace** (1811–72)
US journalist and politician
1 Go West, young man, and grow up with the country. [*Hints toward Reform*]

G24   **Gregory I, Saint** (540–604)
1 *Non Angli sed Angeli.* Not Angles but Angels. [attr. remark on a group of English captives in Rome]

G25   **Gresham, Sir Thomas** (1519?–79) English financier
1 Bad money drives out good. ['Gresham's Law'. A summary of Gresham's theory, but not actually stated by him in this form]

G26   **Grey of Fallodon, Edward, 1st Viscount**
(1862–1933) English statesman
1 The lamps are going out all over Europe; we shall not see them lit again in our lifetime. [remark, 3 August 1914]

G27   **Gwyn, Nell** (1650–87) English actress
1 Pray, good people, be civil. I am the Protestant whore. [remark during anti-Popery disturbances in 1681]

H1 **Hailsham, Lord (Quintin Hogg)** (1907–)
English lawyer and politician
1 [On Labour policies] If the British public falls for this, I say it will be stark, staring bonkers. [remark at press conference, 1964]

H2 **Hale, Nathan** (1755–76) US army officer
1 I only regret that I have but one life to lose for my country. [attr. speech before execution as a spy]

H3 **Hale, Sara Josepha** (1788–1879) US author
1 Mary had a little lamb, / Its fleece was white as snow, / And everywhere that Mary went / The lamb was sure to go. [*Mary's Little Lamb*]

H4 **Halm, Friedrich** (1806–71)
German poet and dramatist
1 Two souls with but a single thought, / Two hearts that beat as one. [*Der Sohn der Wildnis (Ingomar the Barbarian)*, II, trans. Maria Lovell]

H5 **Hammerstein, Oscar** (1895–1960) US librettist
1 Oh, what a beautiful morning / Oh, what a beautiful day. [*Oklahoma,* 'Oh, What a Beautiful Morning']
2 Some enchanted evening, / You may see a stranger / Across a crowded room. [*South Pacific,* 'Some Enchanted Evening']
3 Ol' man river, dat ol' man river, / He must know sumpin', but don't say nothin', / He just keeps rollin', he keeps on rollin' along. [*Show Boat,* 'Ol' Man River']
4 The hills are alive with the sound of music. [*The Sound of Music*]

H6 **Harburg, E. Y.** (1898–) US lyricist
1 Somewhere over the rainbow, / Way up high: / There's a land that I heard of / Once in a lullaby. [*Over the Rainbow*]

H7 **Hardy, Thomas** (1840–1928)
English novelist and poet
1 When the Present has latched its postern behind

my tremulous stay, / And the May month flaps its glad green leaves like wings, / Delicate-filmed as new-spun silk, will the neighbours say, / 'He was a man who used to notice such things'? [*Afterwards*]

2 In a solitude of the sea / Deep from human vanity, / And the Pride of Life that planned her, stilly couches she. [*The Convergence of the Twain*]

3 Till the Spinner of the Years / Said 'Now!' And each one hears, / And consummation comes, and jars two hemispheres. [*do.*]

4 So little cause for carollings / Of such ecstatic sound / Was written on terrestrial things / Afar or nigh around, / That I could think there trembled through / His happy good-night air / Some blessed Hope, whereof he knew / And I was unaware. [*The Darkling Thrush*]

5 Indulge no more may we / In this sweet-bitter pastime: / The love-light shines the last time / Between you, Dear, and me. [*The End of the Episode*]

6 Ache deep; but make no moans: / Smile out; but stilly suffer: / The paths of love are rougher / Than thoroughfares of stones. [*do.*]

7 But Time, to make me grieve, / Part steals, lets part abide; / And shakes this fragile frame at eve / With throbbings of noontide. [*I Look Into My Glass*]

8 Yonder a maid and her wight / Come whispering by: / War's annals will cloud into night / Ere their story die. [*In Time of 'The Breaking of Nations'*]

9 Done because we are too menny. [*Jude the Obscure*, VI, ch. 2]

10 We stood by a pond that winter day, / And the sun was white, as though chidden of God, / And a few leaves lay on the starving sod; / – They had fallen from an ash, and were grey. [*Neutral Tones*]

11 'Justice' was done, and the President of the Immortals (in Aeschylean phrase) had ended his sport with Tess. [*Tess of the D'Urbervilles*, ch. 59]

H8   **Harington, Sir John** (1561–1612)
English courtier and author
1 Treason doth never prosper, what's the reason? / For if it prosper, none dare call it treason. [*Epigrams*, 'Of Treason']

H9   **Hartley, L. P.** (1895–1972) English novelist
1 The past is a foreign country: they do things

differently there. [*The Go-Between*, Prologue]

H10   **Hay, Ian** (1876–1952) Scottish author
1 Funny peculiar, or funny ha-ha?
[*The Housemaster*, III]

H11   **Hayes, J. Milton** (fl. 1911)
1 There's a one-eyed yellow idol to the north of
Khatmandu, / There's a little marble cross below the
town; / There's a broken-hearted woman tends the
grave of Mad Carew / And the Yellow God forever
gazes down. [*The Green Eye of the Yellow God*]

H12   **Hazlitt, William** (1778–1830) English essayist
1 The least pain in our little finger gives us more
concern and uneasiness than the destruction of
millions of our fellow-beings. [*American Literature*]
2 He [i.e Coleridge] talked on for ever; and you
wished him to talk on for ever. [*Lectures on the
English Poets*, 8]
3 There is nothing good to be had in the country, or,
if there is, they will not let you have it. [*Observations
on Mr Wordsworth's 'Excursion'*]
4 We never do anything well till we cease to think
about the manner of doing it. [*Sketches and Essays*,
'On Prejudice']
5 Violent antipathies are always suspicious, and
betray a secret affinity. [*do.*, 'On Vulgarity
and Affectation']

H13   **Healey, Denis** (1917–) English politician
1 [on being criticized by Sir Geoffrey Howe] Like
being savaged by a dead sheep. [speech in the House
of Commons, 14 June 1978]

H14   **Heath, Edward** (1916–) English statesman
1 This would, at a stroke, reduce the rise in prices.
[Conservative Party press release, 1970, commonly
attr. to Heath]
2 It is the unpleasant and unacceptable face of
capitalism. [speech in the House of Commons,
15 May 1973]

H15   **Heber, Reginald** (1783–1826)
English prelate and hymn-writer
1 Though every prospect pleases, / And only man is
vile. [*From Greenland's Icy Mountains*]

H15   **Heller, Joseph** (1923–) US novelist
1 There was only one catch and that was Catch-22, which specified that a concern for one's own safety in the face of dangers that were real and immediate was the process of a rational mind. [*Catch-22*, ch. 5]

H17   **Hellman, Lillian** (1905–84) US dramatist
1 I cannot and will not cut my conscience to fit this year's fashions. [letter to the House Committee on un-American Activities, 1952]

H18   **Hemans, Felicia** (1793–1835) English poet
1 The boy stood on the burning deck / Whence all but he had fled. [*Casabianca*]
2 The stately homes of England, / How beautiful they stand! [*The Homes of England*]

H19   **Hemingway, Ernest** (1899–1961) US author
1 You and me, we've made a separate peace. [*In Our Time*, 'A Very Short Story']
2 No matter how a man alone ain't got no bloody chance. [*To Have and Have Not*, ch. 15]

H20   **Henley, W. E.** (1849–1903) English poet
1 Under the bludgeonings of chance / My head is bloody, but unbowed. [*Invictus*]
2 I am the master of my fate; / I am the captain of my soul. [*do.*]

H21   **Henry II** (1133–89) King of England
1 Will no one free me of this turbulent priest? [attr. remark on Thomas à Becket]

H22   **Henry IV** (1553–1610) King of France
1 Paris is well worth a mass. [attr.]
2 [on King James I] The wisest fool in Christendom. [attr.]

H23   **Henry, Patrick** (1736–99) US statesman
1 I know not what course others may take; but as for me, give me liberty or give me death. [speech to the Virginia Assembly, 23 Mar. 1775]

H24   **Heraclitus** (6th–5th c BC) Greek philosopher
1 Everything flows and nothing stays. [cited by Plato, *Cratylus*]
2 You cannot step twice into the same river. [*do.*]

H25   **Herbert, George** (1593–1633) English poet

1 I struck the board, and cried, 'No more; / I will abroad.' / What, shall I ever sigh and pine? / My lines and life are free; free as the road, / Loose as the wind, as large as store. [*The Collar*]

2 But as I rav'd and grew more fierce and wild / At every word, / Methought I heard one calling, 'Child'; / And I replied, 'My Lord.' [*do.*]

3 Love bade me welcome; yet my soul drew back, / Guilty of dust and sin. [*Love*]

4 'You must sit down,' says Love, 'and taste My meat.' / So I did sit and eat. [*do.*]

5 When God at first made man, / Having a glass of blessings standing by; / Let us (said he) pour on him all we can: / Let the world's riches, which dispersed lie, / Contract into a span. [*The Pulley*]

6 Sweet day, so cool, so calm, so bright, / The bridal of the earth and sky, / The dew shall weep thy fall to-night; / For thou must die. [*Virtue*]

7 Only a sweet and virtuous soul, / Like season'd timber, never gives; / But though the whole world turn to coal, / Then chiefly lives. [*do.*]

H26   Herrick, Robert (1591–1674) English poet

1 A sweet disorder in the dress / Kindles in clothes a wantonness. [*Delight in Disorder*]

2 Fair daffodils, we weep to see / You haste away so soon; / As yet the early-rising sun / Has not attain'd his noon. [*To Daffodils*]

3 Gather ye rosebuds while ye may, / Old time is still a-flying; / And this same flower that smiles today / Tomorrow will be dying. [*To the Virgins, to Make Much of Time*]

4 Whenas in silks my Julia goes, / Then, then, methinks, how sweetly flows / That liquefaction of her clothes. [*Upon Julia's Clothes*]

H27   Hewart, Lord (1870–1943) English jurist

1 Justice should not only be done, but should manifestly and undoubtedly be seen to be done. [judgment in Rex v. Sussex Justices, 9 Nov. 1923]

H28   Hickson, W. E. (1803–70)
English educational writer
1 If at first you don't succeed, / Try, try again. [*Try and Try Again*]

H29   Hill, Joe (1879–1914) US labour leader

1 You'll get pie in the sky when you die. [*The Preacher and the Slave*]

H30 **Hill, Rowland** (1744–1833) English preacher
1 He did not see any good reasons why the devil should have all the good tunes. [E. W. Broome, *Rev. Rowland Hill*]

H31 **Hippocrates** (460?–377? BC) Greek physician
1 The life so short, the craft so long to learn. [*Aphorisms*, I (tr. Chaucer). Often quoted in Latin as *Ars longa, vita brevis*]

H32 **Hitchcock, Alfred** (1899–1980) English film director
1 Actors are cattle. [attr.]

H33 **Hobbes, Thomas** (1588–1679) English philosopher
1 The condition of man . . . is a condition of war of everyone against everyone. [*Leviathan*, pt I, ch. 4]
2 Words are wise men's counters, they do but reckon by them; but they are the money of fools. [*do.*]
3 No arts; no letters; no society; and which is worst of all, continual fear and danger of violent death; and the life of man, solitary, poor, nasty, brutish, and short. [*do.*, ch. 13]
4 I am about to take my last voyage, a great leap in the dark. [attr. last words]

H34 **Homer** (fl. 850? BC) Greek poet
1 Rosy-fingered dawn. [*Iliad*, I *et passim*]
2 Winged words. [*do.*]
3 The wine-dark sea. [*do.*]

H35 **Hood, Thomas** (1799–1845) English poet
1 Ben Battle was a soldier bold, / And used to war's alarms: / But a cannon-ball took off his legs, / So he laid down his arms! [*Faithless Nelly Gray*]
2 I remember, I remember, / The house where I was born, / The little window where the sun / Came peeping in at morn. [*I Remember*]

H36 **Hoover, Herbert** (1874–1964) US president
1 The American system of rugged individualism. [speech in New York, 22 Oct. 1928]

H37 **Hopkins, Gerard Manley** (1844–89) English poet
1 Not, I'll not, carrion comfort, Despair, not feast on thee; / Not untwist – slack they may be – these last strands of man / In me or, most weary, cry *I can no*

more. I can; / Can something, hope, wish day come,
not choose not to be. [*Carrion Comfort*]
2 That night, that year / Of now done darkness I
wretch lay wrestling with (my God!) my God. [*do.*]
3 The world is charged with the grandeur of God.
[*God's Grandeur*]
4 What would the world be, once bereft / Of wet
and of wilderness? Let them be left, / O let them be
left, wildness and wet; / Long live the weeds and the
wilderness yet. [*Inversnaid*]
5 O the mind, mind has mountains; cliffs of
fall / Frightful, sheer, no-man-fathomed. Hold them
cheap / May who ne'er hung there. [*No Worst, There
is None*]
6 Glory be to God for dappled things – / For skies
of couple-colour as a brinded cow; / For rose-moles
all in stipple upon trout that swim. [*Pied Beauty*]
7 Thou art indeed just, Lord, if I contend / With
thee; but, sir, so what I plead is just. / Why do
sinners' ways prosper? and why must /
Disappointment all I endeavour end? [*Thou Art Indeed
Just, Lord*]
8 I caught this morning morning's minion, king-
/ dom of daylight's dauphin, dapple-dawn-drawn
Falcon. [*The Windhover*]

H38 **Horace (Quintus Horatius Flaccus)** (65–8 BC)
Roman poet
1 *Parturient montes, nascetur ridiculus mus.* Mountains
will be in labour, and an absurd little mouse will be
born. [*Ars Poetica*]
2 *Indignor quandoque bonus dormitat Homerus.* I regret
it when sometimes even good Homer nods. [*do.*]
3 *Ira furor brevis est.* Anger is a brief madness.
[*Epistles*, I, 2]
4 *Naturam expellas furca, tamen usque recurret.* You
may drive out nature with a pitchfork, but she'll keep
coming back. [*do.*, 10]
5 *Vitae summa brevis spem nos vetat incohare longam.*
Life's brief span forbids us to embark on far-reaching
hopes. [*Odes*, I, 4]
6 *Dum loquimur, fugerit invida / Aetas: carpe diem,
quam minimum credula postero.* While we're talking,
grudging time will have flown on; seize the day,
relying on the future as little as possible. [*do.*, 11]

7 *Integer vitae scelerisque purus.* A man of upright life and free of guilt. [*do.*, 22]

8 *Eheu fugaces, Postume, Postume, / Labuntur anni.* Alas, Postumus, Postumus, the fleeting years are slipping by. [*do.*, II, 14]

9 *Dulce et decorum est pro patria mori.* It is sweet and seemly to die for one's country. [*do.*, III, 2]

10 *Exegi monumentum aere perennius.* I have completed a monument more lasting than bronze. [*do.*, 30]

H39   **Housman, A. E.** (1859–1936)
English poet and scholar

1 Loveliest of trees, the cherry now / Is hung with bloom along the bough, / And stands about the woodland ride / Wearing white for Eastertide. [*A Shropshire Lad*, 2]

2 Up, lad: thews that lie and cumber / Sunlit pallets never thrive; / Morns abed and daylight slumber / Were not meant for man alive.

Clay lies still, but blood's a rover; / Breath's a ware that will not keep. / Up, lad: when the journey's over / There'll be time enough to sleep. [*do.*, 4, 'Reveille']

3 Oh, when I was in love with you, / Then I was clean and brave, / And miles around the wonder grew / How well did I behave.

And now the fancy passes by, / And nothing will remain, / And miles around they'll say that I / Am quite myself again. [*do.*, 18]

4 Here of a Sunday morning / My love and I would lie, / And see the coloured counties, / And hear the larks so high / About us in the sky. [*do.*, 21, 'Bredon Hill']

5 'Is my team ploughing, / That I was used to drive / And hear the harness jingle / When I was man alive?' [*do.*, 27]

6 On Wenlock Edge the wood's in trouble; / His forest fleece the Wrekin heaves; / The gale, it plies the saplings double, / And thick on Severn snow the leaves. [*do.*, 31]

7 From far, from eve and morning / And yon twelve-winded sky, / The stuff of life to knit me / Blew hither: here am I. [*do.*, 32]

8 Into my heart an air that kills / From yon far

country blows: / What are those blue remembered hills, / What spires, what farms are those?

That is the land of lost content, / I see it shining plain, / The happy highways where I went / And cannot come again. [*do.*, 40]

9 Oh, 'tis jesting, dancing, drinking / Spins the heavy world around. / If young hearts were not so clever, / Oh, they would be young for ever: / Think no more; 'tis only thinking / Lays lads underground. [*do.*, 49]

10 With rue my heart is laden / For golden friends I had, / For many a rose-lipt maiden / And many a lightfoot lad. [*do.*, 54]

11 Oh many a peer of England brews / Livelier liquor than the Muse, / And malt does more than Milton can / To justify God's ways to man. [*do.*, 62]

12 We for a certainty are not the first / Have sat in taverns while the tempest hurled / Their hopeful plans to emptiness, and cursed / Whatever brute and blackguard made the world. [*Last Poems*, 9]

13 The troubles of our proud and angry dust / Are from eternity, and shall not fail. / Bear them we can, and if we can we must. / Shoulder the sky, my lad, and drink your ale. [*do.*]

14 But men at whiles are sober / And think by fits and starts, / And if they think, they fasten / Their hands upon their hearts. [*do.*, 10]

15 The candles burn their sockets, / The blinds let through the day, / The young man feels his pockets / And wonders what's to pay. [*do.*, 21]

16 The stars have not dealt me the worst they could do: / My pleasures are plenty, my troubles are two. / But oh, my two troubles they reave me of rest, / The brains in my head and the heart in my breast. [*Collected Poems*, 'Additional Poems', 9]

H40 **Howe, Julia** (1819–1910) US reformer
1 Mine eyes have seen the glory of the coming of the Lord: / He is trampling out the vintage where the grapes of wrath are stored. [*Battle Hymn of the American Republic*]

H41 **Howitt, Mary** (1799–1888) English author
1 'Will you walk into my parlour?' said a spider to a fly: / ''Tis the prettiest little parlour that ever you did spy.' [*The Spider and the Fly*]

H42 **Hoyle, Edmond** (1672–1769)
English writer on card games
1 When in doubt, win the trick.
[*Hoyle's Games*, 'Whist']

H43 **Hughes, Thomas** (1822–96)
English jurist and author
1 Life isn't all beer and skittles. [*Tom Brown's Schooldays*, pt I, ch. 2]
2 [on cricket] It's more than a game. It's an institution. [*do.*, pt II, ch. 7]

H44 **Hunt, Leigh** (1784–1859) English poet
1 Abou Ben Adham (may his tribe increase!) / Awoke one night from a deep dream of peace.
[*Abou Ben Adhem and the Angel*]
2 'I pray thee then, / Write me as one that loves his fellow-men.' [*do.*]

H45 **Hutcheson, Francis** (1694–1746)
Scottish philosopher
1 That action is best, which procures the greatest happiness for the greatest numbers. [*Inquiry into the Original of our Ideas of Beauty and Virtue*, I]

H46 **Huxley, Aldous** (1894–1963) English author
1 A million million spermatozoa, / All of them alive: / Out of their cataclysm but one poor Noah / Dare hope to survive. [*The Fifth Philosopher's Song*]
2 I can sympathize with people's pains, but not with their pleasures. There is something curiously boring about somebody else's happiness. [*Limbo*, 'Cynthia']

H47 **Huxley, T. H.** (1825–95) English biologist
1 Science is nothing but trained and organized common sense. [*Collected Essays*, 'The Method of Zadig']
2 The great tragedy of Science – the slaying of a beautiful hypothesis by an ugly fact. [*do.*, 'Biogenesis and Abiogenesis']
3 It is the customary fate of new truths to begin as heresies and to end as superstitions. [*Science and Culture*, 12, 'The Coming of Age of the Origin of Species']

I1   **Ibsen, Henrik** (1828–1906)
Norwegian poet and dramatist
1 The minority is always right. [*An Enemy of the People*, IV]
2 A man should never put on his best trousers when he goes out to fight for freedom and truth. [*do.*, V]
3 Mother, give me the sun. [*Ghosts*, III]

I2   **Inge, William Ralph** (1860–1954)
English prelate and author
1 The enemies of Freedom do not argue; they shout and they shoot. [*The End of an Age*, ch. 4]
2 Many people believe that they are attracted by God, or by Nature, when they are only repelled by man. [*More Lay Thoughts of a Dean*, pt III, ch. 1]
3 A nation is a society united by a delusion about its ancestry and by a common hatred of its neighbours. [attr.]

I3   **Isherwood, Christopher** (1904–) English novelist
1 I am a camera with its shutter open, quite passive, recording, not thinking. [*Goodbye to Berlin*]

J1   **James I** (1566–1625) King of Great Britain
1 [on smoking] A custom loathsome to the eye, hateful to the nose, harmful to the brain, dangerous to the lungs, and in the black, stinking fume thereof, nearest resembling the horrible Stygian smoke of the pit that is bottomless. [*A Counterblast to Tobacco*]

J2   **James, Henry** (1843–1916) British (US-born) writer
1 We must grant the artist his subject, his idea, his *donné*: our criticism is applied only to what he makes of it. [*Partial Portraits*, 'The Art of Fiction']
2 Vereker's secret . . . the general intention of his books: the string the pearls were strung on, the buried treasure, the figure in the carpet. [*The Figure*

in the Carpet, ch. 11]

J3 **James, William** (1842–1910)
US psychologist and philosopher
1 The moral flabbiness born of the bitch-goddess
SUCCESS . . . is our national disease. [letter to H. G.
Wells, 11 Sept. 1906]

J4 **Jeans, Sir James** (1877–1946)
English physicist and astronomer
1 Life exists in the universe only because the carbon
atom possesses certain exceptional properties. [*The
Mysterious Universe*, ch. 1]

J5 **Jefferson, Thomas** (1743–1826) US president
1 We hold these truths to be self-evident: that all
men are created equal; that they are endowed by their
Creator with certain unalienable rights; that among
these are life, liberty, and the pursuit of happiness.
[Declaration of Independence, 1776]
2 The tree of liberty must be refreshed from time to
time with the blood of patriots and tyrants. It is its
natural manure. [letter to W. S. Smith, 13 Nov.
1787]

J6 **Jerome, Jerome K.** (1859–1927) English author
1 I like work; it fascinates me. I can sit and look at it
for hours. I love to keep it by me; the idea of getting
rid of it nearly breaks my heart. [*Three Men in a
Boat*, ch. 15]

J7 **Joad, C. E. M.** (1891–1953) English philosopher
1 It all depends what you mean by . . . [repeated
remark on BBC radio programme *The Brains Trust*]

J8 **Johnson, Hiram** (1866–1945) US politician
1 The first casualty when war comes is truth. [speech
in US senate, 1917]

J9 **Johnson, Samuel** (1709–84) English author
1 I'll come no more behind your scenes, David; for
the silk stockings and white bosoms of your actresses
excite my amorous propensities. [remark to David
Garrick. James Boswell's *Life of Johnson*, 1750]
2 This man I thought had been a Lord among wits;
but, I find, he is only a wit among Lords. [on Lord
Chesterfield. *do.*, 1754]
3 They teach the morals of a whore, and the manners

of a dancing master. [on Lord Chesterfield's
Letters. do.]

4 Is not a patron, my Lord, one who looks with
unconcern on a man struggling for life in the water,
and, when he has reached ground, encumbers him
with help? [letter to Lord Chesterfield, *do.*, 1755]

5 Ignorance, Madam, pure ignorance. [remark when
asked the reason for an erroneous definition in his
dictionary. *do.*]

6 If a man does not make new acquaintance as he
advances through life, he will soon find himself left
alone. A man, Sir, should keep his friendship in
constant repair. [*do.*]

7 BOSWELL. I do indeed come from Scotland, but I
cannot help it . . . JOHNSON. That, Sir, I find, is what
a very great many of your countrymen cannot help.
[*do.*, 1763]

8 Yes, Sir, many men, many women, and many
children. [remark when asked whether any modern
man could have written the poem *Ossian. do.*]

9 The noblest prospect which a Scotchman ever sees,
is the high road that leads him to England. [*do.*]

10 A man ought to read just as inclination leads him;
for what he reads as a task will do him little good.
[*do.*]

11 But if he does really think that there is no
distinction between virtue and vice, why, Sir, when
he leaves our houses let us count our spoons. [*do.*]

12 Sir, your levellers wish to level *down* as far as
themselves; but they cannot bear levelling *up* to
themselves. [*do.*]

13 Why, Sir, Sherry [i.e. Thomas Sheridan] is dull,
naturally dull; but it must have taken him a great deal
of pains to become what we now see him. Such an
excess of stupidity, Sir, is not in nature. [*do.*]

14 Sir, a woman's preaching is like a dog's walking
on his hind legs. It is not done well; but you are
surprised to find it done at all. [*do.*]

15 Johnson answered, striking his foot with mighty
force against a large stone, till he rebounded from it,
'I refute it *thus.*' [on Bishop Berkeley's theory of the
non-existence of matter. *do.*]

16 So far is it from being true that men are naturally
equal, that no two people can be half an hour
together, but one shall acquire an evident superiority

over the other. [*do.*, 1766]

17 That fellow seems to me to possess but one idea, and that is a wrong one. [*do.*, 1770]

18 A gentleman who had been very unhappy in marriage, married immediately after his wife died: Johnson said, it was the triumph of hope over experience. [*do.*]

19 I would not give half a guinea to live under one form of government rather than another. It is of no moment to the happiness of an individual. [*do.*, 1772]

20 There are few ways in which a man can be more innocently employed than in getting money. [*do.*, 1775]

21 A man will turn over half a library to make one book. [*do.*]

22 Patriotism is the last refuge of a scoundrel. [*do.*]

23 Politics are now nothing more than a means of rising in the world. [*do.*]

24 There is nothing which has yet been contrived by man, by which so much happiness is produced as by a good tavern or inn. [*do.*, 1776]

25 BOSWELL. Sir, you observed one day . . . that a man is never happy for the present, but when he is drunk. Will you not add, – or when driving rapidly in a post-chaise?

JOHNSON. No, Sir, you are driving rapidly *from* something, or *to* something. [*do.*]

26 No man but a blockhead ever wrote, except for money. [*do.*]

27 Depend upon it, Sir, when a man knows he is to be hanged in a fortnight, it concentrates his mind wonderfully. [*do.*]

28 You find no man, at all intellectual, who is willing to leave London. No, Sir, when a man is tired of London, he is tired of life; for there is in London all that life can afford. [*do.*]

29 BOSWELL. Is not the Giant's-Causeway worth seeing?

JOHNSON. Worth seing? Yes; but not worth going to see. [*do.*, 1779]

30 If you are idle, be not solitary; if you are solitary, be not idle. [letter to Boswell, *do.*]

31 I have two very cogent reasons for not printing any list of subscribers; – one, that I have lost all the names, – the other, that I have spent all the money.

[*do.*, 1781]

32 Sir, there is no settling the point of precedency between a louse and a flea. [remark on being asked which of two minor poets he more approved. *do.*, 1783]

33 [on a violinist's performance] Difficult do you call it, Sir? I wish it were impossible. [*Anecdotes by William Seward*]

34 *Lexicographer*. A writer of dictionaries; a harmless drudge. [*A Dictionary of the English Language*]

35 *Network*. Any thing reticulated or decussated, at equal distances, with interstices between the intersections. [*do.*]

36 *Oats*. A grain, which in England is generally given to horses, but in Scotland supports the people. [*do.*]

37 *Pension*. An allowance made to any one without an equivalent. In England it is generally understood to mean pay given to a state hireling for treason to his country. [*do.*]

38 When two Englishmen meet, their first talk is of the weather. [*The Idler*, 11]

39 The true genius is a mind of large general powers, accidentally determined to some particular direction. [*Lives of the English Poets*, 'Cowley']

40 Language is the dress of thought. [*do.*]

41 I am disappointed by that stroke of death, which has eclipsed the gaiety of nations and impoverished the public stock of harmless pleasure. [on David Garrick's death. *do.*, 'Edmund Smith']

42 Notes are often necessary, but they are necessary evils. [*Plays of William Shakespeare*, Preface]

43 Human life is every where a state in which much is to be endured, and little to be enjoyed. [*Rasselas*, ch. 11]

44 Marriage has many pains, but celibacy has no pleasures. [*do.*, ch. 26]

45 Let observation with extensive view, / Survey mankind, from China to Peru. [*The Vanity of Human Wishes*]

46 He left the name, at which the world grew pale, / To point a moral, or adorn a tale. [*do.*]

J10   Johst, Hanns (1890–) German author
1 Whenever I hear the word 'culture' . . . I release the safety-catch on my pistol. [*Schlageter*, I. 1. Often attr. to Hermann Goering]

J11   **Jolson, Al** (1886–1950) US actor and singer
1 You ain't heard nothin' yet, folks. [*The Jazz Singer* (the first talking film)]

J12   **Jones, John Paul** (1747–92) US naval officer
1 I have not yet begun to fight. [remark on being asked to surrender, as his ship was sinking]

J13   **Jonson, Ben** (1573?–1637) English dramatist
1 Drink to me only with thine eyes, / And I will pledge with mine; / Or leave a kiss but in the cup, / And I'll not look for wine. [*To Celia*]
2 Thou hadst small Latin, and less Greek. [*To the Memory of . . . William Shakespeare*]
3 He was not of an age, but for all time! [*do.*]

J14   **Joyce, James** (1882–1941) Irish novelist
1 Ireland is the old sow that eats her farrow. [*A Portrait of the Artist as a Young Man*, ch. 5]
2 The artist, like the God of the creation, remains within or behind or beyond or above his handiwork, invisible, refined out of existence, indifferent, paring his fingernails. [*do.*]
3 I will try to express myself in some mode of life or art as freely as I can and as wholly as I can, using for my defence the only arms I allow myself to use – silence, exile and cunning. [*do.*]
4 I fear those big words, Stephen said, which make us so unhappy. [*Ulysses*]
5 History, Stephen said, is a nightmare from which I am trying to awake. [*do.*]
6 The heaventree of stars hung with humid nightblue fruit. [*do.*]
7 and yes I said yes I will Yes. [*do.*, closing words]

J15   **Julian of Norwich, Dame** (1343–1443) English mystic
1 It behoved that there should be sin; but all shall be well, and all shall be well, and all manner of thing shall be well. [*Revelations of Divine Love.* ch. 27]

J16   **Juvenal** (60?–140?) Roman poet
1 *Probitas laudatur et alget.* Honesty is praised and left out in the cold. [*Satires*, I]
2 *Rara avis in terris nigroque simillima cycno.* A rare bird on earth, and very like a black swan. [*do.*, VI]
3 *Sed quis custodiet ipsos / Custodes?* But who will guard the guards themselves? [*do.*]

4 *Duas tantum res anxius optat, / Panem et circenses.*
There are only two things he (i.e. the Roman citizen)
longs for – bread and circuses. [*do.*, X]
5 *Orandum est ut sit mens sana in corpore sano.* You
should pray to have a healthy mind in a healthy body.
[*do.*]

K1   **Kant, Immanuel** (1724–1804) German philosopher
1 Two things fill the mind with ever new and
increasing wonder and awe, the more often and the
more seriously reflection concentrates upon them: the
starry heaven above me and the moral law within me.
[*Critique of Pure Reason*, Conclusion]

K2   **Karr, Alphonse** (1808–90) French author
1 *Plus ça change, plus c'est la même chose.* The more it
changes, the more it is the same. [*Les Guêpes*,
Jan. 1849]

K3   **Kavanagh, Ted** (1892–1958) English scriptwriter
1 Can I do you now, sir? [*Itma*, BBC radio
comedy series]
2 Don't forget the diver. [*do.*]
3 I don't mind if I do. [*do.*]
4 'After you, Claude.' 'No, after you, Cecil.' [*do.*]

K4   **Kearney, Denis** (1847–1907) US labour leader
1 Horny-handed sons of toil. [speech in San
Francisco, about 1878]

K5   **Keats, John** (1795–1821) English poet
1 Bright star! would I were steadfast as thou art.
[*Bright Star*]
2 A thing of beauty is a joy for ever: / Its loveliness
increases; it will never / Pass into nothingness.
[*Endymion*, I]
3 St. Agnes' Eve – Ah, bitter chill it was! / The owl,
for all his feathers, was a-cold; / The hare limp'd
trembling through the frozen grass, / And silent was
the flock in woolly fold. [*The Eve of Saint Agnes*]
4 And they are gone: aye, ages long ago / These
lovers fled away into the storm. [*do.*]
5 The poet and the dreamer are distinct, / Diverse,

sheer opposite, antipodes. / The one pours out a balm upon the world, / The other vexes it. [*The Fall of Hyperion*]

6 Ever let the fancy roam, / Pleasure never is at home. [*Fancy*]

7 No stir of air was there, / Not so much life as on a summer's day / Robs not one light seed from the feather'd grass, / But where the dead leaf fell, there did it rest. [*Hyperion*, I]

8 Knowledge enormous makes a God of me. [*do.*, III]

9 Oh, what can ail thee, Knight at arms / Alone and palely loitering; / The sedge is wither'd from the lake, / And no birds sing. [*La Belle Dame Sans Merci*]

10 La belle Dame sans Merci / Hath thee in thrall! [*do.*]

11 Do not all charms fly / At the mere touch of cold philosophy? [*Lamia*, II]

12 Thou still unravish'd bride of quietness, / Thou foster-child of silence and slow time. [*Ode on a Grecian Urn*]

13 Heard melodies are sweet, but those unheard / Are sweeter; therefore, ye soft pipes, play on. [*do.*]

14 'Beauty is truth, truth beauty,' – that is all / Ye know on earth, and all ye need to know. [*do.*]

15 No, no, go not to Lethe, neither twist / Wolf's-bane, tight-rooted, for its poisonous wine. [*Ode on Melancholy*]

16 My heart aches, and a drowsy numbness pains / My sense, as though of hemlock I had drunk. [*Ode to a Nightingale*]

17 O, for a draught of vintage! that hath been / Cool'd a long age in the deep-delved earth, / Tasting of Flora and the country green, / Dance, and Provencal song, and sunburnt mirth! / O for a beaker full of the warm South, / Full of the true, the blushful Hippocrene, / With beaded bubbles winking at the brim, / And purple-stained mouth. [*do.*]

18 Fade far away, dissolve, and quite forget, / What thou among the leaves hast never known, / The weariness, the fever, and the fret, / Here, where men sit and hear each other groan. [*do.*]

19 Where youth grows pale, and spectre-thin, and dies; / Where but to think is to be full of sorrow / And leaden-eyed despairs. [*do.*]

20 Now more than ever seems it rich to die, / To cease upon the midnight with no pain. [*do.*]

21 Thou wast not born for death, immortal Bird! / No hungry generations tread thee down; / The voice I hear this passing night was heard / In ancient days by emperor and clown: / Perhaps the self-same song that found a path / Through the sad heart of Ruth, when, sick for home, / She stood in tears amid the alien corn; / The same that oft-times hath / Charm'd magic casements, opening on the foam / Of perilous seas, in faery lands forlorn. [*do.*]

22 Was it a vision, or a waking dream? / Fled is that music: – Do I wake or sleep? [*do.*]

23 Much have I travell'd in the realms of gold, / And many goodly states and kingdoms seen. [*On First Looking into Chapman's Homer*]

24 Then felt I like some watcher of the skies / When a new planet swims into his ken; / Or like stout Cortez when with eagle eyes / He star'd at the Pacific – and all his men / Look'd at each other with a wild surmise – / Silent, upon a peak in Darien. [*do.*]

25 Season of mists and mellow fruitfulness, / Close bosom-friend of the maturing sun; / Conspiring with him how to load and bless / With fruit the vines that round the thatch-eaves run. [*To Autumn*]

26 Where are the songs of Spring? Ay, where are they? / Think not of them, thou hast thy music too. [*do.*]

27 I am certain of nothing but the holiness of the heart's affections and the truth of imagination – what the imagination seizes as beauty must be truth – whether it existed before or not. [letter to Benjamin Bailey, 22 Nov. 1817]

28 O for a life of sensations rather than of thoughts! [*do.*]

29 Negative Capability, that is, when a man is capable of being in uncertainties, mysteries, doubts, without any irritable reaching after fact and reason. [letter to G. and T. Keats, 21 Dec. 1817]

30 If poetry comes not as naturally as leaves to a tree it had better not come at all. [letter to John Taylor, 27 Feb. 1818]

31 Axioms in philosophy are not axioms until they

are proved upon our pulses; we read fine things but never feel them to the full until we have gone the same steps as the author. [letter to J. H. Reynolds, 3 May 1818]
32 Here lies one whose name was writ in water. [epitaph. Compare **C14.2, S15.99**]

K6 **Kennedy, John F.** (1917–63) US president
1 My fellow Americans: ask not what your country can do for you, ask what you can do for your country. [inaugural address, 20 Jan. 1961]

K7 **Kilmer, Joyce** (1886–1918) US poet
1 I think that I shall never see / A poem lovely as a tree. [*Trees*]

K8 **Kilvert, Francis** (1840–79)
English clergyman and diarist
1 Of all noxious animals, too, the most noxious is a tourist. And of all tourists the most vulgar, ill-bred, offensive and loathsome is the British tourist. [*Diary*, 5 April 1870]

K9 **King, Martin Luther** (1929–68)
US clergyman and civil-rights leader
1 I have a dream that one day this nation will rise up, live out the true meaning of its creed: we hold these truths to be self-evident, that all men are created equal. [speech in Washington, 1963]

K10 **Kingsley, Charles** (1819–75)
English clergyman and author
1 Be good, sweet maid, and let who can be clever. [*A Farewell*]
2 For men must work, and women must weep, / And there's little to earn, and many to keep, / Though the harbour bar be moaning. [*The Three Fishers*]

K11 **Kipling, Rudyard** (1865–1936) English author
1 Oh, East is East, and West is West, and never the twain shall meet. [*The Ballad of East and West*]
2 And a woman is only a woman, but a good cigar is a smoke. [*The Betrothed*]
3 'Oh, where are you going to, all you Big Steamers, / With England's own coal, up and down the salt seas?' / 'We are going to fetch you your bread and your butter, / Your beef, pork, and

mutton, eggs, apples, and cheese.' [*Big Steamers*]

4 We're foot – slog – slog – slog – sloggin' over
Africa – / Foot – foot – foot – foot – sloggin' over
Africa – / (Boots – boots – boots – boots – movin' up
an' down again!) / There's no discharge in the war!
[*Boots*]

5 But the Devil whoops, as he whooped of old: 'It's
clever, but is it art?' [*The Conundrum of the Workshops*]

6 Winds of the World, give answer! They are
whimpering to and fro – / And what should they
know of England who only England know? [*The
English Flag*]

7 For the female of the species is more deadly than
the male. [*The Female of the Species*]

8 For all we have and are, / For all our children's
fate, / Stand up and take the war. / The Hun is at
the gate! [*For All We Have and Are*]

9 Our England is a garden, and such gardens are not
made / By singing: – 'Oh, how beautiful!' and sitting
in the shade. [*The Glory of the Garden*]

10 The uniform 'e wore / Was nothin' much
before, / An' rather less than 'arf o' that be'ind.
[*Gunga Din*]

11 Though I've belted you an' flayed you, / By the
livin' Gawd that made you, / You're a better man
than I am, Gunga Din! [*do.*]

12 If you can keep your head when all about
you / Are losing theirs and blaming it on you. [*If*]

13 If you can fill the unforgiving minute / With
sixty seconds' worth of distance run, / Yours is the
Earth and everything that's in it, / And – which is
more – you'll be a Man, my son! [*do.*]

14 Then ye returned to your trinkets; then ye
contented your souls / With the flannelled fools at
the wicket or the muddied oafs at the goals.
[*The Islanders*]

15 He walked by himself, and all places were alike to
him. [*Just So Stories*, 'The Cat that Walked by
Himself']

16 For the Colonel's Lady an' Judy O'Grady / Are
sisters under their skins! [*The Ladies*]

17 On the road to Mandalay / Where the flyin'-
fishes play; / An' the dawn comes up like thunder
outer China 'crost the Bay! [*Mandalay*]

18 The tumult and the shouting dies; / The

Captains and the Kings depart: / Still stands Thine
ancient sacrifice, / An humble and a contrite
heart. / Lord God of Hosts, be with us yet, / Lest
we forget – lest we forget! [*Recessional*]
19 Oh, it's Tommy this, an' Tommy that, an'
'Tommy, go away'; / But it's 'Thank you, Mister
Atkins,' when the band begins to play. [*Tommy*]
20 It's Tommy this, an' Tommy that, an' 'Chuck
him out, the brute!' / But it's 'Saviour o' 'is country'
when the guns begin to shoot. [*do.*]
21 Take up the White Man's burden – / And reap
his old reward: / The blame of those ye
better, / The hate of those ye guard. [*The White
Man's Burden*]
22 Power without responsibility – the prerogative of
the harlot throughout the ages. [remark]

K12   **Kissinger, Henry** (1923–) US statesman
1 Power is the great aphrodisiac. [*New York Times*,
19 Jan. 1971]

K13   **Kitchener, Earl** (1850–1916) British field marshal
1 You are ordered abroad as a soldier of the King to
help our French comrades against the invasion of a
common enemy . . . It will be your duty not only to
set an example of discipline and perfect steadiness
under fire but also to maintain the most friendly
relations with those whom you are helping in this
struggle. In this new experience you may find
temptations both in wine and women. You must
entirely resist both temptations, and, while treating all
women with perfect courtesy, you should avoid any
intimacy. Do your duty bravely. Fear God. Honour
the King. [message to soldiers of the British
Expeditionary Force, 1914]

K14   **Knox, John** (1514?–72)
Scottish reformer and statesman
1 The First Blast of the Trumpet Against the
Monstrous Regiment [i.e. government] of Women.
[title of pamphlet]

L1   **Lamb, Lady Caroline** (1785–1828)
English author and mistress of Lord Byron
1 [on Byron] Mad, bad, and dangerous to know.
[*Journal*]

L2   **Lamb, Charles** (1775–1834)
English essayist and critic
1 The human species, according to the best theory I
can form of it, is composed of two distinct races, *the
men who borrow*, and *the men who lend*. [*Essays of
Elia*, 'The Two Races of Men']
2 I love to lose myself in other men's minds. When I
am not walking, I am reading; I cannot sit and think.
Books think for me. [*Last Essays of Elia*, 'Detached
Thoughts on Books and Reading']
3 I have had playmates, I have had companions / In
my days of childhood, in my joyful schooldays – /
All, all are gone, the old familiar faces. [*The
Old Familiar Faces*]

L3   **Landor, Walter Savage** (1775–1864) English author
1 I strove with none, for none was worth my strife; /
Nature I loved, and, next to Nature, Art; / I warmed
both hands before the fire of life: / It sinks, and I am
ready to depart. [*Finis*]

L4   **Lang, Julia** (1921–) English broadcaster
1 Are you sitting comfortably? Then I'll begin.
[*Listen With Mother* (BBC radio programme)]

L5   **Langbridge, Frederick** (1849–1923)
1 Two men look out through the same bars: / One
sees the mud, and one the stars. [*A Cluster of
Quiet Thoughts*]

L6   **Langland, William** (1332?–1400?) English poet
1 In a somer season, when soft was the sonne. [*Piers
Plowman*, B text, Prologue]
2 A faire felde ful of folke. [*do.*]

L7   **Larkin, Philip** (1922–) English poet
1 Sexual intercourse began / In nineteen sixty-
three / (Which was rather late for me) – / Between

the end of the *Chatterley* ban / And the Beatles' first
LP. [*Annus Mirabilis*]
2 On me your voice falls as they say love
should, / Like an enormous yes. [*For Sidney Bechet*]
3 They fuck you up, your mum and dad. / They
may not mean to, but they do. / They fill you with
the faults they had / And add some extra, just for
you. [*This Be the Verse*]
4 Why should I let the toad *work* / Squat on my
life? / Can't I use my wit as a pitchfork / And drive
the brute off? [*Toads*]
5 Funny how hard it is to be alone. / I could spend
half my evenings, if I wanted, / Holding a glass of
washing sherry, canted / Over to catch the drivel of
some bitch / Who's read nothing but *Which*.
[*Vers de Société*]

L8   **Latimer, Hugh** (1485?–1555)
English Protestant Martyr
1 Be of good comfort, Master Ridley, and play the
man; we shall this day light such a candle by God's
grace in England, as I trust shall never be put out.
[remark while being burned at the stake, 16 Oct.
1555]

L9   **Lawrence, D. H.** (1885–1930) English novelist
1 How beastly the bourgeois is / especially the male
of the species. [*How Beastly the Bourgeois Is*]
2 Pornography is the attempt to insult sex, to do dirt
on it. [*Phoenix*, 'Pornography and Obscenity']
3 Sex and beauty are inseparable, like life and
consciousness. And the intelligence which goes with
sex and beauty, and arises out of sex and beauty, is
intuition. [*Sex Versus Loveliness*]

L10   **Lazarus, Emma** (1849–87)
US poet and philanthropist
1 Give me your tired, your poor, / Your huddled
masses yearning to breathe free. [*The New Colossus*]

L11   **Leacock, Stephen** (1869–1944) Canadian humorist
1 Lord Ronald said nothing; he flung himself from
the room, flung himself upon his horse and rode
madly off in all directions. [*Nonsense Novels*,
'Gertrude the Governess']
2 Golf may be played on Sunday, not being a game
within the view of the law, but being a form of moral

effort. [*Other Fancies*, 'Why I Refuse to Play Golf']

L12   **Lear, Edward** (1812–88)
English artist and nonsense-poet.
1 There was an Old Man with a beard, / Who said,
'It is just as I feared! – / Two Owls and a
Hen, / Four Larks and a Wren, / Have all built
their nests in my beard!' [*The Book of Nonsense*]
2 On the Coast of Coromandel / Where the early
pumpkins blow, / In the middle of the woods / Lived the
Yonghy-Bonghy-Bo. [*The Courtship of the
Yonghy-Bonghy-Bo*]
3 The Dong! – the Dong! / The wandering Dong
through the forest goes! / The Dong! – the
Dong! / The Dong with a luminous Nose! [*The Dong
with a Luminous Nose*]
4 Far and few, far and few, / Are the lands where
the Jumblies live; / Their heads are green, and their
hands are blue, / And they went to sea in a sieve.
[*do.*]
5 'How pleasant to know Mr Lear!' / Who has
written such volumes of stuff! / Some think him ill-
tempered and queer, / But a few think him pleasant
enough. [*Nonsense Songs*]
6 The Owl and the Pussy-Cat went to sea / In a
beautiful pea-green boat; / They took some honey,
and plenty of money, / Wrapped up in a five-pound
note. / The Owl looked up to the Stars above, / And
sang to a small guitar, / 'O lovely Pussy! O Pussy,
my love, / What a beautiful Pussy you are.' [*The Owl
and the Pussy-Cat*]
7 They sailed away, for a year and a day, / To the
land where the Bong-tree grows, / And there in a
wood a Piggy-wig stood / With a ring at the end of
his nose. [*do.*]
8 They dined on mince, and slices of quince, /
Which they ate with a runcible spoon; /
And hand in hand, on the edge of the sand, /
They danced by the light of the moon. [*do.*]
9 The Pobble who has no toes / Had once as many
as we; / When they said, 'Some day you may lose
them all'; – / He replied, – 'Fish fiddle de-dee!' [*The
Pobble Who Has No Toes*]
10 Two old Bachelors were living in one
house; / One caught a Muffin, the other caught a
Mouse. [*The Two Old Bachelors*]

L13   **Leary, Timothy** (1920–) US author
1 Turn on, tune in, and drop out.
[*The Politics of Ecstasy*]

L14   **Le Carré, John** (1931–) English author
1 The spy who came in from the cold. [title of novel]

L15   **Le Corbusier (C. E. Jeanneret)** (1887–1965)
French architect
1 *La maison est une machine à habiter.* A house is a
machine for living in. [*Vers une architecture*]

L16   **Lee, Nathaniel** (1653?–92) English dramatist
1 When Greeks joined Greeks, then was the tug of
war! [*The Rival Queens*, IV. 2]

L17   **Lennon, John** (1940–80), and **McCartney, Paul**
(1942–) English singers and songwriters
1 All You Need Is Love. [title of song]
2 I don't care too much for money, / Money can't
buy me love. [*Can't Buy Me Love*]
3 All the lonely people, where do they all come
from? / All the lonely people, where do they all
belong? [*Eleanor Rigby*]
4 A Hard Day's Night. [title of song and film]
5 Imagine there's no heaven / It's easy if you
try / No hell below us / Above us only
sky / Imagine all the people / Living for
today – / You may say I'm a dreamer / But I'm not
the only one / And I hope some day you'll join
us / And the world will be as one. [*Imagine* (by
Lennon alone)]
6 I read the news today, oh boy / Four thousand
holes in Blackburn, Lancashire / And though the
holes were rather small / They had to count them
all / Now they know how many holes it takes to fill
the Albert Hall. [*A Life in the Day*]
7 Lovely Rita, meter maid. [*Lovely Rita*]
8 Will you still need me, will you still feed
me, / When I'm sixty-four? [*When I'm Sixty-four*]
9 I'll get by with a little help from my friends. [*With
A Little Help from My Friends*]

L18   **Leno, Dan** (1861–1904) English comedian
1 Ah, what is man? Wherefore does he why? Whence
did he whence? Whither is he withering? [remark in
stage act]

L19   **Léon, Fray Luis Ponce de** (1527–91)
Spanish monk, scholar, and poet
1 *Dicebamus hesterno die.* We were saying yesterday.
[attr. remark on resuming a lecture after five years'
imprisonment]

L20   **Lerner, Alan Jay** (1918–) US dramatist
1 All I want is a room somewhere, / Far away from
the cold night air; / With one enormous
chair – / Oh, wouldn't it be loverly?
[*My Fair Lady*, I. 1]
2 I'm getting married in the morning! / Ding dong!
the bells are gonna chime. / Pull out the
stopper! / Let's have a whopper! / But get me to the
church on time. [*do.*, II. 3]

L21   **Lévis, Duc de** (1764–1830)
French soldier and author
1 *Noblesse oblige.* Nobility has its obligations.
[*Maximes et Réflexions*]

L22   **Lewis, C. S.** (1898–1963) English author
1 Term, holidays, term, holidays, till we leave school,
and then work, work, work till we die. [*Surprised by
Joy*, ch. 4]

L23   **Lewis, Sinclair** (1885–1951) US novelist
1 Our American professors like their literature clear
and cold and pure and very dead. [Nobel Prize
speech, 1930]

L24   **Liberace, Wlaziu Valentino** (1920–) US pianist
1 I cried all the way to the bank. [*Liberace: An
Autobiography*, ch. 2]

L25   **Lincoln, Abraham** (1809–65) US president
1 No man is good enough to govern another man
without that other's consent. [speech, 16 Oct. 1854]
2 The ballot is stronger than the bullet. [speech,
19 May 1856]
3 We here highly resolve . . . that this nation, under
God, shall have a new birth of freedom; and that
government of the people, by the people, and for the
people, shall not perish from the earth. [address at
Gettysburg, 19 Nov. 1863]
4 It is not best to swap horses while crossing the
river. [speech, 9 June 1864]
5 You can fool all the people some of the time, and

Anne

some of the people all the time; but you can't fool all the people all the time. [attr.]

L26 **Litvinov, Maxim** (1876–1951) Russian diplomat
1 Peace is indivisible. [speech to League of Nations, 1 July 1936]

L27 **Lloyd, Marie** (1870–1922)
English music-hall entertainer
1 A little of what you fancy does you good.
[title of song]

L28 **Lloyd, Robert** (1733–64) English poet
1 Slow and steady wins the race.
[*The Hare and the Tortoise*]

L29 **Lloyd George, David** (1863–1945) British statesman
1 What is our task? To make Britain a fit country for heroes to live in. [speech, 24 Nov. 1918]

L30 **Logau, Friedrich von** (1604–55) German poet
1 Though the mills of God grind slowly, yet they grind exceeding small; / Though with patience He stands waiting, with exactness grinds He all.
[*Sinngedichte*, III. 2 (tr. Longfellow)]

L31 **Longfellow, Henry Wadsworth** (1807–82) US poet
1 I shot an arrow into the air, / It fell to earth, I knew not where. [*The Arrow and the Song*]
2 The cares that infest the day, / Shall fold their tents, like the Arabs, / And as silently steal away.
3 The shades of night were falling fast, / As through an Alpine village passed / A youth, who bore, 'mid snow and ice, / A banner with this strange device, / Excelsior! [*Excelsior*]
[*The Day Is Done*]
4 Life is real! Life is earnest! / And the grave is not its goal. [*A Psalm of Life*]
5 Lives of great men all remind us / We can make our lives sublime / And, departing, leave behind us / Footprints on the sands of time. [*do.*]
6 Ships that pass in the night, and speak each other in passing; / Only a signal shown and a distant voice in the darkness; / So on the ocean of life we pass and speak one another, / Only a look and a voice; then darkness again and a silence. [*Tales of a Wayside Inn*, III]
7 There was a little girl / Who had a little

curl / Right in the middle of her forehead; / And
when she was good / She was very, very good, / But
when she was bad she was horrid. [*There Was a
Little Girl*]

8 Under the spreading chestnut tree / The village
smithy stands; / The smith, a mighty man is
he / With large and sinewy hands. [*The Village
Blacksmith*]

9 It was the schooner Hesperus, / That sailed the
wintry sea; / And the skipper had taken his little
daughter, / To bear him company. [*The Wreck
of the Hesperus*]

L32   **Loos, Anita** (1893–) US author
1 Gentlemen always seem to remember blondes.
[*Gentlemen Prefer Blondes*, ch. 1]
2 Kissing your hand may make you feel very very
good but a diamond and safire bracelet lasts forever.
[*do.*, ch. 4]

L33   **Louis XIV** (1638–1715) King of France
1 *L'État c'est moi.* I am the State. [attr.]

L34   **Louis XVIII** (1755–1824) King of France
1 *L'exactitude est la politesse des rois.* Punctuality is
the politeness of kings. [attr.]

L35   **Lovelace, Richard** (1618–58) English poet
1 Stone walls do not a prison make, / Nor iron bars
a cage. [*To Althea, from Prison*]
2 I could not love thee (Dear) so much, / Lov'd I
not honour more. [*To Lucasta, Going to the Wars*]

L36   **Lowell, Robert** (1917–77) US poet
1 The Aquarium is gone. Everywhere, / giant finned
cars nose forward like fish; / a savage servility /
slides by on grease. [*For the Union Dead*]
2 I keep no rank nor station. / Cured, I am frizzled,
stale and small. [*Home after Three Months Away*]
3 I saw the spiders marching through the
air, / Swimming from tree to tree that mildewed
day / In latter August when the hay / Came creaking
to the barn. [*Mr Edwards and the Spider*]

L37   **Lowry, Malcolm** (1909–57) English novelist
1 Sickness is not only in body, but in that part used
to be call: soul. Poor your friend he spend his money
on earth in such continuous tragedies. [*Under the*

Volcano, ch. 1]
2 Come, *amigo*, throw away your mind. [*do.*]

L38 **Lucretius** (96?–55 BC) Roman poet
1 *Nil posse creari / De nilo.* Nothing can be created out of nothing. [*De Rerum Natura*, I]
2 *Suave, mari magno turbantibus aequora ventis, / E terra magnum alterius spectare laborem.* It is sweet, when the winds are lashing the waters on the great sea, to watch from the land the great struggle of someone else.[*do.*, II]

L39 **Luther, Martin** (1483–1546)
German Reformation leader
1 *Hier stehe ich. Ich kann nicht anders. Gott helfe mir. Amen.* Here I stand. I can do nothing else. God help me. Amen. [speech at the Diet of Worms, 1521]
2 *Ein' feste Burg ist unser Gott, / Ein' gute Wehr und Waffen.* A safe stronghold our God is still, / A trusty shield and weapon. [*Ein' feste Burg* (tr. Carlyle)]

L40 **Lyte, H. F.** (1793–1847)
British clergyman and hymn-writer.
1 Abide with me; fast falls the eventide; / The darkness deepens; Lord, with me abide.
[*Abide with Me*]
2 Swift to its close ebbs out life's little day; / Earth's joys grow dim, its glories pass away; / Change and decay in all around I see; / O Thou, who changest not, abide with me. [*do.*]

M1 **Macaulay, Thomas Babington** (1800–59)
English historian and statesman
1 The gallery in which the reporters sit has become a fourth estate of the realm. [*Historical Essays*, 'Hallam's *Constitutional History*']
2 Every schoolboy knows who imprisoned Montezuma, and who strangled Atahualpa. [*do.*, 'Lord Clive']
3 She [i.e. the Roman Catholic Church] may still exist in undiminished vigour when some traveller from New Zealand shall, in the midst of a vast

solitude, take his stand on a broken arch of London Bridge to sketch the ruins of St Paul's.
[*do.*, 'Van Ranke']

4 The Puritan hated bear-baiting, not because it gave pain to the bear, but because it gave pleasure to the spectators. [*History of England*, ch. 2]

5 Now who will stand on either hand, / And keep the bridge with me? [*Lays of Ancient Rome*, 'Horatius']

6 But those behind cried 'Forward!' / And those before cried 'Back!' [*do.*]

7 And even the ranks of Tuscany / Could scarce forbear to cheer. [*do.*]

8 Perhaps no person can be a poet, or can even enjoy poetry, without a certain unsoundness of mind. [*Literary Essays*, 'Milton']

9 We know no spectacle so ridiculous as the British public in one of its periodical fits of morality. [*do.*, 'Moore's *Life of Lord Byron*']

10 Thank you, madam, the agony is abated. [remark made at the age of 4, after being scalded with coffee]

M2   **McGonagall, William** (1830–1902)
Scottish poetaster
1 Beautiful Railway Bridge of the Silv'ry Tay! / Alas, I am very sorry to say / That ninety lives have been taken away / On the last Sabbath day of 1879, / Which will be remember'd for a very long time. [*The Tay Bridge Disaster*]

M3   **Mackintosh, Sir James** (1765–1832)
Scottish philosopher
1 The Commons, faithful to their system, remained in a wise and masterly inactivity. [*Vindiciae Gallicae*]

M4   **McLuhan, Marshall** (1911–80) Canadian author
1 The new electronic interdependence recreates the world in the image of a global village.
[*The Gutenberg Galaxy*]
2 The medium is the message. [*Understanding Media*]

M5   **MacMahon, Comte de** (1808–93)
French marshal and president
1 *J'y suis, j'y reste.* Here I am, and here I stay. [attr. remark at the taking of the Malakoff, 8 Sept. 1855]

M6   **Macmillan, Harold, Earl of Stockton** (1894–)
English statesman

1 Most of our people have never had it so good.
[speech at Bedford, 20 July 1957]
2 Little local difficulties. [remark on a cabinet crisis,
Jan. 1958]
3 The wind of change is blowing through the
continent. Whether we like it or not, this growth of
national consciousness is a political fact. [speech to
the South African Parliament, 3 Feb. 1960]

M7   **Mallory, George Leigh** (1886–1924)
English mountaineer
1 Because it is there. [remark on being asked why he
wanted to climb Mount Everest]

M8   **Malthus, Thomas** (1766–1834) English economist
1 Population, when unchecked, increases in a
geometrical ratio. Subsistence only increases in an
arithmetical ratio. [*The Principle of Population*]

M9   **Mandale, W. R.** (19th c)
1 Up and down the City Road, / In and out the
Eagle, / That's the way the money goes – / Pop
goes the weasel! [*Pop Goes the Weasel*]

M10   **Mao Tse-Tung (Mao Zedong)** (1893–1976)
Chinese Communist leader
1 Political power grows out of the barrel of a gun.
[*Selected Works*, II]
2 All reactionaries are paper tigers. [*do.*, IV]

M11   **Marie Antoinette** (1755–93) Queen of France
1 *Qu'ils mangent de la brioche.* Let them eat cake.
[attr. remark on being told that her people had no
bread]

M12   **Marlowe, Christopher** (1564–93) English dramatist
1 Why this is Hell, nor am I out of it. [*Doctor
Faustus*, I. 3]
2 Was this the face that launch'd a thousand ships, /
And burnt the topless towers of Ilium? /
Sweet Helen, make me immortal with a kiss!
[*do.*, V. 1]
3 Now hast thou but one bare hour to live, / And
then thou must be damn'd perpetually! / Stand still,
you ever-moving spheres of heaven, / That time may
cease, and midnight never come. [*do.*, V. 2]
4 Cut is the branch that might have grown full
straight, / And burned is Apollo's laurel-bough, /

That sometime grew within this learned man. [*do.*, Epilogue]
5 And, as their wealth increaseth, so inclose / Infinite riches in a little room. [*The Jew of Malta*, I. 1]
6 BARNARDINE. Thou hast committed –
BARABAS. Fornication: but that was in another country; / And besides, the wench is dead. [*do.*, IV. 1]
7 Come live with me, and be my love; / And we will all the pleasures prove / That hills and valleys, dales and fields, / Woods or steepy mountain yields. [*The Passionate Shepherd to his Love*]

M13 **Marryat, Frederick** (1792–1848)
English naval commander and novelist
1 If you please, ma'am, it was a very little one. [the nurse's excuse for her illegitimate baby. *Mr. Midshipman Easy*, ch. 3]

M14 **Martial** (*ab* 40 – *ab* 102) Roman poet
1 *Non amo te, Sabidi, nec possum dicere quare: / Hoc tantum possum dicere, non amo te.* I do not love you, Sabidius, and I cannot say why; I can only say this, I do not love you. [*Epigrams*, I, 32]
2 *Rus in urbe.* The country in the town. [*do.*, XII, 57]

M15 **Marvell, Andrew** (1621–78) English poet
1 Annihilating all that's made / To a green thought in a green shade. [*The Garden*]
2 [on the execution of Charles I] He nothing common did or mean / Upon that memorable scene: / But with his keener eye / The axe's edge did try. [*An Horatian Ode upon Cromwell's Return from Ireland*]
3 So much one man can do, / That does both act and know. [*do.*]
4 Had we but world enough, and time, / This coyness, lady, were no crime. [*To his Coy Mistress*]
5 But at my back I always hear / Time's winged chariot hurrying near; / And yonder all before us lie / Deserts of vast eternity. [*do.*]
6 The grave's a fine and private place, / But none, I think, do there embrace. [*do.*]
7 Let us roll all our strength, and all / Our sweetness, up into one ball: / And tear our pleasures

with rough strife / Thorough the iron gates of
life. / Thus, though we cannot make our sun / Stand
still, yet we will make him run. [do.]

M16   **Marx, Groucho** (1895–1977) US comic actor
1 What's a thousand dollars? Mere chicken feed. A
poultry matter. [*The Cocoanuts* (film)]
2 A child of five would understand this. Send
somebody to fetch a child of five. [*Duck Soup* (film)]
3 Look at me: I worked my way up from nothing to
a state of extreme poverty. [*Monkey Business* (film)]
4 Send two dozen roses to Room 424 and put 'Emily,
I love you' on the back of the bill. [*A Night in
Casablanca* (film)]
5 Please accept my resignation. I don't want to
belong to any club that will accept me as a member.
[attr. telegram]

M17   **Marx, Karl** (1818–83) German political philosopher
1 The history of all hitherto existing society is the
history of class struggles. [*The Communist Manifesto*]
2 The workers have nothing to lose but their chains.
They have a world to gain. Workers of the world,
unite! [do.]
3 From each according to his abilities, to each
according to his needs. [*Criticism of the Gotha
Programme*]
4 Religion . . . is the opium of the people. [*Critique
of the Hegelian Philosophy of Right*, Introduction]
5 Hegel says somewhere that all great events and
personalities in world history reappear in one fashion
or another. He forgot to add: the first time as tragedy,
the second as farce. [*The Eighteenth Brumaire of
Louis Napoleon*]

M18   **Mary I** (1516–58) Queen of England
1 When I am dead and opened, you shall find
'Calais' lying in my heart. [cited in Holinshed's
Chronicles, III]

M19   **Masefield, John** (1878–1967) English author
1 I must down to the seas again, to the lonely sea and
the sky, / And all I ask is a tall ship and a star to
steer her by. [*Sea Fever*]

M20   **Maudling, Reginald** (1917–) English politician
1 There comes a time in every man's life when he
must make way for an older man. [remark on being

dismissed from the Shadow Cabinet]

M21   **Maugham, W. Somerset** (1874–1965)
English author
1 Impropriety is the soul of wit. [*The Moon and Sixpence*, ch. 4]
2 People ask you for criticism, but they only want praise. [*Of Human Bondage*, ch. 50]

M22   **Melbourne, Lord (William Lamb)** (1779–1848)
English statesman
1 Nobody ever did anything very foolish except from some strong principle. [remark]
2 Things have come to a pretty pass when religion is allowed to invade the sphere of private life. [remark]

M23   **Melville, Herman** (1819–91) US novelist
1 Call me Ishmael. [*Moby-Dick*, ch. 1]
2 Yes, as everyone knows, meditation and water are wedded forever. [*do.*]
3 Now small fowls flew screaming over the yet yawning gulf; a sullen white surf beat against its steep sides; then all collapsed, and the great shroud of the sea rolled on as it rolled five thousand years ago. [*do.*, 135]

M24   **Menander** (343?–291? BC) Greek dramatist
1 Whom the gods love dies young. [*Dis Exapaton*]

M25   **Mencken, H. L.** (1880–1956) US editor and author
1 I've made it a rule never to drink by daylight and never to refuse a drink after dark. [*New York Post*, 18 Sept. 1945]
2 No one ever went broke underestimating the intelligence of the American people. [attr.]

M26   **Meredith, George** (1828–1909)
English novelist and poet
1 Around the ancient track marched, rank on rank, / The army of unalterable law. [*Lucifer in Starlight*]
2 In tragic life, God wot, / No villain need be! Passions spin the plot: / We are betrayed by what is false within. [*Modern Love*, 43]

M27   **Meredith, Owen (Earl of Lytton)** (1831–91)
English statesman and poet
1 Genius does what it must, and Talent does what it can. [*Last Words of a Sensitive Second-rate Poet*]

M28 **Metellus Macedonicus, Quintus Caecilius**
(d 115 BC) Roman general and statesman
1 *Si sine uxore vivere possemus, Quirites, omnes ea molestia careremus; set quoniam ita Natura tradidit, ut nec cum illis satis commode, nec sine illis ullo modo vivi possit, saluti perpetuae potius quam brevi voluptati consulendum est.* If we could live without a wife, citizens, we would all do without that burden; but since Nature has ordained that life is uncomfortable with them, yet impossible without them, we must look to the continued survival of the race rather than our brief pleasure. [speech on increasing the population, 131 BC]

M29 **Metternich, Prince** (1773–1859) Austrian statesman
1 Italy is a geographical expression.
[letter, 19 Nov. 1849]

M30 **Mikes, George** (1912–)
British (Hungarian-born) author
1 On the Continent people have good food; in England people have good table manners. [*How to be an Alien*]
2 Continental people have sex life; the English have hot-water bottles. [*do.*]

M31 **Mill, John Stuart** (1806–73)
English philosopher and economist
1 Ask yourself whether you are happy, and you cease to be so. [*Autobiography*, ch. 5]
2 No great improvements in the lot of mankind are possible, until a great change takes place in the fundamental constitution of their modes of thought. [*do*, ch.7]
3 The only purpose for which power can be rightfully exercised over any member of a civilized community, against his will, is to prevent harm to others. His own good, either physical or moral, is not a sufficient warrant. [*On Liberty*, ch. 1]
4 If all mankind minus one, were of one opinion, and only one person were of the contrary opinion, mankind would be no more justified in silencing that one person, than he, if he had the power, would be justified in silencing mankind. [*do*, ch. 2]
5 The liberty of the individual must be thus far limited; he must not make himself a nuisance to other people. [*do.*, ch. 3]

M32   **Millett, Kate** (1934–) US feminist
1 Our highly repressive and Puritan tradition has
almost hopelessly confused sexuality with sadism,
cruelty, and that which is in general inhumane and
antisocial. This is a deplorable state of affairs.
[*Sexual Politics*]

M33   **Milne, A. A.** (1882–1956) English author
1 Sir Brian had a battleaxe with great big knobs
on; / He went among the villagers and blipped them
on the head. [*When We Were Very Young*, 'Bad Sir
Brian Botany']
2 They're changing guard at Buckingham
Palace – / Christopher Robin went down with Alice.
[*do.*, 'Buckingham Palace']
3 James James / Morrison Morrison / Weatherby
George Dupree / Took great / Care of his
Mother, / Though he was only three. / James
James / Said to his Mother, / 'Mother,' he said, said
he; / 'You must never go down to the end of the
town, if you don't go down with me.'
[*do.*, 'Disobedience']
4 Hush! Hush! Whisper who dares! / Christopher
Robin is saying his prayers. [*do.*, 'Vespers']
5 How sweet to be a Cloud / Floating in the Blue!
[*Winnie-the-Pooh*, ch. 1]
6 Time for a little something. [*do.*, ch. 6]

M34   **Milton, John** (1608–74) English poet
1 A good book is the precious life-blood of a master
spirit, embalmed and treasured up on purpose to a
life beyond life. [*Areopagitica*]
2 He that can apprehend and consider vice with all
her baits and seeming pleasures, and yet abstain, and
yet distinguish, and yet prefer that which is truly
better, he is the true wayfaring Christian. I cannot
praise a fugitive and cloistered virtue, unexercised and
unbreathed, that never sallies out and sees her
adversary, but slinks out of the race, where that
immortal garland is to be run for, not without dust
and heat. [*do.*]
3 Above the smoke and stir of this dim spot, /
Which men call Earth. [*Comus*]
4 Was I deceived, or did a sable cloud / Turn forth
her silver lining on the night? [*do.*]
5 Beauty is Nature's coin, must not be

hoarded, / But must be current, and the good
thereof / Consists in mutual and partaken bliss. [*do.*]

6 Hence, vain deluding Joys, / The brood of Folly
without father bred! [*Il Penseroso*]

7 Sweet bird, that shunn'st the noise of folly, / Most
musical, most melancholy! [*do.*]

8 Where glowing embers through the room / Teach
light to counterfeit a gloom, / Far from all resort of
mirth, / Save the cricket on the hearth. [*do.*]

9 Hence, loathèd Melancholy, / Of Cerberus, and
blackest Midnight born, / In Stygian cave
forlorn, / 'Mongst horrid shapes, and shrieks, and
sights unholy! [*L'Allegro*]

10 Come, and trip it as you go / On the light
fantastic toe. [*do.*]

11 Yet once more, O ye laurels, and once more / Ye
myrtles brown, with ivy never sere, / I come to pluck
your berries harsh and crude, / And with forced
fingers rude, / Shatter your leaves before the
mellowing year. [*Lycidas*]

12 Fame is the spur that the clear spirit doth
raise / (That last infirmity of noble mind) / To scorn
delights, and live laborious days; / But the fair
guerdon when we hope to find, / And think to burst
out into sudden blaze, / Comes the blind Fury with
th' abhorred shears, / And slits the thin-spun life.
[*do.*]

13 Last came, and last did go, / The Pilot of the
Galilean lake, / Two massy keys he bore of metals
twain, / (The golden opes, the iron shuts amain).
[*do.*]

14 At last he rose, and twitched his mantle blue: /
To-morrow to fresh woods, and pastures new. [*do.*]

15 Of Man's first disobedience, and the fruit / Of
that forbidden tree, whose mortal taste / Brought
death into the World, and all our woe.
[*Paradise Lost*, I]

16 What in me is dark / Illumine, what is low raise
and support: / That to the height of this great
argument / I may assert Eternal Providence, / And
justify the ways of God to men. [*do.*]

17 A dungeon horrible, on all sides round, / As one
great furnace flam'd; yet from those flames / No
light, but rather darkness visible / Serv'd only to
discover sights of woe, / Regions of sorrow, doleful

shades, where peace / And rest can never dwell, hope
never comes / That comes to all. [*do.*]

18 What though the field be lost? / All is not lost –
the unconquerable will, / And study of revenge,
immortal hate, / And courage never to submit or
yield: / And what is else not to be overcome? [*do.*]

19 One who brings / A mind not to be changed by
place or time. / The mind is its own place, and in
itself / Can make a Heaven of Hell, a Hell of
Heaven. [*do.*]

20 To reign is worth ambition, though in
Hell: / Better to reign in Hell than serve in Heaven.
[*do.*]

21 Thick as autumnal leaves that strow the
brooks / In Vallombrosa, where th' Etrurian
shades / High over-arch'd embower. [*do.*]

22 From morn / To noon he fell, from noon to dewy
eve, / A summer's day; and with the setting
sun / Dropped from the zenith like a falling star.
[*do.*]

23 High on a throne of royal state, which far /
Outshone the wealth of Ormus and of Ind, / Or
where the gorgeous East with richest hand / Showers
on her kings barbaric pearl and gold, / Satan exalted
sat, by merit raised / To that bad eminence. [*do.*, II]

24 The other shape, / If shape it might be call'd that
shape had none / Distinguishable in member, joint,
or limb. [*do.*]

25 With ruin upon ruin, rout on rout, / Confusion
worse confounded. [*do.*]

26 Which way I fly is Hell; myself am Hell; / And,
in the lowest deep, a lower deep / Still threat'ning to
devour me opens wide, / To which the Hell I suffer
seems a Heaven. [*do.*, IV]

27 Farewell remorse! All good to me is lost; / Evil,
be thou my Good. [*do.*]

28 But wherefore thou alone? Wherefore with
thee / Came not all hell broke loose? [*do.*]

29 More safe I sing with mortal voice,
unchang'd / To hoarse or mute, though fall'n on evil
days, / On evil days though fall'n, and evil tongues.
[*do.*, VII]

30 Some natural tears they dropped, but wiped them
soon; / The world was all before them, where to
choose / Their place of rest, and Providence their

guide; / They, hand in hand, with wandering steps
and slow, / Through Eden took their solitary way.
[*do.*, XII]

31 Of whom to be dispraised were no small praise.
[*Paradise Regained*, III]

32 A little onward lend thy guiding hand / To these
dark steps, a little further on. [*Samson Agonistes*]

33 Ask for this great deliverer now, and find
him / Eyeless in Gaza at the mill with slaves. [*do.*]

34 O dark, dark, dark, amid the blaze of
noon, / Irrecoverably dark, total eclipse, / Without
all hope of day! [*do.*]

35 To live a life half dead, a living death. [*do.*]

36 Just are the ways of God, / And justifiable to
men; / Unless there be who think not God at all.
[*do.*]

37 My race of glory run, and race of shame, / And I
shall shortly be with them that rest. [*do.*]

38 How soon hath Time, the subtle thief of
youth, / Stolen on his wing my three-and-twentieth
year! [*Sonnet: On his being arrived to the age of
twenty-three*]

39 Avenge, O Lord, thy slaughtered saints, whose
bones / Lie scattered on the Alpine mountains
cold; / Ev'n them who kept thy truth so pure of
old, / When all our fathers worshipped stocks and
stones, / Forget not. [*Sonnet: On the Late Massacre
in Piedmont*]

40 When I consider how my light is spent / Ere half
my days, in this dark world and wide, / And that one
talent which is death to hide, / Lodged with me
useless. [*Sonnet: On his Blindness*]

41 God doth not need / Either man's work or his
own gifts. Who best / Bear his mild yoke, they serve
him best: his state / Is kingly; thousands at his
bidding speed, / And post o'er land and ocean
without rest; / They also serve who only stand and
wait. [*do.*]

42 Methought I saw my late espousèd Saint /
Brought to me like Alcestis from the grave. [*Sonnet:
On His Deceased Wife*]

43 New Presbyter is but old Priest writ large.
[*Sonnet: On the New Forcers of Conscience under the
Long Parliament*]

44 Peace hath her victories / No less renowned than

war. [*Sonnet: To the Lord General Cromwell*]

M35 **Mitchell, Margaret** (1900–49) US novelist
1 After all, tomorrow is another day. [*Gone with the Wind*, closing words]

M36 **Mohr, Joseph** (1792–1848)
Austrian theologian and poet
1 Silent night, holy night, / All is calm, all is bright. [*Stille Nacht (Silent Night)*]

M37 **Molière (Jean Baptiste Poquelin)** (1622–73)
French actor and dramatist
1 *Il faut manger pour vivre et non pas vivre pour manger.* One should eat to live, and not live to eat. [*L'Avare (The Miser)*, III. 5]
2 *Par ma foi! il y a plus de quarante ans que je dis de la prose sans que j'en susse rien.* Good heavens! For more than forty years I have been speaking prose without knowing it. [*Le Bourgeois Gentilhomme*, II. 4]
3 *Que diable allait-il faire dans cette galère?* What the devil was he doing in that galley? [*Les Fourberies de Scapin*, II. 7]
4 *Oui, cela était autrefois ainsi, mais nous avons changé tout cela.* Yes, it used to be so, but we have changed all that. [*Le Médecin malgré lui*, II. 4]

M38 **Montaigne, Michel de** (1533–92) French essayist
1 *Il se faut réserver une arrière boutique toute notre, toute franche, en laquelle nous établissons notre vraie liberté et principale retraite et solitude.* We must keep for ourselves a little back shop, all our own, totally unspoilt, in which we establish our true liberty and chief place of seclusion and solitude. [*Essais*, I, 39]
2 *La plus grande chose du monde, c'est de savoir être à soi.* The greatest thing in the world is to know how to be self-sufficient. [*do.*]
3 *Quand je me joue à ma chatte, qui sait si elle passe son temps de moi plus que je ne fais d'elle?* When I play with my cat, who knows whether she is amusing herself more with me than I am with her? [*do.*, II, 12]
4 *Que sais-je?* What do I know? [*do.*]

M39 **Moore, Edward** (1712–57) English author
1 This is adding insult to injuries. [*The Foundling*, V. 2]
2 I am rich beyond the dreams of avarice. [*The Gamester*, II. 2]

M40 **Moore, Thomas** (1779–1852) Irish poet
1 I never nurs'd a dear gazelle, / To glad me with its soft black eye, / But when it came to know me well, / And love me, it was sure to die! [*Lalla Rookh*]
2 The Minstrel Boy to the war is gone, / In the ranks of death you'll find him; / His father's sword he has girded on, / And his wild harp slung behind him. [*The Minstrel Boy*]
3 'Tis the last rose of summer / Left blooming alone; / All her lovely companions / Are faded and gone. ['*Tis the Last Rose*]

M41 **Morris, Desmond** (1928–) English biologist
1 A naked ape self-named *Homo sapiens*. [*The Naked Ape*, Introduction]

M42 **Morris, William** (1834–96)
English author and artist
1 Dreamer of dreams, born out of my due time, / Why should I strive to set the crooked straight? [*The Earthly Paradise*]
2 Forget six counties overhung with smoke, / Forget the snorting steam and piston stroke, / Forget the spreading of the hideous town; / Think rather of the pack-horse on the down, / And dream of London, small and white and clean, / The clear Thames bordered by its gardens green. [*do.*]
3 Had she come all the way for this, / To part at last without a kiss? [*The Haystack in the Floods*]

M43 **Morton, Thomas** (1764?–1838) English dramatist
1 Always ding, dinging Dame Grundy into my ears – what will Mrs Grundy zay? What will Mrs Grundy think? [*Speed the Plough*, I. 1]

N1 **Nabokov, Vladimir** (1899–1977)
US (Russian-born) novelist
1 Lolita, light of my life, fire of my loins. My sin, my soul. [*Lolita*, pt I, ch. 1]

N2 **Napoleon Bonaparte** (1769–1821) French emperor
1 [on the metric system] Nothing is more contrary to

the organization of the mind, the memory, and the imagination . . . The new system of weights and measures will be a source of awkwardness and difficulties for several generations. [*Mémoires . . . écrits à Ste-Hélène*, IV, ch. 26]
2 It is only one step from the sublime to the ridiculous. [remark after the retreat from Moscow, 1812. Compare **P1.1**]
3 England is a nation of shopkeepers. [attr.]
4 An army marches on its stomach. [attr.]

N3   **Nash, Ogden** (1902–71) US poet
1 Candy / Is dandy / But liquor / Is quicker. [*Reflections on Ice-Breaking*]
2 I think that I shall never see / A billboard lovely as a tree. / Indeed, unless the billboards fall, / I'll never see a tree at all. [*Song of the Open Road.* Compare **K7.1**]

N4   **Nashe, Thomas** (1567–1601) English author
1 Brightness falls from the air; / Queens have died young and fair; / Dust hath closed Helen's eye. / I am sick, I must die. / Lord have mercy on us. [*In Time of Pestilence*]

N5   **Nelson, Horatio** (1758–1805) English admiral
1 I have only one eye – I have a right to be blind sometimes . . . I really do not see the signal. [remark at the Battle of Copenhagen]
2 England expects that every man will do his duty. [signal at the battle of Trafalgar]
3 Kiss me, Hardy. [remark shortly before his death at Trafalgar.]

N6   **Newbolt, Sir Henry** (1862–1938) English author
1 There's a breathless hush in the Close tonight – / Ten to make and the match to win – / A bumping pitch and a blinding light, / An hour to play and the last man in. [*Vitai Lampada*]
2 But his captain's hand on his shoulder smote – / 'Play up! play up! and play the game!' [*do.*]

N7   **Newman, John Henry** (1801–90)
English cardinal and author
1 Praise to the Holiest in the height, / And in the depth be praise; / In all his words most wonderful, / Most sure in all his ways. [*The Dream of Gerontius*]

2 It is almost a definition of a gentleman to say that he is one who never inflicts pain. [*The Idea of a University*, 'Knowledge and Religious Duty']
3 Lead, kindly light, amid the encircling gloom, / Lead thou me on; / The night is dark, and I am far from home, / Lead thou me on. [*Lead Kindly Light*]

N8 **Newton, Sir Isaac** (1642–1727) English scientist
1 If I have seen further it is by standing on the shoulders of giants. [letter to Robert Hooke, 5 Feb. 1675/6]

N9 **Nietzsche, Friedrich** (1844–1900) German philosopher
1 God is dead; but because of the way Man is, perhaps for thousands of years there will be caves in which his shadow will be shown. [*Die Fröhliche Wissenschaft*, III]
2 I teach you the Superman. Man is something that is to be surpassed. [*Thus Spake Zarathustra*, ch. 3]

N10 **Nixon, Richard** (1913–) US president
1 You won't have Nixon to kick around any more, gentlemen. This is my last press conference. [remark, 1962]
2 This is the greatest week in the history of the world since the creation. [remark on man's first moon-landing, 1969]
3 It is time for the great silent majority of Americans to stand up and be counted. [speech, 1970]
4 When the President does it, that means it is not illegal. [remark in TV interview, 1977]

O1 **Oakeley, Frederick** (1802–80) English priest
1 O come all ye faithful, / Joyful and triumphant, / O come ye, O come ye to Bethlehem. [translation of an 18th-century Latin hymn]

O2 **Oates, Captain Lawrence** (1880–1912) English explorer
1 I am just going outside and may be some time. [last words, in R. F. Scott's journal, 16–17 Mar. 1912]

O3   **Ochs, Adolph Simon** (1858–1935)
US newspaper publisher
1 All the news that's fit to print. [motto of the *New York Times*]

O4   **Orczy, Baroness** (1865–1947)
British (Hungarian-born) author
1 We seek him here, we seek him there, / Those Frenchies seek him everywhere. / Is he in heaven? – Is he in hell? / That demmed, elusive Pimpernel? [*The Scarlet Pimpernel*, ch. 12]

O5   **Orwell, George (Eric Blair)** (1903–50)
English author
1 Four legs good, two legs bad. [*Animal Farm*, ch. 3]
2 All animals are equal but some animals are more equal than others. [*do.*, ch. 10]
3 Big Brother is watching you. [*Nineteen Eighty-Four*]
4 *Doublethink* means the power of holding two contradictory beliefs in one's mind simultaneously, and accepting both of them. [*do.*]

O6   **Osborne, John** (1929–) English dramatist
1 Look Back In Anger. [title of play]

O7   **Ovid (Publius Ovidius Naso)** (43 BC–AD 17?)
Roman poet
1 *Gutta cavat lapidem, consumitur anulus usu.* Dripping water hollows out a stone, a ring is worn away by use. [*Epistulae Ex Ponto*, IV]
2 *Medio tutissimus ibis.* You will go most safely in the middle (i.e. the middle path is safest). [*Metamorphoses*, II]
3 *Video meliora, proboque; / Deteriora sequor.* I see the better way, and approve it; but I follow the worse. [*do.*, VII]
4 *Tempus edax rerum.* Time, the devourer of all things. [*do.*, XV]

O8   **Owen, Robert** (1771–1858) Welsh social reformer
1 All the world is queer save thee and me, and even thou art a little queer. [attr. remark to William Allen, on dissolving their business partnership]

O9   **Owen, Wilfred** (1893–1918) English poet
1 What passing-bells for these who die as cattle? / Only the monstrous anger of the guns. [*Anthem for Doomed Youth*]

2 Above all I am not concerned with Poetry. My subject is War, and the pity of War. The Poetry is in the pity. [Preface to *Poems*]

O10   **Oxenstierna, Count Axel** (1583–1654)
Swedish statesman
1 Dost thou not know, my son, with how little wisdom the world is governed? [letter to his son, 1648]

P1   **Paine, Thomas** (1737–1809)
English political philosopher
1 The sublime and the ridiculous are often so nearly related that it is difficult to class them separately. One step above the sublime makes the ridiculous; and one step above the ridiculous makes the sublime again. [*The Age of Reason*, pt II. Compare **N2.2**]
2 Government, even in its best state, is but a necessary evil; in its worst state, an intolerable one. [*Common Sense*, ch. 1]

P2   **Parker, Dorothy** (1893–1967) US author
1 Men seldom make passes / At girls who wear glasses. [*News Item*]
2 Guns aren't lawful; / Nooses give; / Gas smells awful; / You might as well live. [*Résumé*]
3 She ran the whole gamut of the emotions from A to B. [remark on a stage performance by Katharine Hepburn]
4 How could they tell? [remark on being told of the death of President Coolidge]

P3   **Parkinson, C. Northcote** (1909–)
English satirist and historian
1 Work expands so as to fill the time available for its completion. [*Parkinson's Law*]

P4   **Pascal, Blaise** (1623–62)
French mathematician and philosopher
1 *Tout le malheur des hommes vient d'une seule chose, qui est de ne savoir pas demeurer en repos dans une chambre.* All human misfortune stems from one thing,

which is not knowing how to stay quietly in a room.
[*Pensées*]
2 *Le nez de Cléopâtre: s'il eût été plus court, toute la
face de la terre aurait changé.* If Cleopatra's nose had
been shorter, the whole face of the world would have
changed. [*do.*]
3 *Le silence eternel de ces espaces infinis m'effraie.* The
eternal silence of these infinite spaces (i.e. the
heavens) terrifies me. [*do.*]
4 *Le coeur a ses raisons que la raison ne connaît point.*
The heart has its reasons, of which reason knows
nothing. [*do.*]
5 *L'homme n'est qu'un roseau, le plus faible de la
nature; mais c'est un roseau pensant.* Man is only a
reed, the weakest thing in nature; but he is a thinking
reed. [*do.*]

P5   **Pater, Walter** (1839–94) English essayist and critic
1 She [i.e. Mona Lisa] is older than the rocks among
which she sits; like the vampire, she has been dead
many times, and learned the secrets of the grave; and
has been a diver in deep seas, and keeps their fallen
day about her; and trafficked for strange webs with
Eastern merchants. [*Studies in the History of the
Renaissance*, 'Leonardo da Vinci']
2 All art constantly aspires towards the condition of
music. [*do.*, 'The School of Giorgione']
3 To burn always with this hard, gemlike flame, to
maintain this ecstasy, is success in life. [*do.*,
'Conclusion']

P6   **Paterson, Andrew** (1864–1941) Australian author
1 Once a jolly swagman camped by a billabong, /
Under the shade of a kulibar tree, / And he sang
as he sat and waited for his billy-boil, / 'You'll come
a-waltzing, Matilda, with me.' [*Waltzing Matilda*]

P7   **Payne, John Howard** (1791–1852)
1 Mid pleasures and palaces though we may
roam, / Be it ever so humble, there's no place like
home . . . Home, home, sweet, sweet, home! [*Clari,
the Maid of Milan*]

P8   **Peacock, Thomas Love** (1785–1866)
English novelist
1 Not drunk is he who from the floor / Can rise
alone and still drink more; / But drunk is he, who

prostrate lies, / Without the power to drink or rise.
[*The Misfortunes of Elphin*, ch. 3, heading]
2 He was sent, as usual, to a public school, where a
little learning was painfully beaten into him, and from
thence to the university, where it was carefully taken
out of him. [*Nightmare Abbey*, ch. 1]

P9   **Pepys, Samuel** (1633–1703)
English diarist and Admiralty official
1 And so to bed. [*Diary*, 20 Apr. 1660 and *passim*]
2 Music and women I cannot but give way to,
whatever my business is. [*do.*, 9 Mar. 1666]
3 I bless God I do find that I am worth more than
ever I yet was, which is £6,200, for which the Holy
Name of God be praised! [*do.*, 31 Oct. 1666]

P10 **Pétain, Henri** (1856–1951) French marshal
1 *Ils ne passeront pas.* They shall not pass. [attr.
remark at Verdun, 1916. Probably based on an Order
of the Day by General Nivelle]

P11 **Peter, Laurence** (1919–) Canadian author
1 *The Peter Principle*: In a Hierarchy Every Employee
Tends to Rise to his Level of Incompetence. [*The
Peter Principle*, ch. 1]

P12 **Petronius** (1st c AD) Roman author
1 *Cave canem.* Beware of the dog. [*Satyricon*]

P13 **Philip, Prince, Duke of Edinburgh** (1921–)
1 Dontopedalogy is the science of opening your
mouth and putting your foot in it, a science which I
have practised for a good many years. [remark]

P14 **Phillips, Wendell** (1811–84) US reformer
1 Every man meets his Waterloo at last. [lecture at
Brooklyn, 1 Nov. 1859]

P15 **Pitt, William (The Younger)** (1759–1806)
English statesman
1 Roll up that map [i.e. of Europe]; it will not be
wanted these ten years. [remark on hearing news of
the Battle of Austerlitz in 1805]

P16 **Plato** (427?–347 BC) Greek philosopher
1 The good is the beautiful. [*Lysis*]
2 Our object in the construction of the state is the
greatest happiness of the whole, and not that of any
one class. [*Republic*, 4]

P17   **Pliny (The Elder)** (23–79) Roman scholar
1 *In vino veritas.* Truth comes out in wine. [*Historia Naturalis*, XIV]

P18   **Poe, Edgar Allan** (1809–49) US author
1 The fever call'd 'Living' / Is conquer'd at last. [*For Annie*]
2 Once upon a midnight dreary, while I pondered, weak and weary, / Over many a quaint and curious volume of forgotten lore, / While I nodded, nearly napping, suddenly there came a tapping, / As of some one gently rapping, rapping at my chamber door. [*The Raven*]
3 Take thy beak from out my heart, and take thy form from off my door! / Quoth the Raven, 'Nevermore.' [*do.*]
4 On desperate seas long wont to roam, / Thy hyacinth hair, thy classic face, / Thy Naiad airs have brought me home, / To the glory that was Greece / And the grandeur that was Rome. [*To Helen*]

P19   **Pompadour, Madame de** (1721–64) mistress of Louis XV
1 *Après nous le déluge.* After us the deluge. [remark after the Battle of Rossbach, 1757]

P20   **Pope, Alexander** (1688–1744) English poet
1 The right divine of kings to govern wrong. [*The Dunciad*, IV]
2 Lo! thy dread Empire, Chaos! is restor'd; / Light dies before thy uncreating word: / Thy hand, great Anarch! lets the curtain fall; / And Universal Darkness buries All. [*do.*]
3 As yet a child, nor yet a fool to fame, / I lisp'd in numbers, for the numbers came. / I left no calling for this idle trade, / No duty broke, nor father disobey'd. / The Muse but serv'd to ease some friend, not wife, / To help me through this long disease, my life. [*An Epistle to Dr Arbuthnot*]
4 Peace to all such! But were there one whose fires / True genius kindles, and fair fame inspires, / Blest with each talent and each art to please, / And born to write, converse, and live with ease: / Should such a man, too fond to rule alone, / Bear, like the Turk, no brother near the throne, / View him with scornful,

yet with jealous eyes, / And hate for arts that caus'd himself to rise; / Damn with faint praise, assent with civil leer, / And, without sneering, teach the rest to sneer. [*do.*]

5 Satire or sense alas! can Sporus feel? / Who breaks a butterfly upon a wheel? [*do.*]

6 The ruling passion, be it what it will, / The ruling passion conquers reason still. [*Epistles to Several Persons (Moral Essays)*, III]

7 Nature, and Nature's laws lay hid in night. / God said, *Let Newton be!* and all was light. [*Epitaph. Intended for Sir Isaac Newton*]

8 'Tis with our judgments as our watches, none / Go just alike, yet each believes his own. [*An Essay on Criticism*]

9 A little learning is a dangerous thing; / Drink deep, or taste not the Pierian spring: / There shallow draughts intoxicate the brain, / And drinking largely sobers us again. [*do.*]

10 Whoever thinks a faultless piece to see, / Thinks what ne'er was, nor is, nor e'er shall be. [*do.*]

11 True wit is nature to advantage drest, / What oft was thought, but ne'er so well exprest. [*do.*]

12 True ease in writing comes from art, not chance, / As those move easiest who have learn'd to dance. / 'Tis not enough no harshness gives offence, / The sound must seem an echo to the sense. [*do.*]

13 To err is human; to forgive, divine. [*do.*]

14 All seems infected that th' infected spy, / As all looks yellow to the jaundic'd eye. [*do.*]

15 For fools rush in where angels fear to tread. [*do.*]

16 Hope springs eternal in the human breast: / Man never is, but always to be blest. [*An Essay on Man*, I]

17 Lo! the poor Indian, whose untutor'd mind / Sees God in clouds, or hears him in the wind. [*do.*]

18 And, spite of pride, in erring reason's spite, / One truth is clear, 'Whatever IS, is RIGHT.' [*do.*]

19 Know then thyself, presume not God to scan; / The proper study of Mankind is Man. [*do.*, II]

20 Created half to rise, and half to fall; / Great lord of all things, yet a prey to all; / Sole judge of truth, in endless error hurl'd: / The glory, jest, and riddle of the world! [*do.*]

21 Worth makes the man, and want of it, the fellow; / The rest is all but leather or prunella. [*do.*, IV]

22 True friendship's laws are by this rule express'd, / Welcome the coming, speed the parting guest. [*Odyssey*, XV]

23 Where'er you walk, cool gales shall fan the glade, / Trees, where you sit, shall crowd into a shade. [*Pastorals*, 'Summer']

24 What dire offence from am'rous causes springs, / What mighty contests rise from trivial things. [*The Rape of the Lock*, I]

25 Here thou, great Anna! whom three realms obey, / Dost sometimes counsel take – and sometimes Tea. [*do.*, III]

26 The hungry judges soon the sentence sign, / And wretches hang that jury-men may dine. [*do.*]

P21   **Porter, Cole** (1891–1964)
US songwriter and composer

1 I get no kick from champagne. / Mere alcohol doesn't thrill me at all, / So tell me why should it be true / That I get a kick out of you. [*I Get a Kick out of You*]

2 I've Got You Under My Skin. [title of song]

3 It was great fun, / But it was just one of those things. [*Just One of Those Things*]

4 Let's Do It; Let's Fall in Love. [title of song]

5 Well, did you evah! What a swell party this is. [*Well, Did You Evah!*]

P22   **Potter, Stephen** (1900–69) English author

1 Gamesmanship or The Art of Winning Games Without Actually Cheating. [title of book]

2 *How to be one up* – how to make the other man feel that something has gone wrong, however slightly. [*Lifemanship*]

P23   **Pottier, Eugène** (1816–87)
French song-writer and politician

1 *Debout! les damnés de la terre!* Arise, the damned ones of the earth! [*L'Internationale*]

2 *C'est la lutte finale / Groupons-nous, et, demain, / L'Internationale / Sera le genre humain.* This is the final struggle; let us group ourselves and, tomorrow, the International will unite the human race. [*do.*]

P24   **Pound, Ezra** (1885–1972) US poet
1 Pull down thy vanity, it is not man / Made
courage, or made order, or made grace. / Pull down
thy vanity, I say pull down. [*Cantos*, 81]
2 For three years, out of key with his time, / He
strove to resuscitate the dead art / Of poetry; to
maintain 'the sublime' / In the old sense. Wrong
from the start. [*Hugh Selwyn Mauberley*, I]
3 There died a myriad, / And of the best, among
them, / For an old bitch gone in the teeth, / For a
botched civilization. [*do.*, V]
4 The apparition of these faces in the crowd; / Petals
on a wet, black bough. [*In a Station of the Metro*]

P25   **Powell, J. Enoch** (1912–) English politician
1 As I look ahead, I am filled with foreboding. Like
the Roman I seem to see 'the river Tiber foaming
with much blood'. [speech in Birmingham, 1968]

P26   **Prayer, The Book of Common**
1 We have left undone those things which we ought
to have done; and we have done those things we
ought not to have done. [*Morning Prayer*, 'General
Confession']
2 And forgive us our trespasses. As we forgive them
that trespass against us. [*do.*, The Lord's Prayer]
3 As it was in the beginning, is now, and ever shall
be: world without end [*Gloria*]
4 I believe in God the Father Almighty, Maker of
heaven and earth: And in Jesus Christ his only Son
our Lord, Who was conceived by the Holy Ghost,
Born of the Virgin Mary, Suffered under Pontius
Pilate, Was crucified, dead, and buried, He descended
into hell; The third day he rose again from the dead,
He ascended into heaven, And sitteth on the right
hand of God the Father Almighty; From thence he
shall come to judge the quick and the dead. I believe
in the Holy Ghost; The holy Catholick Church; The
Communion of Saints; The Forgiveness of sins; The
Resurrection of the body, And the life everlasting.
Amen. [*The Apostles' Creed*]
5 Give peace in our time, O Lord. [*Versicles*]
6 Lighten our darkness, we beseech thee, O Lord.
[*Evening Prayer*, Third Collect]

7 Read, mark, learn and inwardly digest. [*Collect, 2nd Sunday in Advent*]

8 If any of you know cause, or just impediment. [*Solemnization of Matrimony*]

9 Let him now speak, or else hereafter for ever hold his peace. [*do.*]

10 To have and to hold from this day forward, for better for worse, for richer for poorer, in sickness and in health, to love and to cherish, till death us do part. [*do.*]

11 Those whom God hath joined together let no man put asunder. [*do.*]

12 In the midst of life we are in death. [*Burial of the Dead*, First Anthem]

13 We therefore commit his body to the ground; earth to earth, ashes to ashes, dust to dust; in sure and certain hope of the Resurrection to eternal life. [*do.*, Interment]

P27 **Prescott, William** (1726–95) US Soldier
1 Don't fire until you see the whites of their eyes. [remark at Bunker Hill, 17 June 1775. Also attr. to Israel Putnam (1718–90)]

P28 **Proudhon, Pierre-Joseph** (1809–65) French journalist
1 *La propriété c'est le vol.* Property is theft. [*Qu'est-ce que la propriété?*, ch. 1]

P29 **Proust, Marcel** (1871–1922) French novelist
1 *Impossible venir, mensonge suit.* Cannot come, lie follows. [*A la recherche du temps perdu*, 'Le Temps retrouvé', I, ch. 1]
2 *Les vrais paradis sont les paradis qu'on a perdus.* The true paradises are the paradises we have lost. [*do.*, II, ch. 3]

P30 **Puzo, Mario** (1920–) US author
1 I'll make him an offer he can't refuse. [*The Godfather*]

R1 **Rabelais, François** (1494?–1553) French author
1 *L'appétit vient en mangeant.* The appetite grows by
eating. [*Gargantua*, I, ch. 5]
2 *Fay ce que vouldras.* Do what thou wilt. [*do.*, ch.
57]
3 *Je vais quérir un grand peut-être.* I am going to seek
a great perhaps. [attr. last words]
4 *Tirez le rideau, la farce est jouée.* Bring down the
curtain, the farce is over. [*do.*]

R2 **Raleigh, Sir Walter** (1552?–1618)
English courtier, navigator, and historian
1 Our graves that hide us from the searching
sun, / Are like drawn curtains when the play is
done. / Thus march we playing to our latest
rest, / Only we die in earnest, that's no jest. [*What is
our Life?*]
2 Fain would I climb, yet fear I to fall. [written on a
windowpane]

R3 **Reade, Charles** (1814–84) English author
1 Make 'em laugh; make 'em cry; make 'em wait.
[attr. formula for a serialized novel]

R4 **Reagan, Ronald** (1911–) US president
1 My fellow Americans, I am pleased to tell you I've
just signed legislation which outlaws Russia forever.
The bombing begins in five minutes. [remark in a
microphone test, Aug. 1984]

R5 **Reed, Henry** (1914–) English poet and dramatist
1 Today we have naming of parts. Yesterday / We
had daily cleaning. And tomorrow morning, / We
shall have what to do after firing. But today, / Today
we have naming of parts. [*Naming of Parts*]

R6 **Remarque, Erich** (1898–1970) German novelist
1 *Im Westen nichts Neues.* All Quiet on the Western
Front. [title of novel]

R7 **Reynolds, Malvina** (1900–78) US song-writer

1 They're all made out of ticky-tacky, / And they all look just the same. [*Little Boxes*]

R8   **Rhodes, Cecil** (1853–1902)
English administrator in South Africa
1 So little done, so much to do. [last words. Compare **T4.14**]

R9   **Rice-Davies, Mandy** (1944–) English entertainer
1 He would, wouldn't he? [remark on being told that Lord Astor had denied her allegations of sexual intimacy]

R10   **Roche, Sir Boyle** (1743–1807) Irish politician
1 Mr Speaker, I smell a rat; I see him forming in the air and darkening the sky; but I'll nip him in the bud. [attr. remark in the Irish parliament]

R11   **Rochester, Earl of (John Wilmot)** (1647–80) English poet
1 Here lies our sovereign lord the King, / Whose word no man relies on; / He never said a foolish thing, / Nor ever did a wise one. [*Epitaph on Charles II*]

R12   **Roland, Marie-Jeanne** (1754–93) French revolutionary
1 Oh liberty, what crimes are committed in your name! [remark before her execution]

R13   **Roosevelt, Franklin D.** (1882–1945) US president
1 I pledge you, I pledge myself, to a new deal for the American people. [speech in Chicago, 2 July 1932]
2 The only thing we have to fear is fear itself. [Inaugural Address, 4 March 1933]
3 A radical is a man with both feet firmly planted in the air. [broadcast, 26 Oct. 1939]

R14   **Roosevelt, Theodore** (1858–1919) US president
1 I wish to preach, not the doctrine of ignoble ease, but the doctrine of the strenuous life. [speech in Chicago, 10 Apr. 1899]
2 Every reform movement has a lunatic fringe. [speech, 1913]

R15   **Ross, Alan S. C.** (1907–) English linguist
1 U and Non-U, An Essay in Sociological Linguistics. [title of essay]

R16 **Rossetti, Christina** (1830–94) English poet
1 Does the road wind up-hill all the way? / Yes, to the very end. [*Up-Hill*]
2 In the bleak mid-winter / Frosty wind made moan, / Earth stood hard as iron, / Water like a stone; / Snow had fallen, snow on snow, / Snow on snow, / In the bleak mid-winter, / Long ago. [*Mid-Winter*]

R17 **Rosten, Leo C.** (1908–) US humorist
1 Any man who hates dogs and babies can't be all bad. [on W. C. Fields, to whom it is often wrongly attr. Speech at Masquers' Club dinner, 1939]

R18 **Rouget de Lisle, Claude Joseph** (1760–1836) French army officer
1 *Allons, enfants de la patrie, / Le jour de gloire est arrivé.* Come, children of our native land, / The day of glory has arrived. [*La Marseillaise*]

R19 **Rousseau, Jean Jacques** (1712–78) French (Swiss-born) philosopher
1 *L'homme est né libre, et partout il est dans les fers.* Man was born free, and everywhere he is in chains. [*Du Contrat Social (The Social Contract)*, ch. 1]

R20 **Routh, Martin** (1755–1854) English scholar
1 You will find it a very good practice always to verify your references, sir! [remark to a young scholar]

R21 **Ruskin, John** (1819–1900) English essayist and critic
1 I have seen, and heard, much of Cockney impudence before now; but never expected to hear a coxcomb ask two hundred guineas for flinging a pot of paint in the public's face. [on Whistler's painting 'Nocturne in Black and Gold.' *Fors Clavigera*, letter 79. See **W19.2**]
2 Remember that the most beautiful things in the world are the most useless; peacocks and lilies for instance. [*The Stones of Venice*, I, ch. 2]

R22 **Russell, Bertrand** (1872–1970) English mathematician and philosopher
1 Three passions, simple but overwhelmingly strong, have governed my life: the longing for love, the search for knowledge, and unbearable pity for the

suffering of mankind. [*Autobiography*, I, Prologue]
2 Mathematics . . . possesses not only truth, but supreme beauty – a beauty cold and austere, like that of sculpture. [*Mysticism and Logic*, ch. 4]

S1   **Saki (Hector Hugh Munro)** (1870–1916)
British author
1 'The man is a common murderer.' 'A common murderer, possibly, but a very uncommon cook.' [*Beasts and Super-Beasts*, 'The Blind Spot']
2 The cook was a good cook, as cooks go; and as cooks go she went. [*Reginald*, 'Reginald on Besetting Sins']

S2   **Salisbury, Lord** (1830–1903) English statesman
1 By office boys for office boys. [remark on the *Daily Mail*]

S3   **Santayana, George** (1863–1952)
US poet and philosopher
1 Those who cannot remember the past are condemned to repeat it. [*The Life of Reason*, I]

S4   **Sartre, Jean-Paul** (1905–80)
French philosopher and author
1 *L'Enfer, c'est les autres.* Hell is other people. [*Huis Clos*]

S5   **Schelling, Friedrich von** (1775–1854)
German philosopher
1 Architecture in general is frozen music. [*Philosophie der Kunst (Philosophy of Art)*]

S6   **Schumacher, E. F.** (1911–77) German economist
1 Small is beautiful. [title of book]

S7   **Scott, C. P.** (1846–1932) English journalist
1 Comment is free, but facts are sacred. [*Manchester Guardian*, 6 May 1926]

S8   **Scott, Robert Falcon** (1868–1912) English explorer
1 [on the South Pole] Great God! this is an awful place. [*Journal*, 17 Jan. 1912]

2 For God's sake look after our people. [*do.*, last entry, 29 March 1912]

S9 **Scott, Sir Walter** (1771–1832)
Scottish poet and novelist
1 Breathes there the man, with soul so dead, / Who never to himself hath said, / This is my own, my native land! [*The Lay of the Last Minstrel*, VI]
2 O what a tangled web we weave, / When first we practise to deceive! [*Marmion*, VI]
3 When pain and anguish wring the brow, / A ministering angel thou! [*do.*]

S10 **Seeger, Pete** (1919–) US singer and songwriter
1 Where have all the flowers gone? / The young girls picked them every one. [*Where Have All the Flowers Gone*]

S11 **Selden, John** (1584–1654)
English jurist and antiquarian
1 Preachers say, Do as I say, not as I do. [*Table Talk*]
2 Ignorance of the law excuses no man; not that all men know the law, but because 'tis an excuse every man will plead, and no man can tell how to confute him. [*do.*]

S12 **Sellar, W. C.** (1898–1951) and **Yeatman, R. J.** (1897–1968) English authors
1 1066 And All That. [title of book]

S13 **Service, Robert** (1874–1958) Canadian poet
1 This is the Law of the Yukon, that only the Strong shall thrive; / That surely the Weak shall perish, and only the Fit survive. [*The Law of the Yukon*]

S14 **Shadwell, Thomas** (1642?–92) English dramatist
1 'Tis the way of all flesh. [*The Sullen Lovers*, V. 2]

S15 **Shakespeare, William** (1564–1616)
English dramatist and poet
1 A young man married is a man that's marred. [*All's Well That Ends Well*, II. 3]
2 The web of our life is of a mingled yarn, good and ill together. [*do.*, IV. 3]
3 The triple pillar of the world transform'd / Into a strumpet's fool. [*Antony and Cleopatra*, I. 1]
4 There's beggary in the love that can be reckon'd.

[*do.*]

5 Eternity was in our lips and eyes, / Bliss in our brows' bent. [*do.*, I. 3]

6 My salad days, / When I was green in judgment, cold in blood, / To say as I said then! [*do.*, I. 5]

7 The barge she sat in, like a burnish'd throne, / Burn'd on the water; the poop was beaten gold; / Purple the sails, and so perfumed that / The winds were love-sick with them; the oars were silver, / Which to the tune of flutes kept stroke, and made / The water which they beat to follow faster, / As amorous of their strokes. For her own person, / It beggar'd all description. [*do.*, II. 2]

8 Age cannot wither her, nor custom stale / Her infinite variety. Other women cloy / The appetites they feed, but she makes hungry / Where most she satisfies. [*do.*]

9 Let's have one other gaudy night: call to me / All my sad captains; fill our bowls once more; / Let's mock the midnight bell. [*do.*, III. 11]

10 To business that we love we rise betime, / And go to't with delight. [*do.*, IV. 4]

11 Unarm, Eros; the long day's task is done, / And we must sleep. [*do.*, IV. 12]

12 I am dying, Egypt, dying; only / I here importune death awhile, until / Of many thousand kisses the poor last / I lay upon thy lips. [*do.*, IV. 13]

13 O! wither'd is the garland of the war, / The soldier's pole is fall'n; young boys and girls / Are level now with men; the odds is gone, / And there is nothing left remarkable / Beneath the visiting moon. [*do.*]

14 Finish, good lady; the bright day is done, / And we are for the dark. [*do.*, V. 2]

15 Give me my robe, put on my crown; I have / Immortal longings in me. [*do.*]

16 Well said; that was laid on with a trowel. [*As You Like It*, I. 2]

17 Sweet are the uses of adversity, / Which like the toad, ugly and venomous, / Wears yet a precious jewel in his head. [*do.*, II. 1]

18 Under the greenwood tree / Who loves to lie with me, / And turn his merry note / Unto the sweet bird's throat, / Come hither, come hither, come hither: / Here shall he see / No enemy / But winter and rough weather. [*do.*, II. 5]

19 And so, from hour to hour, we ripe and
ripe, / And then, from hour to hour, we rot and
rot; / And thereby hangs a tale. [*do.*, II. 7]

20 All the world's a stage, / And all the men and
women merely players: / They have their exits and
their entrances; / And one man in his time plays
many parts, / His acts being seven ages. At first the
infant, / Mewling and puking in the nurse's
arms. / And then the whining schoolboy, with his
satchel, / And shining morning face, creeping like
snail / Unwillingly to school. [*do.*]

21 The sixth age shifts / Into the lean and slipper'd
pantaloon. [*do.*]

22 Last scene of all, / That ends this strange
eventful history, / Is second childishness and mere
oblivion; / Sans teeth, sans eyes, sans taste, sans
every thing. [*do.*]

23 Blow, blow, thou winter wind, / Thou art not so
unkind / As man's ingratitude. [*do.*]

24 Men have died from time to time, and worms
have eaten them, but not for love. [*do.*, IV. 1]

25 It was a lover and his lass, / With a hey, and a
ho, and a hey nonino, / That o'er the green cornfield
did pass, / In the spring time, the only pretty ring
time, / When birds do sing, hey ding a ding,
ding; / Sweet lovers love the spring. [*do.*, V. 3]

26 An ill-favoured thing, sir, but mine own. [*do.*, V.
4. Often quoted as 'a poor thing . . .']

27 If it be true that good wine needs no bush, 'tis
true that a good play needs no epilogue.
[*do.*, Epilogue]

28 Fear no more the heat o' the sun / Nor the
furious winter's rages; / Thou thy worldly task hast
done, / Home art gone, and ta'en thy wages. /
Golden lads and girls all must, / As chimney-
sweepers, come to dust. [*Cymbeline*, IV. 2]

29 For this relief much thanks; 'tis bitter cold, / And
I am sick at heart. [*Hamlet*, I. 1]

30 And then it started like a guilty thing / Upon a
fearful summons. [*do.*]

31 A little more than kin, and less than kind.
[*do.*, I. 2]

32 O! that this too too solid flesh would
melt, / Thaw, and resolve itself into a dew; / Or that

the Everlasting had not fix'd / His canon 'gainst self-slaughter! O God! O God! / How weary, stale, flat, and unprofitable / Seem to me all the uses of this world! [*do.*]

33 Frailty, thy name is woman! [*do.*]

34 It is not, nor it cannot come to good. [*do.*]

35 We'll teach you to drink deep ere you depart. [*do.*]

36 He was a man, take him for all in all, / I shall not look upon his like again. [*do.*]

37 A countenance more in sorrow than in anger. [*do.*]

38 Do not, as some ungracious pastors do, / Show me the steep and thorny way to heaven, / Whiles, like a puff'd and reckless libertine, / Himself the primrose path of dalliance treads / And recks not his own rede. [*do.*, I. 3]

39 Costly thy habit as thy purse can buy, / But not express'd in fancy; rich, not gaudy; / For the apparel oft proclaims the man. [*do.*]

40 Neither a borrower, nor a lender be; / For loan oft loses both itself and friend, / And borrowing dulls the edge of husbandry. / This above all – to thine own self be true, / And it must follow, as the night the day, / Thou canst not then be false to any man. [*do.*]

41 But to my mind, though I am native here / And to the manner born, it is a custom / More honour'd in the breach than the observance. [*do.*, I. 4]

42 Something is rotten in the state of Denmark. [*do.*]

43 Murder most foul, as in the best it is; / But this most foul, strange, and unnatural. [*do.*, I. 5]

44 HAMLET. There's ne'er a villain dwelling in all Denmark, / But he's an arrant knave.

HORATIO. There needs no ghost, my lord, come from the grave, / To tell us this. [*do.*]

45 There are more things in heaven and earth, Horatio, / Than are dreamt of in your philosophy. [*do.*]

46 The time is out of joint; O cursed spite, / That ever I was born to set it right! [*do.*]

47 Brevity is the soul of wit. [*do.*, II. 2]

48 To be honest, as this world goes, is to be one man pick'd out of ten thousand. [*do.*]

49 Though this be madness, yet there is method in't. [*do.*]

50 There is nothing either good or bad, but thinking

makes it so. [*do.*]

51 O God! I could be bounded in a nut-shell, and count myself a king of infinite space, were it not that I have bad dreams. [*do.*]

52 What a piece of work is a man! How noble in reason! how infinite in faculty, in form and moving, how express and admirable! in action, how like an angel! in apprehension, how like a god! the beauty of the world! the paragon of animals! And yet, to me, what is this quintessence of dust? Man delights not me – no, nor woman neither. [*do.*]

53 I am but mad north-north-west; when the wind is southerly, I know a hawk from a handsaw. [*do.*]

54 The play, I remember, pleas'd not the million; 'twas caviare to the general. [*do.*]

55 Use every man after his desert, and who should 'scape whipping? [*do.*]

56 The play's the thing / Wherein I'll catch the conscience of the King. [*do.*]

57 To be, or not to be – that is the question; / Whether 'tis nobler in the mind to suffer / The slings and arrows of outrageous fortune, / Or to take arms against a sea of troubles, / And by opposing end them? To die, to sleep – / No more; and by a sleep to say we end / The heart-ache and the thousand natural shocks / That flesh is heir to, 'tis a consummation / Devoutly to be wish'd. To die, to sleep; / To sleep, perchance to dream. Ay, there's the rub; / For in that sleep of death what dreams may come, / When we have shuffled off this mortal coil, / Must give us pause. [*do.*, III. 1]

58 The dread of something after death – / The undiscover'd country, from whose bourn / No traveller returns. [*do.*]

59 Thus conscience does make cowards of us all; / And thus the native hue of resolution / Is sicklied o'er with the pale cast of thought. [*do.*]

60 O! what a noble mind is here o'erthrown: / The courtier's, soldier's, scholar's, eye, tongue, sword; / The expectancy and rose of the fair state, / The glass of fashion, and the mould of form, / The observed of all observers, quite, quite, down! [*do.*]

61 Marry, this is miching mallecho; it means

mischief. [*do.*, III. 2]

62 The lady doth protest too much, methinks. [*do.*]

63 What! frighted with false fire? [*do.*]

64 Very like a whale. [*do.*]

65 Thou wretched, rash, intruding fool, farewell! / I took thee for thy better. [*do.*, III. 4]

66 A king of shreds and patches. [*do.*]

67 I must be cruel only to be kind. [*do.*]

68 How all occasions do inform against me, / And spur my dull revenge! What is a man, / If his chief good and market of his time / Be but to sleep and feed? a beast, no more. / Sure he that made us with such large discourse, / Looking before and after, gave us not / That capability and god-like reason / To fust in us unus'd. [*do.*, IV. 4]

69 Some craven scruple / Of thinking too precisely on th' event. [*do.*, IV. 4]

70 Alas, poor Yorick! I knew him, Horatio; a fellow of infinite jest, of most excellent fancy. [*do.*, V. 1]

71 There's a divinity that shapes our ends, / Rough-hew them how we will. [*do.*, V. 2]

72 A hit, a very palpable hit. [*do.*]

73 The rest is silence. [*do.*]

74 Now cracks a noble heart. Good-night, sweet prince, / And flights of angels sing thee to thy rest! [*do.*]

75 If all the year were playing holidays, / To sport would be as tedious as to work; / But when they seldom come, they wish'd for come. [*Henry IV, Part 1*, I. 2]

76 By heaven, methinks it were an easy leap / To pluck bright honour from the pale-fac'd moon, / Or dive into the bottom of the deep, / Where fathom-line could never touch the ground, / And pluck up drowned honour by the locks. [*do.*, I. 3]

77 Falstaff sweats to death, / And lards the lean earth as he walks along. [*do.*, II. 2]

78 Out of this nettle, danger, we pluck this flower, safety. [*do.*, II. 3]

79 GLENDOWER. I can call spirits from the vasty deep. HOTSPUR. Why, so can I, or so can any man; / But will they come when you do call for them? [*do.*, III. 1]

80 I have more flesh than another man, and therefore more frailty. [*do.*, III. 3]

81 The better part of valour is discretion; in the

which better part I have saved my life. [*do.*, V. 4]

82 I am not only witty in myself, but the cause that wit is in other men. [*Henry IV, Part 2*, I. 2]

83 It was always yet the trick of our English nation, if they have a good thing, to make it too common. [*do.*]

84 He hath eaten me out of house and home. [*do.*, II. 1]

85 Is it not strange that desire should so many years outlive performance? [*do.*, II. 4]

86 Uneasy lies the head that wears a crown. [*do.*, III. 1]

87 We have heard the chimes at midnight. [*do.*, III. 2]

88 I know thee not, old man: fall to thy prayers; / How ill white hairs become a fool and jester! / I have long dream'd of such a kind of man, / So surfeit-swell'd, so old, and so profane. [*do.*, V. 5]

89 I dare not fight; but I will wink and hold out mine iron. [*Henry V*, II. 1]

90 His nose was as sharp as a pen, and a' babbled of green fields. [*do.*, II. 3]

91 Once more unto the breach, dear friends, once more; / Or close the wall up with our English dead! / In peace there's nothing so becomes a man / As modest stillness and humility: / But when the blast of war blows in our ears, / Then imitate the action of the tiger; / Stiffen the sinews, summon up the blood, / Disguise fair nature with hard-favour'd rage. [*do.*, III. 1]

92 Old men forget; yet all shall be forgot, / But he'll remember, with advantages, / What feats he did that day. [*do.*, IV. 3]

93 We few, we happy few, we band of brothers. [*do.*]

94 There is occasions and causes why and wherefore in all things. [*do.*, V. 1]

95 O tiger's heart wrapp'd in a woman's hide! [*Henry VI, Part 3*, I. 4]

96 O God! methinks it were a happy life, / To be no better than a homely swain; / To sit upon a hill, as I do now, / To carve out dials, quaintly, point by point, / Thereby to see the minutes how they run, / How many make the hour full complete; / How many hours bring about the day; / How many days will finish up the year; / How many years a mortal man may live. [*do.*, II. 5]

97 Farewell! a long farewell, to all my greatness! / This is the state of man: to-day he puts forth / The tender leaves of hope; to-morrow blossoms, / And bears his blushing honours thick upon him; / The third day comes a frost, a killing frost; / And when he thinks, good easy man, full surely / His greatness is a-ripening, nips his root, / And then he falls, as I do. [*Henry VIII*, III. 2]

98 Had I but serv'd my God with half the zeal / I serv'd my King, he would not in mine age / Have left me naked to mine enemies. [*do.* Compare **W34.1**]

99 Men's evil manners live in brass; their virtues / We write in water. [*do.*, IV. 2]

100 Beware the ides of March. [*Julius Caesar*, I. 2]

101 Why, man, he doth bestride the narrow world / Like a Colossus. [*do.*]

102 Men at some time are masters of their fates: / The fault, dear Brutus, is not in our stars, / But in ourselves, that we are underlings. [*do.*]

103 Let me have men about me that are fat; / Sleek-headed men, and such as sleep o' nights. / Yond Cassius has a lean and hungry look; / He thinks too much: such men are dangerous. [*do.*]

104 Cowards die many times before their deaths; / The valiant never taste of death but once. [*do.*, II. 2]

105 *Et tu, Brute*? [*do.*, III. 1]

106 O mighty Caesar! dost thou lie so low? / Are all thy conquests, glories, triumphs, spoils, / Shrunk to this little measure? [*do.*]

107 O, pardon me, thou bleeding piece of earth, / That I am meek and gentle with these butchers! / Thou art the ruins of the noblest man / That ever lived in the tide of times. [*do.*]

108 Cry 'Havoc!' and let slip the dogs of war. [*do.*]

109 Not that I lov'd Caesar less, but that I lov'd Rome more. [*do.*, III. 2]

110 Friends, Romans, countrymen, lend me your ears; / I come to bury Caesar, not to praise him. / The evil that men do lives after them; / The good is oft interred with their bones. [*do.*]

111 For Brutus is an honourable man; / So are they all, all honourable men. [*do.*]

112 When that the poor have cried, Caesar hath

wept; / Ambition should be made of sterner stuff. [*do.*]

113 If you have tears, prepare to shed them now. [*do.*]

114 This was the most unkindest cut of all. [*do.*]

115 There is a tide in the affairs of men, / Which, taken at the flood, leads on to fortune; / Omitted, all the voyage of their life / Is bound in shallows and in miseries. / On such a full sea are we now afloat, / And we must take the current when it serves, / Or lose our ventures. [*do.*, IV. 3]

116 This was the noblest Roman of them all. [*do.*, V. 5]

117 His life was gentle; and the elements / So mix'd in him that Nature might stand up / And say to all the world 'This was a man!' [*do.*]

118 Well, whiles I am a beggar, I will rail, / And say there is no sin, but to be rich; / And, being rich, my virtue then shall be, / To say there is no vice, but beggary. [*King John*, II. 2]

119 Life is as tedious as a twice-told tale, / Vexing the dull ear of a drowsy man. [*do.*, III. 4]

120 To gild refined gold, to paint the lily, / To throw a perfume on the violet, / To smooth the ice, or add another hue / Unto the rainbow, or with taper-light / To seek the beauteous eye of heaven to garnish, / Is wasteful and ridiculous excess. [*do.*, IV. 2]

121 Nothing will come of nothing: speak again. [*King Lear*, I. 1]

122 Ingratitude, thou marble-hearted fiend, / More hideous when thou show'st thee in a child / Than the sea-monster! [*do.*, I. 4]

123 How sharper than a serpent's tooth it is / To have a thankless child! [*do.*]

124 O, let me not be mad, not mad, sweet heaven! / Keep me in temper; I would not be mad! [*do.*, I. 5]

125 O, reason not the need! Our basest beggars / Are in the poorest thing superfluous: / Allow not nature more than nature needs, / Man's life is cheap as beast's. [*do.*, II. 4]

126 I will have such revenges on you both / That all the world shall – I will do such things, – / What they are, yet I know not, – but they shall be / The terrors of the earth. [*do.*]

127 Blow, winds, and crack your cheeks; rage, blow! / You cataracts and hurricanoes, spout / Till you have drench'd our steeples, drown'd the cocks. [*do.*, III. 2]

128 I am a man / More sinn'd against than sinning. [*do.*]

129 O! that way madness lies; let me shun that. [*do.*, III. 4]

130 The worst is not, / So long as we can say, 'This is the Worst.' [*do.*, IV. 1]

131 As flies to wanton boys are we to the gods; / They kill us for their sport. [*do.*]

132 Ay, every inch a king. [*do.*, IV. 6]

133 Through tatter'd clothes small vices do appear; / Robes and furr'd gowns hide all. [*do.*]

134 When we are born, we cry that we are come / To this great stage of fools. [*do.*]

135 You do me wrong, to take me out of the grave. / Thou art a soul in bliss; but I am bound / Upon a wheel of fire, that mine own tears / Do scald like molten lead. [*do.*, IV. 7]

136 I am a very foolish, fond old man, / Fourscore and upward, not an hour more or less; / And, to deal plainly, / I fear I am not in my perfect mind. [*do.*]

137 Men must endure / Their going hence, even as their coming hither: / Ripeness is all. [*do.*, V. 2]

138 The gods are just, and of our pleasant vices / Make instruments to plague us. [*do.*, V. 3]

139 Her voice was ever soft, / Gentle and low, an excellent thing in woman. [*do.*]

140 And my poor fool is hang'd! No, no, no life! / Why should a dog, a horse, a rat, have life, / And thou no breath at all? Thou'lt come no more, / Never, never, never, never, never. [*do.*]

141 Vex not his ghost: O! let him pass; he hates him / That would upon the rack of this tough world / Stretch him out longer. [*do.*]

142 Small have continual plodders ever won, / Save base authority from others' books. [*Love's Labour's Lost*, I. 1]

143 At Christmas I no more desire a rose / Than wish a snow in May's new fangled shows. [*do.*]

144 They have been at a great feast of languages, and stolen the scraps. [*do.*, V. 1]

145 When icicles hang by the wall, / And Dick the

shepherd blows his nail, / And Tom bears logs into the hall, / And milk comes frozen home in pail, / When blood is nipp'd, and ways be foul, /
Then nightly sings the staring owl: / 'Tu-who; / Tu-whit, Tu-who' – A merry note, / While greasy Joan doth keel the pot. [*do.*, V. 2]

146 When shall we three meet again / In thunder, lightning, or in rain? [*Macbeth*, I. 1]

147 Fair is foul, and foul is fair: / Hover through the fog and filthy air. [*do.*]

148 A drum! a drum! / Macbeth doth come. [*do.*, I. 3]

149 So foul and fair a day I have not seen. [*do.*]

150 Present fears / Are less than horrible imaginings. [*do.*]

151 Nothing in his life / Became him like the leaving it: he died / As one that had been studied in his death / To throw away the dearest thing he ow'd / As 'twere a careless trifle. [*do.*, I. 4]

152 Yet do I fear thy nature; / It is too full o' the milk of human kindness / To catch the nearest way. [*do.*, I. 5]

153 If it were done when 'tis done, then 'twere well / It were done quickly. [*do.*, I. 7]

154 That but this blow / Might be the be-all and the end-all here – / But here upon this bank and shoal of time – / We'd jump the life to come. [*do.*]

155 I have no spur / To prick the sides of my intent, but only / Vaulting ambition, which o'er-leaps itself, / And falls on the other. [*do.*]

156 I dare do all that may become a man; / Who dares do more is none. [*do.*]

157 But screw your courage to the sticking-place, / And we'll not fail. [*do.*]

158 Is this a dagger which I see before me, / The handle toward my hand? Come, let me clutch thee: / I have thee not, and yet I see thee still. [*do.*, II. 1]

159 Methought I heard a voice cry, 'Sleep no more! / Macbeth does murder sleep,' the innocent sleep, / Sleep that knits up the ravell'd sleave of care, / The death of each day's life, sore labour's bath, / Balm of hurt minds, great nature's second course, / Chief nourisher in life's feast. [*do.*, II. 2]

160 Will all great Neptune's ocean wash this

blood / Clean from my hand? No, this my hand will rather / The multitudinous seas incarnadine, / Making the green one red. [do.]

161 Lechery, sir, it [i.e. drink] provokes, and unprovokes: it provokes the desire, but it takes away the performance. Therefore, much drink may be said to be an equivocator with lechery: it makes him, and it mars him; it sets him on, and it takes him off; it persuades him, and disheartens him; makes him stand to, and not stand to. [do., II. 3]

162 Confusion now hath made his masterpiece! [do.]

163 We have scotch'd the snake, not killed it. [do., III. 2]

164 Duncan is in his grave; / After life's fitful fever he sleeps well. [do.]

165 I had else been perfect, / Whole as the marble, founded as the rock, / As broad and general as the casing air, / But now I am cabin'd, cribb'd, confin'd, bound in / To saucy doubts and fears. [do., III. 4]

166 Stand not upon the order of your going, / But go at once. [do.]

167 I am in blood / Stepp'd in so far that, should I wade no more, / Returning were as tedious as go o'er. [do.]

168 Double, double toil and trouble; / Fire burn and cauldron bubble. [do., IV. 1]

169 By the pricking of my thumbs, / Something wicked this way comes. [do.]

170 Be bloody, bold, and resolute; laugh to scorn / The power of man, for none of woman born / Shall harm Macbeth. [do.]

171 Out, damned spot! out, I say! [do., V. 1]

172 Here's the smell of the blood still: all the perfumes of Arabia will not sweeten this little hand. [do.]

173 I have liv'd long enough: my way of life / Is fall'n into the sear, the yellow leaf; / And that which should accompany old age, / As honour, love, obedience, troops of friends, / I must not look to have. [do., V. 3]

174 I have supp'd full with horrors. [do., V. 5]

175 Tomorrow, and tomorrow and tomorrow, / Creeps in this petty pace from day to day, / To the last syllable of recorded time; / And all our yesterdays have lighted fools / The way to dusty

death. Out, out, brief candle! / Life's but a walking
shadow, a poor player, / That struts and frets his
hour upon the stage, / And then is heard no more; it
is a tale / Told by an idiot, full of sound and
fury, / Signifying nothing. [*do.*]

176 I bear a charmed life, which must not yield / To
one of woman born. [*do.*, V. 7]

177 Lay on, Macduff; / And damn'd be him that
first cries, 'Hold, enough!' [*do.*, V. 7. Often quoted as
'Lead on, Macduff']

178 A man whose blood / Is very snow-broth; one
who never feels / The wanton stings and motions of
the sense, / But doth rebate and blunt his natural
edge / With profits of the mind, study and fast.
[*Measure for Measure*, I. 5]

179 We must not make a scarecrow of the law, /
Setting it up to fear the birds of prey, / And let it
keep one shape, till custom make it / Their perch
and not their terror. [*do.*, II. 1]

180 But man, proud man, / Dress'd in a little brief
authority, / Most ignorant of what he's most
assur'd, / His glassy essence, like an angry
ape, / Plays such fantastic tricks before high
heaven / As makes the angels weep. [*do.*, II. 2]

181 Be absolute for death; either death or life / Shall
thereby be the sweeter. Reason thus with life: / If I
do lose thee, I do lose a thing / That none but fools
would keep: a breath thou art, / Servile to all the
skyey influences, / That dost this habitation, where
thou keep'st, / Hourly afflict. Merely, thou art
death's fool; / For him thou labour'st by thy flight to
shun, / And yet run'st toward him still. [*do.*, III. 1]

182 Ay, but to die, and go we know not where; / To
lie in cold obstruction, and to rot; / This sensible
warm motion to become / A kneaded clod; and the
delighted spirit / To bathe in fiery floods or to
reside / In thrilling region of thick-ribbed ice. [*do.*]

183 In sooth, I know not why I am so sad: / It
wearies me; you say it wearies you; / But how I
caught it, found it, or came by it, / What stuff 'tis
made of, whereof it is born, / I am to learn. [*The
Merchant of Venice*, I. 1]

184 Gratiano speaks an infinite deal of nothing, more
than any man in all Venice. His reasons are as two
grains of wheat hid in two bushels of chaff: you shall

seek all day ere you find them; and, when you have them, they are not worth the search. [*do.*]

185 By my troth, Nerissa, my little body is aweary of this great world. [*do.*, I. 2]

186 The devil can cite Scripture for his purpose. [*do.*, I. 3]

187 It is a wise father that knows his own child. [*do.*, II. 2]

188 I will not choose what many men desire, / Because I will not jump with common spirits, / And rank me with the barbarous multitudes. [*do.*, II. 9]

190 Hath not a Jew eyes? Hath not a Jew hands, organs, dimensions, senses, affections, passions? fed with the same food, hurt with the same weapons, subject to the same diseases, healed by the same means, warmed and cooled by the same winter and summer, as a Christian is? If you prick us, do we not bleed? If you tickle us, do we not laugh? If you poison us, do we not die? And if you wrong us, shall we not revenge? [*do.*, III. 1]

191 I am not bound to please thee with my answer. [*do.*, IV. 1]

192 The quality of mercy is not strain'd; / It droppeth as the gentle rain from heaven / Upon the place beneath: it is twice blest; / It blesseth him that gives and him that takes. [*do.*]

193 A Daniel come to judgment! yea, a Daniel! / O wise young judge, how I do honour thee! [*do.*]

194 I thank thee, Jew, for teaching me that word. [*do.*]

195 How sweet the moonlight sleeps upon this bank! / Here will we sit, and let the sounds of music / Creep in our ears. [*do.*, V. 1]

196 The man that hath no music in himself, / Nor is not mov'd with concord of sweet sounds, / Is fit for treasons, stratagems, and spoils. [*do.*]

197 How far that little candle throws his beams! / So shines a good deed in a naughty world. [*do.*]

198 Why, then the world's mine oyster, / Which I with sword will open. [*The Merry Wives of Windsor*, II. 2]

199 They say there is divinity in odd numbers, either in nativity, chance, or death. [*do.*, V. 1]

200 For aught that I could ever read, / Could ever hear by tale or history, / The course of true love never did run smooth. [*A Midsummer Night's Dream*, I. 1]

201 I'll put a girdle round about the earth / In forty minutes. [*do.*, II. 2]

202 I know a bank whereon the wild thyme blows, / Where oxlips and the nodding violet grows; / Quite over-canopied with luscious woodbine, / With sweet musk-roses, and with eglantine. [*do.*]

203 Lord, what fools these mortals be! [*do.*, III. 2]

204 The eye of man hath not heard, the ear of man hath not seen, man's hand is not able to taste, his tongue to conceive, nor his heart to report, what my dream was. [*do.*, IV. 1]

205 The lunatic, the lover, and the poet, / Are of imagination all compact. [*do.*, V. 1]

206 The poet's eye, in a fine frenzy rolling, / Doth glance from heaven to earth, from earth to heaven; / And, as imagination bodies forth / The forms of things unknown, the poet's pen / Turns them to shapes, and gives to airy nothing / A local habitation, and a name. [*do.*]

207 I see a voice. [*do.*]

208 Sigh no more, ladies, sigh no more, / Men were deceivers ever. [*Much Ado About Nothing*, II. 3]

209 Doth not the appetite alter? A man loves the meat in his youth, that he cannot endure in his age. [*do.*]

210 Comparisons are odorous. [*do.*, III. 5]

211 For there was never yet philosopher / That could endure the toothache patiently, / However they have writ the style of gods / And made a push at chance and sufferance. [*do.*, V. 1]

212 Though in the trade of war I have slain men, / Yet do I hold it very stuff o' the conscience / To do no contriv'd murder: I lack iniquity / Sometimes, to do me service. [*Othello*, I. 2]

213 Keep up your bright swords, for the dew will rust them. [*do.*]

214 My story being done, / She gave me for my pains a world of sighs: / She swore, in faith, 'twas strange, 'twas passing strange; / 'Twas pitiful, 'twas wondrous pitiful. [*do.*, I. 3]

215 She lov'd me for the dangers I had pass'd, / And I lov'd her that she did pity them. [*do.*]

216 Put money in thy purse. [*do.*]

217 Do not put me to't, / For I am nothing if not critical. [*do.*, II. 1]

218 To suckle fools and chronicle small beer. [*do.*]

219 I have very poor and unhappy brains for drinking: I could well wish courtesy would invent some other custom of entertainment. [*do.*, II. 3]

220 Reputation, reputation, reputation! O, I have lost my reputation! I have lost the immortal part of myself, and what remains is bestial. [*do.*]

221 Excellent wretch! Perdition catch my soul / But I do love thee! and when I love thee not, / Chaos is come again. [*do.*, III. 3]

222 Good name in man and woman, dear my lord, / Is the immediate jewel of their souls: / Who steals my purse steals trash; 'tis something, nothing; / 'Twas mine, 'tis his, and has been slave to thousands; / But he that filches from me my good name / Robs me of that which not enriches him, / And makes me poor indeed. [*do.*]

223 O! beware my lord, of jealousy; / It is the green-ey'd monster, which doth mock / The meat it feeds on. [*do.*]

224 I had been happy, if the general camp, / Pioners and all, had tasted her sweet body, / So I had nothing known. O! now, for ever / Farewell the tranquil mind; farewell content! / Farewell the plumed troop and the big wars / That make ambition virtue! O, farewell! / Farewell the neighing steed and the shrill trump, / The spirit-stirring drum, the ear-piercing fife, / The royal banner, and all quality, / Pride, pomp, and circumstance of glorious war! / And, O you mortal engines, whose rude throats / The immortal Jove's dread clamours counterfeit, / Farewell! Othello's occupation's gone! [*do.*]

225 Put out the light, and then put out the light. / If I quench thee, thou flaming minister, / I can again thy former light restore, / Should I repent me; but once put out thy light, / Thou cunning'st pattern of excelling nature, / I know not where is that Promethean heat / That can thy light relume. [*do.*, V. 2]

226 I have done the state some service, and they know 't; / No more of that. I pray you, in your letters, / When you shall these unlucky deeds

relate, / Speak of me as I am; nothing
extenuate, / Nor set down aught in malice: then
must you speak / Of one that lov'd not wisely, but
too well; / Of one not easily jealous, but, being
wrought, / Perplex'd in the extreme; of one whose
hand, / Like the base Indian, threw a pearl
away / Richer than all his tribe; of one whose
subdu'd eyes / Albeit unused to the melting
mood, / Drop tears as fast as the Arabian
trees / Their med'cinable gum. [*do.*]
227 I kiss'd thee ere I kill'd thee: no way but
this, / Killing myself to die upon a kiss. [*do.*]
228 Crabbed age and youth cannot live together: /
Youth is full of pleasance, age is full of care; /
Youth like summer morn, age like winter weather; /
Youth like summer brave, age like winter bare.
[*The Passionate Pilgrim*, 12]
229 3RD FISHERMAN. Master, I marvel how the fishes
live in the sea.
1ST FISHERMAN. Why, as men do a-land: the great ones
eat up the little ones.[*Pericles*, II. 1]
230 The purest treasure mortal times afford /
Is spotless reputation; that away, / Men are but gilded
loam or painted clay. [*Richard II*, I. 1]
231 Methinks I am a prophet new inspir'd, / And
thus expiring do foretell of him: / His rash fierce
blaze of riot cannot last, / For violent fires soon burn
out themselves; / Small showers last long, but sudden
storms are short; / He tires betimes that spurs too
fast betimes. [*do.*, II. 1]
232 This royal throne of kings, this scepter'd
isle, / This earth of majesty, this seat of Mars, /
This other Eden, demi-paradise, / This fortress built
by Nature for herself / Against infection and the
hand of war; / This happy breed of men, this little
world, / This precious stone set in the silver
sea, / Which serves it in the office of a wall, / Or as
a moat defensive to a house, / Against the envy of
less happier lands; / This blessed plot, this earth, this
realm, this England, / This nurse, this teeming
womb of royal kings, / Fear'd by their breed, and
famous by their birth, / Renowned for their deeds as
far from home, – / For Christian service and true
chivalry, – / As is the sepulchre in stubborn
Jewry / Of the world's ransom, blessed Mary's

Son: / This land of such dear souls, this dear, dear land, / Dear for her reputation through the world. [*do.*]

233 That England, that was wont to conquer others, / Hath made a shameful conquest of itself. [*do.*]

234 Of comfort no man speak: / Let's talk of graves, of worms, and epitaphs; / Make dust our paper, and with rainy eyes / Write sorrow on the bosom of the earth. / Let's choose executors, and talk of wills. [*do.*, III. 2]

235 For God's sake, let us sit upon the ground / And tell sad stories of the death of kings: / How some have been depos'd, some slain in war, / Some haunted by the ghosts they have depos'd, / Some poison'd by their wives, some sleeping kill'd; / All murder'd: for within the hollow crown / That rounds the mortal temples of a king / Keeps Death his court, and there the antick sits, / Scoffing his state, and grinning at his pomp. [*do.*]

236 How sour sweet music is, / When time is broke and no proportion kept! / So is it in the music of men's lives. [*do.*, V. 5]

237 Now is the winter of our discontent / Made glorious summer by this sun of York. [*Richard III*, I. 1]

238 Why, I, in this weak piping time of peace, / Have no delight to pass away the time. [*do.*]

239 And therefore, since I cannot prove a lover, / To entertain these fair well-spoken days, / I am determined to prove a villain, / And hate the idle pleasures of these days. [*do.*]

240 Was ever woman in this humour woo'd? / Was ever woman in this humour won? [*do.*, I. 2]

241 Since every Jack became a gentleman, / There's many a gentle person made a Jack. [*do.*, I. 3]

242 I am not in the giving vein to-day. [*do.*, IV. 2]

243 A horse! a horse! my kingdom for a horse! [*do.*, V. 4]

244 From forth the fatal loins of these two foes / A pair of star-cross'd lovers take their life. [*Romeo and Juliet*, Prologue]

245 O! then, I see, Queen Mab hath been with you. / She is the fairies' midwife, and she comes / In shape no bigger than an agate-stone / On the forefinger of an alderman, / Drawn with a team of little atomies / Over men's noses as they lie asleep. [*do.*, I. 4]

246 He jests at scars, that never felt a wound. / But, soft! what light through yonder window breaks? / It is the east, and Juliet is the sun. [*do.*, II. 2]

247 O Romeo, Romeo! wherefore art thou Romeo? [*do.*]

248 What's in a name? That which we call a rose / By any other name would smell as sweet. [*do.*]

249 O, swear not by the moon, the inconstant moon, / That monthly changes in her circled orb, / Lest that thy love prove likewise variable. [*do.*]

250 Good night, good night! Parting is such sweet sorrow / That I shall say good night till it be morrow. [*do.*]

251 A plague o' both your houses! [*do.*, III. 1]

252 From fairest creatures we desire increase, / That thereby beauty's rose might never die. [*Sonnets*, 1]

253 Shall I compare thee to a summer's day? / Thou art more lovely and more temperate: / Rough winds do shake the darling buds of May, / And summer's lease hath all too short a date. [*do.*, 18]

254 When, in disgrace with fortune and men's eyes, / I all alone beweep my outcast state, / And trouble deaf heaven with my bootless cries, / And look upon myself, and curse my fate. [*do.*, 29]

255 When to the sessions of sweet silent thought / I summon up remembrance of things past, / I sigh the lack of many a thing I sought, / And with old woes new wail my dear time's waste. [*do.*, 30]

256 Full many a glorious morning have I seen / Flatter the mountain-tops with sovereign eye, / Kissing with golden face the meadows green, / Gilding pale streams with heavenly alchemy. [*do.*, 33]

257 Like as the waves make towards the pebbled shore, / So do our minutes hasten to their end. [*do.*, 60]

258 No longer mourn for me when I am dead / Than you shall hear the surly sullen bell / Give warning to the world that I am fled / From this vile world, with vilest worms to dwell. [*do.*, 71]

259 That time of year thou mayst in me behold / When yellow leaves, or none, or few, do hang /

Upon those boughs which shake against the cold, /
Bare ruin'd choirs, where late the sweet birds sang.
[*do.*, 73]

260 Farewell! thou art too dear for my
possessing, / And like enough thou know'st thy
estimate. [*do.*, 87]

261 They that have power to hurt and will do
none, / That do not do the thing they most do
show, / Who, moving others, are themselves as
stone, / Unmoved, cold, and to temptation slow; /
They rightly do inherit heaven's graces, /
And husband nature's riches from expense. [*do.*, 94]

262 For sweetest things turn sourest by their deeds: /
Lilies that fester smell far worse than weeds. [*do.*]

263 When in the chronicle of wasted time / I see
descriptions of the fairest wights. [*do.*, 106]

264 My nature is subdu'd / To what it works in,
like the dyer's hand. [*do.*, 111]

265 Let me not to the marriage of true minds /
Admit impediments. Love is not love / Which alters
when it alteration finds, / Or bends with the remover
to remove. / O, no! it is an ever-fixed mark, / That
looks on tempests and is never shaken. [*do.*, 116]

266 The expense of spirit in a waste of shame / Is
lust in action; and till action, lust / Is perjur'd,
murderous, bloody, full of blame, / Savage, extreme,
rude, cruel, not to trust; / Enjoyed no sooner but
despised straight; / Past reason hunted; and no
sooner had, / Past reason hated, as a swallow'd
bait, / On purpose laid to make the taker mad: /
Mad in pursuit, and in possession so; / Had, having,
and in quest to have, extreme; / A bliss in
proof, – and prov'd, a very woe; / Before, a joy
propos'd; behind, a dream. / All this the world well
knows; yet none knows well / To shun the heaven
that leads men to this hell. [*do.*, 129]

267 My mistress' eyes are nothing like the sun; /
Coral is far more red than her lips' red.
[*do.*, 130]

268 Two loves I have, of comfort and despair, /
Which like two spirits do suggest me still; /
The better angel is a man right fair, / The worser
spirit a woman colour'd ill. [*do.*, 144]

269 Kiss me Kate, we will be married o' Sunday.
[*The Taming of the Shrew*, II. 1]

270 This is a way to kill a wife with kindness.
[*do.*, IV. 1]

271 What seest thou else / In the dark backward and
abysm of time? [*The Tempest*, I. 2]

272 Full fathom five thy father lies; / Of his bones
are coral made; / Those are pearls that were his
eyes; / Nothing of him that doth fade / But doth
suffer a sea-change / Into something rich and strange.
[*do.*]

273 Misery acquaints a man with strange bedfellows.
[*do.*, II. 2]

274 Be not afeard: the isle is full of noises, / Sounds
and sweet airs, that give delight, and hurt not.
[*do.*, III. 2]

275 Our revels now are ended. These our actors, /
As I foretold you, were all spirits, and / Are melted
into air, into thin air; / And, like the baseless fabric
of this vision, / The cloud-capp'd towers, the
gorgeous palaces, / The solemn temples, the great
globe itself, / Yea, all which it inherit, shall
dissolve, / And, like this insubstantial pageant
faded, / Leave not a rack behind. We are such stuff /
As dreams are made on, and our little life /
Is rounded with a sleep. [*do.*, IV. 1]

276 But this rough magic / I here abjure. [*do.*, V. 1]

277 Where the bee sucks, there suck I; / In a
cowslip's bell I lie; / There I couch when owls do
cry. / On the bat's back I do fly / After summer
merrily: / Merrily, merrily shall I live now / Under
the blossom that hangs on the bough. [*do.*]

278 How beauteous mankind is! O brave new
world, / That has such people in't! [*do.*]

279 My long sickness / Of health and living now
begins to mend, / And nothing brings me all things.
[*Timon of Athens*, V. 1]

280 To be wise and love / Exceeds man's might.
[*Troilus and Cressida*, III. 2]

281 Time hath, my lord, a wallet at his back, /
Wherein he puts alms for oblivion, / A great-siz'd
monster of ingratitudes: / Those scraps are good
deeds past; which are devour'd / As fast as they
are made, forgot as soon / As done. [*do.*, III. 3]

282 Lechery, lechery! Still wars and lechery! Nothing
else holds fashion. [*do.*, V. 2]

283 Words, words, mere words, no matter from the

heart. [*do.*, V. 3]

284 If music be the food of love, play on; / Give me excess of it, that, surfeiting, / The appetite may sicken and so die. [*Twelfth Night*, I. 1]

285 Many a good hanging prevents a bad marriage. [*do.*, I. 5]

286 What is love? Tis not hereafter; / Present mirth hath present laughter; / What's to come is still unsure. / In delay there lies no plenty; / Then come kiss me, sweet and twenty, / Youth's a stuff will not endure. [*do.*, II. 3]

287 Dost thou think, because thou art virtuous, there shall be no more cakes and ale? [*do.*]

288 Some are born great, some achieve greatness, and some have greatness thrust upon 'em. [*do.*, II. 5]

289 Love sought is good, but given unsought is better. [*do.*, III. 1]

290 Thus the whirligig of time brings in his revenges. [*do.*, V. 1]

291 When that I was and a little tiny boy, / With hey, ho, the wind and the rain; / A foolish thing was but a toy, / For the rain it raineth every day. [*do.*]

292 Who is Silvia? What is she, / That all our swains commend her? / Holy, fair, and wise is she. [*The Two Gentlemen of Verona*, IV. 2]

293 *Exit, pursued by a bear.* [*The Winter's Tale*, III. 3 (stage direction)]

294 I would there were no age between ten and three and twenty, or that youth would sleep out the rest; for there is nothing in the between but getting wenches with child, wronging the ancientry, stealing, fighting. [*do.*]

295 A snapper-up of unconsidered trifles. [*do.*, IV. 2]

296 Though I am not naturally honest, I am so sometimes by chance. [*do.*, IV. 3]

S16   **Shaw, George Bernard** (1856–1950)
Irish dramatist and critic

1 You can always tell an old soldier by the inside of his holsters and cartridge boxes. The young ones carry pistols and cartridges: the old ones, grub. [*Arms and the Man*, I]

2 You're not a man, you're a machine. [*do.*, III]

3 When a stupid man is doing something he is ashamed of, he always declares that it is his duty.

[*Caesar and Cleopatra*, III]

4 I'm only a beer teetotaller, not a champagne teetotaller. [*Candida*, III]

5 The worst sin towards our fellow creatures is not to hate them, but to be indifferent to them. [*The Devil's Disciple*, II]

6 All professions are conspiracies against the laity. [*The Doctor's Dilemma*, I]

7 The greatest of evils and the worst of crimes is poverty. [*Major Barbara*, Preface]

8 I am a Millionaire. That is my religion. [*do.*, I]

9 Nothing is ever done in this world until men are prepared to kill one another if it is not done. [*do.*, III]

10 A lifetime of happiness! No man alive could bear it: it would be hell on earth. [*Man and Superman*, I]

11 Hell is full of musical amateurs: music is the brandy of the damned. [*do.*, III]

12 An Englishman thinks he is moral when he is only uncomfortable. [*do.*]

13 There are two tragedies in life. One is not to get your heart's desire. The other is to get it. [*do.*, IV]

14 Democracy substitutes election by the incompetent many for appointment by the corrupt few. [*do.*, 'Maxims for Revolutionists']

15 He who can, does. He who cannot, teaches. [*do.*]

16 Home is the girl's prison and the woman's workhouse. [*do.*]

17 There is only one religion, though there are a hundred versions of it. [*Plays Pleasant and Unpleasant*, II, Preface]

18 Walk! Not bloody likely. I am going in a taxi. [*Pygmalion*, III]

19 We were not fairly beaten, my lord. No Englishman is ever fairly beaten. [*St. Joan*, 4]

S17   Shelley, Percy Bysshe (1792–1822) English poet
1 He has outsoared the shadow of our night; / Envy and calumny, and hate and pain, / And that unrest which men miscall delight, / Can touch him not and torture not again; / From the contagion of the world's slow stain / He is secure, and now can never mourn / A heart grown cold, a head grown grey in vain. [*Adonais*]

2 He is made one with Nature: there is heard / His voice in all her music, from the moan / Of thunder, to the song of night's sweet bird. [*do.*]

3 The One remains, the many change and pass; / Heaven's light for ever shines, Earth's shadows fly; / Life, like a dome of many-coloured glass, / Stains the white radiance of Eternity, / Until Death tramples it to fragments. [*do.*]

4 Poetry lifts the veil from the hidden beauty of the world, and makes familiar objects be as if they were not familiar. [*A Defence of Poetry*]

5 Poets are the unacknowledged legislators of the world. [*do.*]

6 I never was attached to that great sect, / Whose doctrine is, that each one should select / Out of the crowd a mistress or a friend, / And all the rest, though fair and wise, commend / To cold oblivion. [*Epipsychidion*]

7 I urged and questioned still: she told me how / All happened – but the cold world shall not know. [*Julian and Maddalo*]

8 O world! O life! O time! / On whose last steps I climb, / Trembling at that where I had stood before. [*A Lament*]

9 Many a green isle needs must be in the wide sea of misery. [*Lines Written among the Euganean Hills*]

10 I met Murder on the way – / He had a mask like Castlereagh. [*The Masque of Anarchy*]

11 O Wild West Wind, thou breath of Autumn's being, / Thou, from whose unseen presence the leaves dead / Are driven, like ghosts from an enchanter fleeing, / Yellow, and black, and pale, and hectic red, / Pestilence-stricken multitudes. [*Ode to the West Wind*]

12 Oh, lift me as a wave, a leaf, a cloud! / I fall upon the thorns of life! I bleed! / A heavy weight of hours has chained and bowed / One too like thee: tameless, and swift, and proud. [*do.*]

13 O, Wind, / If Winter comes, can Spring be far behind? [*do.*]

14 I met a traveller from an antique land / Who said: Two vast and trunkless legs of stone / Stand in the desert. [*Ozymandias*]

15 'My name is Ozymandias, king of kings: / Look on my works, ye Mighty, and despair!' / Nothing beside remains. Round the decay / Of that colossal wreck, boundless and bare / The lone and level sands stretch far away. [*do.*]

16 Lift not the painted veil which those who live / Call Life. [*Sonnet*]

17 Music, when soft voices die, / Vibrates in the memory. [*To – *]

18 Hail to thee, blithe Spirit! / Bird thou never wert, / That from Heaven, or near it, / Pourest thy full heart / In profuse strains of unpremeditated art. [*To a Skylark*]

19 We look before and after, / And pine for what is not; / Our sincerest laughter / With some pain is fraught; / Our sweetest songs are those that tell of saddest thought. [*do.*]

20 Art thou pale for weariness / Of climbing heaven, and gazing on the earth, / Wandering companionless / Among the stars that have a different birth, – / And ever changing, like a joyless eye / That finds no object worth its constancy? [*To the Moon*]

S18 **Sheridan, Philip Henry** (1831–88)
US army commander
1 The only good Indian is a dead Indian. [attr.]

S19 **Sheridan, R. B.** (1751–1816) Irish dramatist
1 The Spanish fleet thou *canst* not see because – / It is not yet in sight! [*The Critic*, II. 2]
2 MRS MALAPROP. He is the very pine-apple of politeness! [*The Rivals*, III. 3]
3 MRS MALAPROP. If I reprehend any thing in this world, it is the use of my oracular tongue, and a nice derangement of epitaphs. [*do.*]
4 MRS MALAPROP. She's as headstrong as an allegory on the banks of the Nile. [*do.*]
5 The Right Honourable gentleman is indebted to his memory for his jests, and to his imagination for his facts. [speech in the House of Commons]
6 A man may surely be allowed to take a glass of wine by his own fireside. [remark while drinking in the street when the Drury Lane Theatre, which he owned, burnt down]

S20 **Sherman, William T.** (1820–91)
US army commander
1 There is many a boy here today who looks on war as all glory, but, boys, it is all hell. [speech at

Columbus, Ohio, 11 Aug. 1880]

S21 **Shirley, James** (1596–1666) English dramatist
1 Sceptre and crown / Must tumble down, / And in
the dust be equal made / With the poor crooked
scythe and spade. [*The Contention of Ajax and Ulysses*,
I. 3]

S22 **Sidney, Sir Philip** (1554–86)
English poet, soldier, and statesman
1 My true love hath my heart and I have his, / By
just exchange one for the other giv'n. [*The
Arcadia*, bk 3]
2 With how sad steps, O Moon, thou climb'st the
skies! / How silently, and with how wan a face!
[*Astrophel and Stella*, Sonnet 31]
3 With a tale forsooth he cometh unto you, with a
tale which holdeth children from play, and old men
from the chimney corner. [*The Defence of Poesy*]

S23 **Simon, Paul** (1942–) US singer and songwriter
1 Bridge over Troubled Water. [title of song]
2 The Sound of Silence. [title of song]

S24 **Sims, George R.** (1847–1922)
English journalist and playwright
1 It is Christmas Day in the Workhouse.
[*Dagonet Ballads*]

S25 **Smith, Logan Pearsall** (1865–1946) US essayist
1 The indefatigable pursuit of an unattainable
perfection, even though it consist in nothing more
than in the pounding of an old piano, is what alone
gives a meaning to our life on this unavailing star.
[*Afterthoughts*]
2 We need two kinds of acquaintances, one to
complain to, while we boast to the others. [*All Trivia*]

S26 **Smith, Stevie** (1902–71) English poet
1 I was much too far out all my life, / And not
waving but drowning. [*Not Waving But Drowning*]

S27 **Smith, Sydney** (1771–1845) English clergyman and
essayist
1 Dame Partington . . . was seen . . . with mop and
pattens . . . vigorously pushing away the Atlantic
Ocean. The Atlantic Ocean beat Mrs Partington.
[*Peter Plymley's Letters*]

2 We shall generally find that the triangular person has got into the square hole, the oblong into the triangular, and a square person has squeezed himself into the round hole. The officer and the office, the doer and the thing done, seldom fit so exactly that we can say they were almost made for each other. [*Sketches of Moral Philosophy*, lecture 9]

3 [on T. B. Macaulay] He has occasional flashes of silence, that make his conversation perfectly delightful. [remark]

4 I have no relish for the country; it is a kind of healthy grave. [letter to Miss G. Harcourt, 1838]

5 I never read a book before reviewing it; it prejudices a man so. [remark]

6 Let the Dean and Canons lay their heads together and the thing will be done. [remark on the proposal to lay a wooden pavement round St Paul's]

7 What a pity it is that we have no amusements in England but vice and religion. [remark]

S28   **Smollett, Tobias** (1721–71) British novelist
1 Some folks are wise and some are otherwise. [*Roderick Random*, ch. 6]

S29   **Snow, C. P.** (1905–80)
English novelist and physicist
1 The official world, the corridors of power. [*Homecomings*, ch. 22]
2 The Two Cultures [i.e. science and the humanities. Title of book]

S30   **Socrates** (470?–399 BC) Greek philosopher
1 There is only one good, knowledge, and one evil, ignorance. [cited in Diogenes Laertius, *Lives of Eminent Philosophers*]
2 I know nothing except the fact of my ignorance. [*do.*]

S31   **Solon** (638?–559? BC) Athenian lawgiver
1 Call no man happy until he dies; he is at best fortunate. [cited in Herodotus, *Histories*]

S32   **Sophocles** (496?–406 BC) Greek dramatist
1 Wonders are many, and none is more wonderful than man. [*Antigone*]

S33   **Soule, J. B. L.** (1815–91) US editor and author
1 Go west, young man. [editorial in the *Terre Haute*

(Indiana) *Express*, 1851]

S34   **Southey, Robert** (1774–1843) English poet
1 It was a summer evening, / Old Kaspar's work was
done, / And he before his cottage door / Was sitting
in the sun. [*The Battle of Blenheim*]
2 'But what good came of it at last?' / Quoth little
Peterkin. / 'Why that I cannot tell,' said he, / 'But
'twas a famous victory.' [*do.*]

S35   **Spencer, Herbert** (1820–1903) English philosopher
1 Science is organized knowledge. [*Education*, ch. 2]
2 Survival of the fittest. [*Principles of Biology*,
pt III, ch. 12]
3 Education has for its object the formation of
character. [*Social Statics*, pt II, ch. 17]
4 Opinion is ultimately determined by the feelings,
and not by the intellect. [*do.*, pt IV, ch. 30]
5 To play billiards well is a sign of an ill-spent
youth. [attr., but Spencer stated the remark was made
by a friend of his]

S36   **Spenser, Edmund** (1552–99) English poet
1 Sleep after toil, port after stormy seas, / Ease after
war, death after life does greatly please. [*The Faerie
Queene*, bk I, canto 9]
2 Sweet Thames, run softly, till I end my Song.
[*Prothalamion*]

S37   **Spooner, W. A.** (1844–1930)
English clergyman and scholar
1 Sir, you have tasted two whole worms; you have
hissed all my mystery lectures and have been caught
fighting a liar in the quad; you will leave Oxford by
the next town drain. [attr.]
2 I remember your name perfectly, but I just can't
think of your face. [attr.]

S38   **Squire, Sir John** (1884–1958) English author
1 But I'm not so think as you drunk I am. [*Ballade of
Soporific Absorption*]

S39   **Stanley, H. M.** (1841–1904) English explorer
1 Dr Livingstone, I presume? [remark on meeting
Livingstone at Ujiji, Central Africa, 10 Nov. 1871]

S40   **Steffens, Lincoln** (1866–1936) US journalist
1 I have seen the future, and it works. [remark after

visiting Moscow in 1919]

S41   **Stein, Gertrude** (1874–1946) US author
  1 Rose is a rose is a rose is a rose. [*Sacred Emily*]
  2 What is the answer? . . . In that case, what is the
  question? [last words]

S42   **Sterne, Laurence** (1713–68) English novelist
  1 They order, said I, this matter better in France. [*A
  Sentimental Journey*, opening words]
  2 There are worse occupations in this world than
  feeling a woman's pulse. [*do.*, 'The Pulse']
  3 God tempers the wind, said Maria, to the shorn
  lamb. [*do.*, 'Maria']
  4 So that when I stretched out my hand, I caught
  hold of the fille de chambre's – [*do.*, 'The Case of
  Delicacy']
  5 I wish either my father or my mother, or indeed
  both of them, as they were in duty both equally
  bound to it, had minded what they were about when
  they begot me. [*Tristram Shandy*, I, ch. 1]
  6 'Pray, my dear', quoth my mother, 'have you not
  forgot to wind up the clock?' – 'Good G–!' cried my
  father, making an exclamation, but taking care to
  moderate his voice at the same time, – 'Did ever
  woman, since the creation of the world, interrupt a
  man with such a silly question?' [*do.*]
  7 I'll not hurt thee, says my uncle Toby, rising from
  his chair, and going across the room, with the fly in
  his hand, – I'll not hurt a hair of thy head: – Go, says
  he, lifting up the sash, and opening his hand as he
  spoke, to let it escape; – go, poor devil, get thee gone,
  why should I hurt thee? – This world surely is wide
  enough to hold both thee and me. [*do.*, II, ch. 12]
  8 My uncle Toby laid down his pipe as gently upon
  the fender as if it had been spun from the
  unravellings of a spider's web – Let us go to my
  brother Shandy's, said he. [*do.*, IX, ch. 31]
  9 L–d! said my mother, what is all this story
  about? – A COCK and a BULL, said Yorick – And
  one of the best of its kind I ever heard. [*do.*, IX, ch.
  33]

S43   **Stevens, Wallace** (1879–1955) US poet
  1 Let be be finale of seem. / The only emperor is
  the emperor of ice-cream. [*The Emperor of Ice-Cream*]

2 Poetry is the supreme fiction, madame. [*A High-toned Old Christian Woman*]

3 Beauty is momentary in the mind – / The fitful tracing of a portal; / But in the flesh it is immortal. [*Peter Quince at the Clavier*]

S44 **Stevenson, Robert Louis** (1850–94) Scottish author
1 Politics is perhaps the only profession for which no preparation is thought necessary. [*Familiar Studies of Men and Books*]
2 Fifteen men on the dead man's chest / Yo-ho-ho, and a bottle of rum! [*Treasure Island*, ch. 1]
3 Under the wide and starry sky / Dig the grave and let me lie. / Glad did I live and gladly die, / And I laid me down with a will. [*Underwoods*, 'Requiem']
4 Home is the sailor, home from sea, / And the hunter home from the hill. [*do.*]
5 Extreme busyness, whether at school or college, kirk or market, is a symptom of deficient vitality. [*Virginibus Puerisque*, 'An Apology for Idlers']
6 To travel hopefully is a better thing than to arrive, and the true success is to labour. [*do.*, 'El Dorado']

S45 **Stoppard, Tom** (1937–)
English (Czech-born) dramatist
1 The scientific approach to the examination of phenomena is a defence against the pure emotion of fear. [*Rosencrantz and Guildenstern Are Dead*, I]

S46 **Stowe, Harriet Beecher** (1811–96) US author
1 'Do you know who made you?' 'Nobody as I knows on,' said the child [Topsy], with a short laugh ... 'I 'spect I grow'd.' [*Uncle Tom's Cabin*, ch. 20]

S47 **Stubbes, Philip** (1583–91)
English Puritan pamphleteer
1 [On football] A develishe pastime ... and hereof groweth envy, rancour and malice, and sometimes brawling, murther, homicide, and great effusion of blood, as experience daily teacheth. [*The Anatomie of Abuses*]

S48 **Suckling, Sir John** (1609–42) English poet
1 Why so pale and wan, fond lover? / Prithee, why so pale? [*Aglaura*, IV. 1]
2 Out upon it, I have loved / Three whole days together; / And am like to love three more, / If it

prove fair weather. [*A Poem with the Answer*]

S49 **Suetonius** (69?–140?)
Roman biographer and historian
1 *Festina lente.* Hasten slowly. [*The Lives of the Caesars*, 'Augustus']
2 *Ave, Caesar, morituri te salutant.* Hail, Emperor, those about to die salute you. [*do.*, 'Claudius']

S50 **Swift, Jonathan** (1667–1745) Irish author
1 Satire is a sort of glass, wherein beholders do generally discover everybody's face but their own. [*The Battle of the Books*, Preface]
2 Instead of dirt and poison, we have rather chosen to fill our hives with honey and wax; thus furnishing mankind with the two noblest of things, which are sweetness and light. [*do.*]
3 I cannot but conclude the bulk of your natives to be the most pernicious race of little odious vermin that nature ever suffered to crawl upon the surface of the earth. [*Gulliver's Travels: Voyage to Brobdingnag*, ch. 6]
4 Whoever could make two ears of corn, or two blades of grass to grow upon a spot of ground where only one grew before, would deserve better of mankind, and do more essential service to his country, than the whole race of politicians put together. [*do.*, ch. 7]
5 He had been eight years upon a project for extracting sun-beams out of cucumbers, which were to be put into vials hermetically sealed, and let out to warm the air in raw inclement summers. [*do.*, *Voyage to Laputa*, ch. 5]
6 Proper words in proper places make the true definition of a style. [letter to a young clergyman, 9 Jan. 1720]
7 I have ever hated all nations, professions and communities, and all my love is towards individuals . . . But principally I hate and detest that animal called man; although I heartily love John, Peter, Thomas, and so forth. [letter to Alexander Pope, 29 Sept. 1725]
8 I have been assured by a very knowing American of my acquaintance in London, that a young healthy child well nursed is at a year old a most delicious, nourishing, and wholesome food, whether stewed,

roasted, baked, or boiled, and I make no doubt that it will equally serve in a fricassee, or a ragout. [*A Modest Proposal*]

9 So, naturalists observe, a flea / Hath smaller fleas that on him prey, / And these have smaller fleas to bite 'em, / And so proceed *ad infinitum*. [*On Poetry*]

10 Yet malice never was his aim; / He lash'd the vice, but spared the name; / No individual could resent, / Where thousands equally were meant. [*On the Death of Dr Swift*]

11 Why every one as they like; as the good woman said when she kissed her cow. [*Polite Conversation*]

12 Last week I saw a woman flayed, and you will hardly believe, how much it altered her person for the worse. [*A Tale of a Tub*, ch. 9]

13 When a true genius appears in this world, you may know him by this sign, that the dunces are all in confederacy against him. [*Thoughts on Various Subjects*]

14 Hated by fools, and fools to hate, / Be that my motto and my fate. [*To Mr Delany*]

15 Laws are like cobwebs, which may catch small flies, but let wasps and hornets break through. [*A Tritical Essay upon the Faculties of the Mind*]

16 [on *A Tale of a Tub*] Good God! What a genius I had when I wrote that book. [attr.]

17 *Ubi saeva indignatio ulterius cor lacerare nequit.* Where fierce indignation can no longer tear his heart. [Swift's epitaph]

S51   **Swinburne, A. C.** (1837–1909) English poet

1 When the hounds of spring are on winter's traces. [*Atalanta in Calydon*]

2 From too much love of living, / From hope and fear set free, / We thank with brief thanksgiving / Whatever gods may be / That no man lives forever, / That dead men rise up never; / That even the weariest river / Winds somewhere safe to sea. [*The Garden of Proserpine*]

T1 **Talleyrand, Charles-Maurice de** (1754–1838)
French statesman
1 *Voilà le commencement de la fin.* This is the
beginning of the end. [attr. remark on Napoleon's
defeat at Borodino, 1812]
2 They have learnt nothing, and forgotten nothing.
[attr.]
3 Speech was given to man to disguise his thoughts.
[attr.]
4 War is much too serious a thing to be left to
military men. [attr. Also attr. to Georges Clemenceau]
5 *Pas trop de zèle.* Not too much zeal. [attr. Also
quoted as *Point de zèle* ('Not the slightest zeal')]

T2 **Tate, Nahum** (1652–1715) and **Brady, Nicholas**
(1659–1726) British authors
1 While shepherds watch'd their flocks by
night, / All seated on the ground, / The Angel of
the Lord came down, / And glory shone around.
[*While Shepherds Watched*]

T3 **Taylor, Jane** (1783–1824) English poet
1 Twinkle, twinkle, little star, / How I wonder what
you are! / Up above the world so high, / Like a
diamond in the sky! [*The Star*]

T4 **Tennyson, Alfred, Lord** (1809–92) English poet
1 Break, break, break, / On thy cold grey stones, O
Sea! / And I would that my tongue could utter /
The thoughts that arise in me. [*Break, Break, Break*]
2 For men may come and men may go, / But I go
on for ever. [*The Brook*]
3 Half a league, half a league, / Half a league
onward, / All in the valley of Death / Rode the six
hundred. [*The Charge of the Light Brigade*]
4 Their's not to make reply, / Their's not to reason
why, / Their's but to do and die. [*do.*]
5 Cannon to right of them, / Cannon to left of
them, / Cannon in front of them / Volley'd and
thunder'd. [*do.*]

6 Sunset and evening star, / And one clear call for
me! / And may there be no moaning of the
bar, / When I put out to sea. [*Crossing the Bar*]
7 For tho' from out our bourne of Time and Place /
The flood may bear me far, / I hope to see my Pilot
face to face / When I have crost the bar. [*do.*]
8 It is the little rift within the lute, / That by and by
will make the music mute, / And ever widening
slowly silence all. [*The Idylls of the King*, 'Merlin
and Vivien']
9 And slowly answer'd Arthur from the barge: /
'The old order changeth, yielding place to new, /
And God fulfils himself in many ways, / Lest one
good custom should corrupt the world.' [*do.*, 'The
Passing of Arthur']
10 Believing where we cannot prove.
[*In Memoriam*, Prologue]
11 I hold it true, whate'er befall; / I feel it, when I
sorrow most; / 'Tis better to have loved and
lost / Than never to have loved at all. [*do.*, 27]
12 Behold, we know not anything; / I can but trust
that good shall fall / At last – far off – at last, to
all, / And every winter change to spring. / So runs
my dream: but what am I? / An infant crying in the
night: / An infant crying for the light: / And with
no language but a cry. [*do.*, 54]
13 Nature, red in tooth and claw / With ravine.
[*do.*, 56]
14 So many worlds, so much to do, / So little done,
such things to be. [*do.*, 73]
15 Ring out, wild bells, to the wild sky, / The flying
cloud, the frosty light: / The year is dying in the
night; / Ring out, wild bells, and let him die.
[*do.*, 106]
16 One God, one law, one element, / And one far-off
divine event, / To which the whole creation moves.
[*do.*, 131]
17 Kind hearts are more than coronets, / And simple
faith than Norman blood. [*Lady Clara Vere de Vere*]
18 On either side the river lie / Long fields of barley
and of rye, / That clothe the wold and meet the
sky; / And thro' the field the road runs by / To
many-tower'd Camelot. [*The Lady of Shalott*]
19 'The curse is come upon me,' cried / The Lady
of Shalott. [*do.*]

20 In the Spring a young man's fancy lightly turns to thoughts of love. [*Locksley Hall*]

21 Music that gentlier on the spirit lies, / Than tir'd eyelids upon tir'd eyes. [*The Lotos-Eaters*]

22 Surely, surely, slumber is more sweet than toil, the shore / Than labour in the deep mid-ocean, wind and wave and oar; / Oh rest ye, brother mariners, we will not wander more. [*do.*]

23 She only said, 'My life is dreary, / He cometh not,' she said; / She said, 'I am aweary, aweary, / I would that I were dead!' [*Mariana*]

24 Come into the garden, Maud, / For the black bat, night, has flown, / Come into the garden, Maud, / I am here at the gate alone. [*Maud*, I]

25 It is better to fight for the good than to rail at the ill. [*do.*, III]

26 You must wake and call me early, call me early, mother dear. [*The May Queen*]

27 The splendour falls on castle walls / And snowy summits old in story. [*The Princess*, IV]

28 Tears, idle tears, I know not what they mean, / Tears from the depth of some divine despair. [*do.*]

29 My strength is as the strength of ten, / Because my heart is pure. [*Sir Galahad*]

30 The woods decay, the woods decay and fall, / The vapours weep their burthen to the ground, / Man comes and tills the field and lies beneath, / And after many a summer dies the swan. [*Tithonus*]

31 I cannot rest from travel: I will drink / Life to the lees: all times I have enjoy'd / Greatly, have suffered greatly. [*Ulysses*]

32 I am a part of all that I have met; / Yet all experience is an arch wherethro' / Gleams that untravell'd world, whose margin fades / For ever and for ever when I move. [*do.*]

T5   **Terence** (190?–159 BC) Roman dramatist

1 *Homo sum: humani nil a me alienum puto.* I am a man; I consider nothing human foreign to me. [*Heauton Timorumenos*]

2 *Fortis fortuna adiuvat.* Fortune favours the brave. [*Phormio*]

3 *Quot homines tot sententiae.* There are as many opinions as there are men. [*do.*]

T6   **Tertullian** (160?–230?) Carthaginian church father

1 *Certum est quia impossibile.* It is certain because it is impossible. [*De Carne Christi*, 5]

T7   **Thackeray, William Makepeace** (1811–63)
English author
1 'No business before breakfast, Glum!' says the King. 'Breakfast first, business next.' [*The Rose and the Ring*, ch. 11]
2 If a man's character is to be abused, say what you will, there's nobody like a relation to do the business. [*Vanity Fair*, ch. 19]
3 Ah! Vanitas Vanitatum! which of us is happy in this world? Which of us has his desire? or, having it, is satisfied? – Come, children, let us shut up the box and the puppets, for our play is played out. [*do.*, ch. 67]

T8   **Thatcher, Margaret** (1925–) English politician
1 There is no alternative. [repeated remark on her economic policy]

T9   **Thomas à Kempis** (1380–1471) German ecclesiastic
1 *O quam cito transit gloria mundi.* O how quickly the glory of the world passes away. [*The Imitation of Christ*, I. 3. Often quoted as *Sic transit gloria mundi* ('Thus the glory of the world passes away')]
2 *Nam homo proponit, sed Deus disponit.* For man proposes, but God disposes. [*do.*, 19]

T10   **Thomas, Brandon** (1857–1914) English dramatist
1 I'm Charley's aunt from Brazil, where the nuts come from. [*Charley's Aunt*, I]

T11   **Thomas, Dylan** (1914–53) Welsh poet
1 Do not go gentle into that good night, / Old age should burn and rave at close of day; / Rage, rage, against the dying of the light. [*Do Not Go Gentle into that Good Night*]
2 Now as I was young and easy under the apple boughs / About the lilting house and happy as the grass was green. [*Fern Hill*]
3 Time held me green and dying / Though I sang in my chains like the sea. [*do.*]
4 The force that through the green fuse drives the flower / Drives my green age. [*The Force that through the Green Fuse Drives the Flower*]
5 After the first death, there is no other. [*A Refusal*

to Mourn the Death, by Fire, of a Child in London]

T12   Thomas, Edward (1878–1917) English poet
1 Yes, I remember Adlestrop – / The name, because
one afternoon / Of heat the express train drew up
there / Unwontedly. It was late June. [*Adlestrop*]

T13   Thompson, Francis (1859–1907) English poet
1 I fled Him, down the nights and down the
days; / I fled Him, down the arches of the years; / I
fled Him, down the labyrinthine ways / Of my own
mind. [*The Hound of Heaven*]

T14   Thompson, William Hepworth (1810–66)
English scholar
1 We are none of us infallible – not even the
youngest of us. [remark on a junior don at
Cambridge]

T15   Thomson, James (1700–48) Scottish poet
1 When Britain first, at Heaven's command, / Arose
from out the azure main, / This was the charter of
the land, / And guardian angels sung this strain: /
'Rule, Britannia, rule the waves: / Britons never will
be slaves.' [*Alfred: A Masque*, II. 5]

T16   Thomson of Fleet, Lord (1894–1976)
Canadian newspaper proprietor
1 A stake in commercial television is the equivalent
of having a licence to print money. [remark]

T17   Thoreau, Henry David (1817–62) US author
1 Government is at best but an expedient; but most
governments are usually, and all governments are
sometimes, inexpedient. [*Civil Disobedience*]
2 The mass of men lead lives of quiet desperation.
[*Walden*, 'Economy']
3 Most of the luxuries, and many of the so-called
comforts of life, are not only not indispensable, but
positive hindrances to the elevation of mankind. [*do.*]
4 The life which men praise and regard as successful
is but one kind. Why should we exaggerate any one
kind at the expense of the others? [*do.*]
5 Our inventions are wont to be pretty toys, which
distract our attention from serious things. They are
but improved means to an unimproved end ... We
are in great haste to construct a magnetic telegraph
from Maine to Texas; but Maine and Texas, it may

be, have nothing important to communicate. [*do.*]
6 Our life is frittered away by detail . . . Simplify,
simplify. [*do.*, 'Where I Lived and What I Lived For']
7 A man sits as many risks as he runs.
[*do.*, 'Visitors']
8 We should be blessed if we lived in the present
always, and took advantage of every accident that
befell us, like the grass which confesses the influence
of the slightest dew that falls on it; and did not spend
our time in atoning for the neglect of past
opportunities, which we call doing our duty.
[*do.*, 'Spring']
9 It is easier to sail many thousand miles through
cold and storm and cannibals, in a government ship,
with five hundred men and boys to assist one, than it
is to explore the private sea, the Atlantic and Pacific
Ocean of one's being alone. [*do.*, 'Conclusion']

T18   **Thurber, James** (1894–1961)
US author and cartoonist
1 It's a naive domestic Burgundy, without any
breeding, but I think you'll be amused by its
presumption. [cartoon caption]
2 Well, if I called the wrong number, why did you
answer the phone? [*do.*]

T19   **Toffler, Alvin** (1928–) US author
1 Future shock . . . the shattering stress and
disorientation that we induce in individuals by
subjecting them to too much change in too short a
time. [*Future Shock*, ch. 1]

T20   **Tolstoy, Leo** (1828–1910) Russian author
1 All happy families resemble one another, but each
unhappy family is unhappy in its own way. [*Anna
Karenina*, pt I, ch. 1]

T21   **Truman, Harry S.** (1884–1972) US president
1 The buck stops here. [notice on his desk]
2 If you can't stand the heat, get out of the kitchen.
[*Mr Citizen*, ch. 15]

T22   **Twain, Mark (S. L. Clemens)** (1835–1910)
US author
1 There was things which he stretched, but mainly
he told the truth. [*The Adventures of Huckleberry
Finn*, ch. 1]

2 The report of my death was an exaggeration. [cable from Europe to the Associated Press. Also quoted as 'Reports of my death are greatly exaggerated']

V1   **Vaughan, Henry** (1622–95) British poet
1 Happy those early days, when I / Shin'd in my angel infancy. [*The Retreat*]
2 They are all gone into the world of light, / And I alone sit lingering here. [*They Are All Gone*]
3 I saw Eternity the other night, / Like a great ring of pure and endless light, / All calm, as it was bright. [*The World*]

V2   **Vergil (Publius Vergilius Maro)** (70–19 BC) Roman poet
1 *Arma virumque cano.* I sing of arms and the man. [*Aeneid*, I]
2 *Forsan et haec olim meminisse juvabit.* Perhaps one day it will be pleasant to remember even these things. [*do.*]
3 *Sunt lacrimae rerum et mentem mortalia tangunt.* The world is full of tears, and mortality touches the heart. [*do.*]
4 *Timeo Danaos et dona ferentis.* I fear the Greeks even when they bring gifts. [*do.*, II]
5 *Dis aliter visum.* The gods decreed otherwise. [*do.*]
6 *Facilis descensus Averno: / Noctes atque dies patet atri ianua Ditis; / Sed revocare gradum superasque evadere ad auras, / Hoc opus, hic labor est.* The way down to Hell is easy; night and day the doorway of black Dis stands open; but to retrace one's steps and regain the upper air, that is the task and the labour. [*do.*, VI]
7 *Procul, o procul este, profani.* Keep far, far off, uninitiated ones. [*do.*]
8 *Sic itur ad astra.* That is the way to the stars. [*do.*, IX]
9 *Audentis Fortuna iuvat.* Fortune assists the bold. [*do.*, X]

10 *Experto credite*. Trust one who has tried it.
[*do.*, XI]
11 *Latet anguis in herba*. A snake lies hidden in the grass. [*Eclogues*, III]

V3 **Victoria** (1819–1901) Queen of Great Britain
1 We are not amused. [attr.]
2 [on Gladstone] He speaks to Me as if I was a public meeting. [attr.]

V4 **Villiers de L'Isle-Adam, Comte Auguste de** (1838–89) French author
1 *Vivre? les serviteurs feront cela pour nous.* Living? The servants will do that for us. [*Axel*, IV]

V5 **Villon, François** (1431–after 1462) French poet
1 *Mais où sont les neiges d'antan?* But where are the snows of yesteryear? [*Ballade des Dames du Temps Jadis*]

V6 **Voltaire (François Marie Arouet)** (1694–1778) French author
1 *Tout est pour le mieux dans le meilleur des mondes possibles.* All is for the best in the best of all possible worlds. [*Candide*, ch. 1]
2 *Dans ce pays-ci il est bon de tuer de temps en temps un amiral pour encourager les autres.* In this country [i.e. England] it is thought good to kill an admiral from time to time to encourage the others.
[*do.*, ch. 23]
3 *Il faut cultiver notre jardin.* We must tend our garden (i.e. we must mind our own affairs).
[*do.*, ch. 30]
4 *Si Dieu n'existait pas, il faudrait l'inventer.* If God did not exist, it would be necessary to invent him.
[*Epîtres*, 'A l'Auteur du Livre des Trois Imposteurs']
5 I disapprove of what you say, but I will defend to the death your right to say it. [attr.]

W1   **Wallace, Henry** (1888–1965)
US agriculturist and politician
1 The century on which we are entering – the
century which will come out of this war – can be and
must be the century of the common man.
[address, 1942]

W2   **Waller, Edmund** (1606–87) English poet
1 The soul's dark cottage, batter'd and decay'd /
Lets in new light through chinks that time has made.
[*On the Foregoing Divine Poems*]
2 Go, lovely rose, / Tell her, that wastes her time
and me, / That now she knows, / When I resemble
her to thee, / How sweet and fair she seems to be.
[*Song*]

W3   **Waller, Fats** (1904–43)
US jazz pianist and composer
1 Lady, if you has to ask, you ain't got it. [attr. reply
to a question on what rhythm was]

W4   **Walpole, Horace** (1717–97) English author
1 Every drop of ink in my pen ran cold. [letter to
Montagu, 3 July 1752]
2 The world is a comedy to those who think, a
tragedy to those who feel. [letter to the Countess of
Upper Ossory, 16 Aug. 1776]
3 I do not dislike the French from the vulgar
antipathy between neighbouring nations, but for their
insolent and unfounded airs of superiority. [letter to
Hannah More, 14 Oct. 1787]

W5   **Walpole, Sir Robert** (1676–1745) English statesman
1 They now ring the bells, but they will soon wring
their hands. [remark on the declaration of war with
Spain in 1739]
2 The balance of power. [speech in the House of
Commons, 13 Feb. 1741]
3 All those men have their price. [attr.]

W6   **Walton, Izaak** (1593–1683) English author
1 Angling may be said to be so like the mathematics,
that it can never be fully learnt. [*The Compleat
Angler*, 'Epistle to the Reader']
2 We may say of angling as Dr Boteler said of
strawberries, 'Doubtless God could have made a
better berry, but doubtless God never did.'

[*do.*, ch. 5]
3 [on hooking a live frog for use as bait] In so doing,
use him as though you loved him. [*do.*, ch. 8]

W7   **Warhol, Andy** (1931–) US artist and filmmaker
1 In the future everyone will be world-famous for
fifteen minutes. [catalogue of photo exhibition, 1968]

W8   **Washington, George** (1732–99) US president
1 Father, I cannot tell a lie. I did it with my little
hatchet. [attr.]

W9   **Watts, Isaac** (1674–1748)
English theologian and hymn-writer
1 How doth the little busy bee / Improve each
shining hour, / And gather honey all the day / From
every opening flower! [*Divine Songs for Children*,
'Against Idleness and Mischief']
2 For Satan finds some mischief still / For idle
hands to do. [*do.*]
3 'Tis the voice of the sluggard, I heard him
complain: / 'You have waked me too soon, I must
slumber again.' [*Moral Songs*, 'The Sluggard']

W10   **Waugh, Evelyn** (1903–66) English novelist
1 We class schools, you see, into four grades: Leading
School, First-rate School, Good School, and School.
[*Decline and Fall*, pt I, ch. 1]
2 Anyone who has been to an English public school
will always feel comparatively at home in prison. [*do.*,
pt III, ch. 4]
3 Up to a point, Lord Copper. [*Scoop*, ch. 1
and *passim*]

W11   **Webster, Daniel** (1782–1852) US statesman
1 The people's government, made for the people,
made by the people, and answerable to the people.
[speech in the US Senate, 26 Jan. 1830]
2 There is always room at the top. [remark when
advised not to become a lawyer]

W12   **Webster, John** (1580?–1625?) English dramatist
1 I am Duchess of Malfi still. [*The Duchess of
Malfi*, IV. 2]
2 Cover her face; mine eyes dazzle: she died young.
[*do.*]
3 We are merely the stars' tennis-balls, struck and
bandied / Which way please them. [*do.*, V. 4]

W13 **Weiss, Peter** (1916–) German dramatist
1 What's the use of a revolution / Without general copulation? [*The Marat/Sade*]

W14 **Wellington, 1st Duke of** (1769–1852)
English general and statesman
1 Ours [i.e. our army] is composed of the scum of the earth. [remark]
2 Up, Guards, and at 'em. [attr. order at the Battle of Waterloo]
3 The battle of Waterloo was won on the playing fields of Eton. [attr.]
4 Publish and be damned. [attr.]
5 If you believe that you will believe anything. [attr. remark on being addressed by a stranger as 'Mr Jones, I believe?']

W15 **Wells, H. G.** (1866–1946) English author
1 In the country of the blind the one-eyed man is king. [*The Country of the Blind*]
2 The Shape of Things to Come. [title of book]

W16 **Wesker, Arnold** (1932–) English dramatist
1 You breed babies and you eat chips with everything. [*Chips with Everything*, I. 2]

W17 **Wesley, John** (1703–91)
English theologian and evangelist
1 I look upon all the world as my parish. [*Journal*, 11 June 1739]

W18 **West, Mae** (1893–1980) US film actress
1 Beulah, peel me a grape. [*I'm No Angel* (film)]
2 It's not the men in your life that matter – it's the life in your men. [*do.*]
3 'Goodness, what beautiful diamonds.' 'Goodness had nothing to do with it, dearie.'
[*Night After Night* (film)]
4 Why don't you come up sometime and see me? [*She Done Him Wrong* (film). Often quoted as 'Come up and see me sometime']
5 When I'm good, I'm very very good; but when I'm bad, I'm better. [attr.]

W19 **Whistler, James** (1834–1903) US artist
1 I am not arguing with you – I am telling you. [*The Gentle Art of Making Enemies*]
2 'For two days' labour, you ask two hundred

guineas?' 'No, I ask it for the knowledge of a
lifetime.' [reply in his libel suit against John Ruskin
(see **R21.1**)]
3 OSCAR WILDE. I wish I had said that.
WHISTLER. You will, Oscar, you will. [attr.]

W20 **Whitefield, George** (1714–70) English evangelist
1 I had rather wear out than rust out. [attr. Also attr.
to Richard Cumberland (1631–1718)]

W21 **Whitehead, Alfred North** (1861–1947)
English mathematician and philosopher
1 Art is the imposing of a pattern on experience, and
our aesthetic enjoyment is recognition of the pattern.
[*Dialogues*]

W22 **Whitman, Walt** (1819–92) US poet
1 O Captain! my Captain! our fearful trip is
done, / The ship has weather'd every rack, the prize
we sought is won, / The port is near, the bells I
hear, the people all exulting. [*O Captain! My
Captain!*]
2 I celebrate myself, and sing myself, / And what I
assume you shall assume, / For every atom belonging
to me as good belongs to you. [*Song of Myself*, 1]
3 I am the man, I suffer'd, I was there. [*do.*, 33]
4 Do I contradict myself? / Very well then I
contradict myself, / (I am large, I contain
multitudes). [*do.*, 51]

W23 **Whittington, Robert** (fl. 1519) English grammarian
1 [on Sir Thomas More] As time requireth, a man of
marvellous mirth and pastimes, and sometime of as
sad gravity, as who say: a man for all seasons.
[*Vulgaria*]

W24 **Wilcox, Ella Wheeler** (1850–1919) US poet
1 Laugh, and the world laughs with you; / Weep,
and you weep alone, / For the sad old earth must
borrow its mirth, / But has trouble enough of its
own. [*Solitude*]

W25 **Wilde, Oscar** (1854–1900)
English (Irish-born) author
1 I never saw a man who looked / With such a
wistful eye / Upon that little tent of blue / Which
prisoners call the sky. [*The Ballad of Reading Gaol*, I]
2 Yet each man kills the thing he loves, / By each let

this be heard, / Some do it with a bitter
look, / Some with a flattering word / The coward
does it with a kiss, / The brave man with a sword!
[*do.*]

3 Something was dead in each of us, / And what was
dead was Hope. [*do.*, III]

4 A little sincerity is a dangerous thing, and a great
deal of it is absolutely fatal. [*The Critic as Artist*]

5 The truth is rarely pure, and never simple. [*The
Importance of Being Earnest*, I]

6 LANE. There were no cucumbers in the market this
morning, sir. I went down twice.
ALGERNON. No cucumbers!
LANE. No, sir. Not even for ready money. [*do.*]

7 To lose one parent, Mr Worthing, may be regarded
as a misfortune; to lose both looks like carelessness.
[*do.*]

8 I never travel without my diary. One should always
have something sensational to read in the train.
[*do.*, II]

9 No woman should ever be quite accurate about her
age. It looks so calculating. [*do.*, III]

10 JACK. In a hand-bag.
LADY BRACKNELL. A hand-bag? [*do.*]

11 Over the piano was printed a notice: Please do not
shoot the pianist. He is doing his best. [*Impressions of
America*, 'Leadville']

12 I can resist everything except temptation. [*Lady
Windermere's Fan*, I]

13 We are all in the gutter, but some of us are
looking at the stars. [*do.*, III]

14 A man who knows the price of everything and the
value of nothing. [definition of a cynic. *do.*]

15 All Art is quite useless. [*The Picture of Dorian
Gray*, Preface]

16 There is only one thing in the world worse than
being talked about, and that is not being talked about.
[*do.*, ch. 1]

17 The only way to get rid of a temptation is to yield
to it. [*do.*, ch. 2]

18 A cigarette is the perfect type of a perfect
pleasure. It is exquisite, and it leaves one unsatisfied.
What more can one want? [*do.*, ch. 6]

19 One knows so well the popular idea of health.
The English country gentleman galloping after a

fox – the unspeakable in full pursuit of the uneatable.
[*A Woman of No Importance*, I]
20 Moderation is a fatal thing, Lady Hunstanton.
Nothing succeeds like excess. [*do.*, III]
21 I have nothing to declare except my genius.
[remark at the New York Custom House]
22 I suppose that I shall have to die beyond my
means. [remark on being told the high cost of an
operation]
23 Work is the curse of the drinking classes. [attr.]

W26   **Wilhelm II** (1859–1941)
King of Prussia and Emperor of Germany
1 [on the British Expeditionary Force] A
contemptible little army. [Order from HQ, 19 Aug.
1914. The original German should probably be
translated as 'contemptibly small army']

W27   **William III** (1650–1702) King of Great Britain
1 Every bullet has its billet. [cited in John Wesley's
Journal, 6 June 1765]

W28   **William of Wykeham** (1324–1404) English prelate
1 Manners maketh man. [motto of Winchester
College and New College, Oxford, which he founded]

W29   **Williams, Harry** (1874–1924)
1 It's a long way to Tipperary, it's a long way to
go; / It's a long way to Tipperary, to the sweetest
girl I know! / Goodbye, Piccadilly, farewell, Leicester
Square, / It's a long, long way to Tipperary, but my
heart's right there! [*Tipperary*]

W30   **Wilson, Sir Harold** (1916–) English statesman
1 All these financiers, all the little gnomes of Zurich
and the other financial centres, about whom we keep
on hearing. [speech in the House of Commons, 1956]
2 A week is a long time in politics. [speech, 1964]
3 From now, the pound is worth 14 per cent or so
less in terms of other currencies. It does not mean, of
course, that the pound here in Britain, in your pocket
or purse or in your bank, has been devalued.
[broadcast on devaluation, 20 Nov. 1967]
4 One man's wage increase is another man's price
increase. [speech, 1970]

W31   **Wilson, Thomas Woodrow** (1856–1924)
US president

1 The world must be made safe for democracy.
[address to Congress, 2 Apr. 1917]

W32   **Wittgenstein, Ludwig** (1889–1951)
British (Austrian-born) philosopher
1 *Die Welt ist alles, was der Fall ist.* The world is
everything that is the case. [*Tractatus Logico-Philosophicus*, 1]

W33   **Wodehouse, P. G.** (1881–1975)
US (English-born) author
1 Jeeves shimmered out and came back with a
telegram. [*Carry on Jeeves*]
2 He spoke with a certain what-is-it in his voice, and
I could see that, if not actually disgruntled, he was far
from being gruntled. [*The Code of the Woosters*]

W34   **Wolsey, Thomas** (1475?–1530)
English cardinal and statesman
1 Had I but served God as diligently as I have served
the King, he would not have given me over in my
grey hairs. [remark on his death bed]

W35   **Wood, Mrs Henry** (1814–87) English novelist
1 Dead! and . . . never called me mother. [*East Lynne*
(dramatized version by T. A. Palmer)]

W36   **Wordsworth, William** (1770–1850) English poet
1 Ah! then, if mine had been the Painter's
hand, / To express what then I saw; and add the
gleam, / The light that never was, on sea or
land, / The consecration, and the Poet's dream.
[*Elegiac Stanzas*]
2 The good die first, / And they whose hearts are
dry as summer dust / Burn to the socket. [*The
Excursion*, I]
3 I travelled among unknown men, / In lands
beyond the sea; / Nor, England! did I know till
then / What love I bore to thee. [*I Travelled among
Unknown Men*]
4 I wandered lonely as a cloud / That floats on high
o'er vales and hills, / When all at once I saw a
crowd, / A host of golden daffodils. [*I Wandered
Lonely as a Cloud*]
5 For oft when on my couch I lie / In vacant or in
pensive mood, / They flash upon that inward
eye / Which is the bliss of solitude; / And then my

heart with pleasure fills, / And dances with the daffodils. [*do.*]

6 That best portion of a good man's life, / His little, nameless, unremembered acts / Of kindness and of love. [*Lines Composed a Few Miles above Tintern Abbey*]

7 That blessed mood, / In which the burthen of the mystery, / In which the heavy and the weary weight / Of all this unintelligible world, / Is lightened. [*do.*]

8 I have learned / To look on nature, not as in the hour / Of thoughtless youth; but hearing oftentimes / The still, sad music of humanity, / Nor harsh nor grating, though of ample power / To chasten and subdue. And I have felt / A presence that disturbs me with the joy / Of elevated thoughts; a sense sublime / Of something far more deeply interfused, / Whose dwelling is the light of setting suns, / And the round ocean and the living air, / And the blue sky, and in the mind of man. [*do.*]

9 Nature never did betray / The heart that loved her. [*do.*]

10 And much it grieved my heart to think / What man has made of man. [*Lines Written in Early Spring*]

11 Poetry is the spontaneous overflow of powerful feelings: it takes its origin from emotion recollected in tranquillity. [*Lyrical Ballads*, Preface]

12 There is a comfort in the strength of love; / 'Twill make a thing endurable, which else / Would overset the brain, or break the heart. [*Michael*]

13 My heart leaps up when I behold / A rainbow in the sky: / So was it when my life began; / So is it now I am a man; / So be it when I shall grow old, / Or let me die! / The child is father of the man; / And I could wish my days to be / Bound each to each by natural piety. [*My Heart Leaps Up*]

14 There was a time when meadow, grove, and stream, / The earth, and every common sight, / To me did seem / Apparelled in celestial light, / The glory and the freshness of a dream. [*Ode, Intimations of Immortality from Recollections of Early Childhood*]

15 Our birth is but a sleep and a forgetting: / The soul that rises with us, our life's star, / Hath had elsewhere its setting, / And cometh from afar: / Not in entire forgetfulness, / And not in utter nakedness, / But trailing clouds of glory do we come / From God, who is our home: / Heaven lies about us in our infancy! / Shades of the prison-house begin to close / Upon the growing boy. [*do.*]

16 Thanks to the human heart by which we live, / Thanks to its tenderness, its joys, and fears, / To me the meanest flower that blows can give / Thoughts that do often lie too deep for tears. [*do.*]

17 Fair seed-time had my soul, and I grew up / Fostered alike by beauty and by fear. [*The Prelude*, I]

18 Where the statue stood / Of Newton, with his prism and silent face, / The marble index of a mind for ever / Voyaging through strange seas of Thought, alone. [*do.*, III]

19 Bliss was it in that dawn to be alive, / But to be young was very Heaven! [*do.*, XI]

20 She was a phantom of delight / When first she gleamed upon my sight. [*She was a Phantom of Delight*]

21 A slumber did my spirit seal; / I had no human fears: / She seemed a thing that could not feel / The touch of earthly years. / No motion has she now, no force; / She neither hears nor sees; / Rolled round in earth's diurnal course, / With rocks, and stones, and trees. [*A Slumber did my Spirit Seal*]

22 Behold her, single in the field, / Yon solitary Highland lass! [*The Solitary Reaper*]

23 Love had he found in huts where poor men lie; / His daily teachers had been woods and rills, / The silence that is in the starry sky, / The sleep that is among the lonely hills. [*Song at the Feast of Brougham Castle*]

24 Earth has not anything to show more fair: / Dull would he be of soul who could pass by / A sight so touching in its majesty: / This city now doth, like a garment, wear / The beauty of the morning; silent, bare, / Ships, towers, domes, theatres, and temples lie / Open unto the fields, and to the sky; / All bright and glittering in the smokeless air. [*Sonnet*, 'Composed upon Westminster Bridge']

25 Dear God! the very houses seem asleep; / And all that mighty heart is lying still! [*do.*]

26 It is a beauteous evening, calm and free; / The holy time is quiet as a nun, / Breathless with adoration. [*Sonnet*, 'It is a Beauteous Evening']

27 Milton! thou shouldst be living at this hour: / England hath need of thee; she is a fen / Of stagnant waters: altar, sword, and pen, / Fireside, the heroic wealth of hall and bower, / Have forfeited their ancient English dower / Of inward happiness.
[*Sonnet*, 'Milton! thou shouldst']

28 Nuns fret not at their convent's narrow room; / And hermits are contented with their cells.
[*Sonnet*, 'Nuns fret not']

29 Two Voices are there; one is of the sea, / One of the mountains; each a mighty Voice, / In both from age to age thou didst rejoice, / They were thy chosen music, Liberty! [*Sonnet*, 'Two Voices Are There']

30 The world is too much with us; late and soon, / Getting and spending, we lay waste our powers: / Little we see in Nature that is ours.
[*Sonnet*, 'The World is Too Much with Us']

31 Come forth into the light of things, / Let nature be your teacher. [*The Tables Turned*]

32 One impulse from a vernal wood / May teach you more of man, / Of moral evil and of good, / Than all the sages can. [*do.*]

33 Our meddling intellect / Misshapes the beauteous forms of things: − / We murder to dissect. [*do.*]

34 I've measured it from side to side: / 'Tis three feet long and two feet wide. [*The Thorn* (original version)]

35 O blithe new-comer! I have heard, / I hear thee and rejoice. / O Cuckoo! Shall I call thee bird, / Or but a wandering voice? [*To the Cuckoo*]

W37 **Wotton, Sir Henry** (1568–1639)
English diplomat and poet
1 An Ambassador is an honest man sent to lie abroad for the good of his country. [written in a friend's album]

W38 **Wren, Sir Christopher** (1632–1723)
English architect
1 *Si monumentum requiris, circumspice*. If you seek his monument, look around. [inscription, written by his son, in St Paul's Cathedral]

W39 **Wyatt, Sir Thomas** (1503–43)
English poet and diplomat
1 They flee from me that sometime did me

seek, / With naked foot, stalking in my chamber. / I
have seen them gentle, tame, and meek, / That now
are wild, and do not remember / That sometime they
put themselves in danger / To take bread at my
hand. [*Remembrance*]

X1 **Xenophon** (434?–355? BC)
Greek historian and soldier
1 The sea! the sea! [*Anabasis*, IV]

Y1 **Yeames, W. F.** (1835–1918)
1 And when did you last see your father?
[title of painting]

Y2 **Yeats, W. B.** (1865–1939) Irish poet
1 O body swayed to music, O brightening
glance, / How can we know the dancer from the
dance? [*Among School Children*]
2 A starlit or a moonlit dome disdains / All that man
is, / All mere complexities, / The fury and the mire
of human veins. [*Byzantium*]
3 That dolphin-torn, that gong-tormented sea. [*do.*]
4 The intellect of man is forced to choose /
Perfection of the life, or of the work. [*The Choice*]
5 Now that my ladder's gone, / I must lie down
where all the ladders start, / In the foul rag-and-bone
shop of the heart. [*The Circus Animals' Desertion*]
6 Though leaves are many, the root is one; /
Through all the lying days of my youth / I
swayed my leaves and flowers in the sun; / Now I
may wither into the truth. [*The Coming of Wisdom
with Time*]
7 But love has pitched his mansion in / The place of
excrement. [*Crazy Jane Talks with the Bishop*]
8 Down by the salley gardens my love and I did

meet; / She passed the salley gardens with little snow-white feet. / She bid me take love easy, as the leaves grow on the tree; / But I, being young and foolish, with her would not agree. [*Down by the Salley Gardens*]

9 All changed, changed utterly: / A terrible beauty is born. [*Easter 1916*]

10 But I, being poor, have only my dreams; / I have spread my dreams under your feet; / Tread softly because you tread on my dreams. [*He Wishes for the Cloths of Heaven*]

11 I balanced all, brought all to mind, / The years to come seemed waste of breath, / A waste of breath the years behind / In balance with this life, this death. [*An Irish Airman Foresees His Death*]

12 I will arise and go now, and go to Innisfree, / And a small cabin build there, of clay and wattles made: / Nine bean rows will I have there, a hive for the honey-bee, / And live alone in the bee-loud glade. [*The Lake Isle of Innisfree*]

13 Like a long-legged fly upon the stream / His mind moves upon silence. [*Long-legged Fly*]

14 A pity beyond all telling / Is hid in the heart of love. [*The Pity of Love*]

15 That is no country for old men. [*Sailing to Byzantium*]

16 An aged man is but a paltry thing, / A tattered coat upon a stick, unless / Soul clap its hands and sing. [*do.*]

17 Things fall apart; the centre cannot hold; / Mere anarchy is loosed upon the world, / The blood-dimmed tide is loosed, and everywhere / The ceremony of innocence is drowned; / The best lack all conviction, while the worst / Are full of passionate intensity. [*The Second Coming*]

18 And what rough beast, its hour come round at last, / Slouches towards Bethlehem to be born? [*do.*]

19 Romantic Ireland's dead and gone, / It's with O'Leary in the grave. [*September, 1913*]

20 Cast a cold eye / On life, on death. / Horseman, pass by! [*Under Ben Bulben* (Yeats' epitaph)]

21 When you are old and grey and full of sleep, / And nodding by the fire, take down this book, / And slowly read, and dream of the soft look / Your eyes had once, and of their shadows deep.

[*When You Are Old*]

Y3   **Young, Edward** (1683–1765) English poet
1 Be wise with speed; / A fool at forty is a fool
indeed. [*Love of Fame*]
2 Procrastination is the thief of time.
[*Night Thoughts*]

Z1   **Zangwill, Israel** (1864–1926)
English dramatist and novelist
1 America is God's Crucible, the great Melting-Pot
where all the races of Europe are melting and re-
forming! [*The Melting-Pot*, I]

Z2   **Zapata, Emiliano** (1879–1919)
Mexican revolutionary leader
1 It is better to die on your feet than to live on your
knees! [attr.]

Index

subject **J2.**1
Artistic: ~ temperament is a disease **C23.**5
Arts: No ~; no letters; no society **H33.**3
Ash: They had fallen from an ~ **H7.**10
Ashamed: stupid man is doing something he is ~ of **S16.**3
Ashes: earth to earth, ~ to ~, dust to dust **P26.**13
Ask: ~ and it shall be given you **B23.**147
if you has to ~ you ain't got it **W3.**1
Ass: law is a ~ **D13.**24
Assyrian: ~ came down like the wolf **B62.**10
Astra: *Sic itur ad* ~ **V2.**8
Asunder: let no man put ~ **P26.**11
let not man put ~ **B23.**163
Atheist: ~ is a man **B49.**1
Atlantic: ~ Ocean beat Mrs Partington **S27.**1
Atom: carbon ~ possesses certain exceptional properties **J4.**1
Attracted: ~ by God, or by Nature **I2.**2
Audentis: ~ *Fortuna iuvat* **V2.**9
Aunt: Charley's ~ from Brazil **T10.**1
Authority: Dress'd in a little brief ~ **S15.**180
Avarice: rich beyond the dreams of ~ **M39.**2
Ave: ~ *atque vale* **C14.**3
~ *Caesar, morituri te salutant* **S49.**2
Avenge: ~ O Lord, thy slaughtered saints **M34.**39
Averno: *Facilis descensus* ~ **V2.**6
A-waltzing: ~ Matilda **P6.**1

Babes: Out of the mouth of ~ and sucklings **B23.**57
Babies: Any man who hates dogs and ~ **R17.**1
putting milk into ~ **C25.**14
Babylon: By the rivers of ~ **B23.**77
Bachelors: Two old ~ were living in one house **L12.**10
Back: at my ~ from time to time I hear **E8.**29
at my ~ I always hear **M15.**5
One who never turned his ~ **B48.**2
those before cried ~ **M1.**6
Bad: Defend the ~ against the worse **D5.**1
when I'm ~ I'm better **W18.**5
Balance: ~ of power **W5.**2
Balances: weighed in the ~ and

art found wanting **B23.**120
Ballot: ~ is stronger than the bullet **L25.**2
Band: we ~ of brothers **S15.**93
Bang: Not with a ~ but a whimper **E8.**13
Bank: ~ whereon the wild thyme blows **S15.**202
How sweet the moonlight sleeps upon this ~ **S15.**195
I cried all the way to the ~ **L24.**1
Banks: ~ and braes o' bonnie Doon **B56.**17
Banner: ~ with this strange device **L31.**3
Bar: may there be no moaning of the ~ **T4.**6
When I have crost the ~ **T4.**7
Barbarians: ~, Philistines, and Populace **A22.**1
Barber: she very imprudently married the ~ **F11.**1
Barge: ~ she sat in **S15.**7
Barkis: ~ is willin' **D13.**7
Barley: Long fields of ~ and of rye **T4.**18
Bars: Two men look out through the same ~ **L5.**1
Bat: Twinkle, twinkle little ~ **C12.**7
Battle: ~ of Britain **C25.**8
~ of Waterloo was won on the playing fields of Eton **W14.**3
Ben ~ was a solder bold **H35.**1
Bauble: What shall we do with this ~ **C52.**2
Beaker: O for a ~ full of the warm South **K5.**17
Be-all: Might be the ~ and the end-all **S15.**154
Beam: ~ that is in thine own eye **B23.**145
Bean: Nine ~ rows will I have there **Y2.**12
Bear: *Exit, pursued by a* ~ **S15.**293
Bear-baiting: Puritan hated ~ **M1.**4
Beard: singed the Spanish king's ~ **D23.**1
There was an Old Man with a ~ **L12.**1
Beast: count the number of the ~ **B23.**268
Man's life is cheap as ~'s **S15.**125
what rough ~ **Y2.**18
Beastie: Wee, sleekit, cow'rin', tim'rous ~ **B56.**15
Beastly: Don't let's be ~ to the

Be: To ~ or not to ~ – that is the question **S15.**57

Man doth not live by ~ only
B23.33
Man shall not live by ~ alone
B23.130
Break: ~, ~, ~ **T**4.1
Never Give a Sucker an Even
~ **F**5.2
Breakfast: ~ first, business next
T7.1
Breast: Hope springs eternal in
the human ~ **P**20.16
Breath: ~'s a ware that will not
keep **H**39.2
Breed: This happy ~ of men
S15.232
Brevity: ~ is the soul of wit
S15.47
Brian: Sir ~ had a battleaxe
M33.1
Brick: found it ~ and left it
marble **A**28.1
Bride: Thou still unravish'd ~ of
quietness **K**5.12
Bridge: And keep the ~ with me
M1.5
~ over Troubled Water **S**23.1
Bright: All things ~ and beautiful
A10.1
young lady named ~ **B**51.1
Brightness: ~ falls from the air
N4.1
Brillig: Twas ~ and the slithy
toves **C**12.18
Britain: battle of ~ **C**25.8
~ has lost an empire **A**1.1
When ~ first **T**15.1
Britannia: Rule, ~, rule the
waves **T**15.1
British: liquidation of the ~
Empire **C**25.13
so ridiculous as the ~ public
M1.9
The maxim of the ~ people
C25.2
Britons: ~ never will be slaves
T15.1
Broken-hearted: We had ne'er
been ~ **B**56.2
Brother: Am I my ~'s keeper?
B23.10
Big ~ is watching you **O**5.3
Brothers: we band of ~ **S**15.93
Brown: John ~'s body **B**28.
Brute: Et tu, ~ **C**2.5
Et tu, ~ **S**15.105
Whatever ~ and blackguard
made the world **H**39.12
Brutes: Exterminate all ~ **C**38.2
Brutus: ~ is an honourable man
S15.111
fault, dear ~, is not in our
stars **S**15.102
Buck: ~ stops here **T**21.1
Buckingham: They're changing

guard at ~ Palace **M**33.2
Builded: He ~ better than he
knew **E**12.8
Builders: stone which the ~
refused **B**23.74
BULL: COCK and a ~ **S**42.9
Bullet: ballot is stronger than the
~ **L**25.2
Every ~ has its billet **W**27.1
Bunk: History is more or less ~
F12.1
Burden: Take up the White
Man's ~ **K**11.21
Burg: Ein' feste ~ ist unser Gott
L39.2
Burgundy: naive domestic ~
T18.1
Burn: better to marry than to ~
B23.234
Bury: I come to ~ Caesar, not
to praise him **S**15.110
Bush: good wine needs no ~
S15.27
Business: 'Breakfast first, ~
next.' **T**7.1
~ as usual **C**25.2
I must be about my Father's ~
B23.190
No ~ Like Show Business
B20.2
To ~ that we love **S**15.10
true ~ precept **D**13.17
Busyness: Extreme ~ **S**44.5
Butter: ~ will only make us fat
G16.1
Butterfly: Float like a ~ **A**11.2
Who breaks a ~ upon a
wheel? **P**20.5
Byzantium: Soldan of ~ is
smiling **C**23.6

Cabbages: Of ~ –and kings
C12.23
Cabin: small ~ build there **Y**2.12
Cabin'd: ~, cribb'd, confin'd
S15.165
Caesar: ~'s wife must be above
suspicion **C**2.4
I come to bury ~, not to
praise him **S**15.110
Not that I lov'd ~ less
S15.109
O mighty ~, dost thou lie so
low? **S**15.106
Render therefore unto ~
B23.169
Cake: Let them eat ~ **M**11.1
Cakes: no more ~ and ale
S15.287
Calais: ~ lying in my heart
M18.1
Calf: Bring hither the fatted ~
B23.198
Call: ~ me early, mother dear

T4.26
Called: many are ~ but few are chosen **B23.168**
Calm: All is ~, all is bright **M36.1**
Came: I ~ and no one answered **D9.4**
I ~, I saw, I conquered **C2.2**
Camel: ~ to go through the eye of a needle **B23.164**
Camelot: many-tower'd ~ **T4.18**
Camera: I am a ~ **I3.1**
Cammin: *Nel mezzo del ~ di nostra vita* **D2.1**
Candle: we shall this day light such a ~ **L8.1**
Candles: ~ burn their sockets **H39.15**
Candy: ~/Is dandy **N3.1**
Cannon: ~ to right of them **T4.5**
Cannon-ball: ~ took off his legs **H35.1**
Capability: Negative ~ **K5.29**
Capitalism: unpleasant and unacceptable face of ~ **H14.2**
Captain: I am the ~ of my soul **H20.2**
O ~ my ~ **W22.1**
Captains: All my sad ~ **S15.9**
~ and the Kings depart **K11.18**
~ of industry **C10.8**
Care: I ~ for nobody **B24.2**
Sleep that knits up the ravell'd sleave of ~ **S15.159**
Carelessness: to lose both looks like ~ **W25.7**
Carollings: So little cause for ~ **H7.4**
Carpe: ~ *diem* **H38.6**
Carpet: figure in the ~ **J2.2**
Carrion: ~ comfort, Despair **H37.1**
Carthago: *Delenda est ~* **C13.1**
Castle: man's house is his ~ **C31.1**
splendour falls on ~ walls **T4.27**
Castlereagh: He had a mask like ~ **S17.10**
Casualty: first ~ when war comes is truth **J8.1**
Cat: ~ n. A soft indestructible automaton **B25.3**
Hanging of his ~ on Monday **B39.1**
When I play with my ~ **M38.3**
Catch-22: only one catch and that was ~ **H15.1**
Cattle: What passing-bells for these who die as ~ **O9.1**
Cause: ~ or just impediment **P26.8**

Causes: Home of lost ~ **A22.4**
occasions and ~ why and wherefore in all things **S15.94**
Cavaliero: perfect ~ **B62.1**
Cave: ~ *canem* **P12.1**
Caverns: ~ measureless to man **C32.7**
Caviare: ~ to the general **S15.54**
Cedant: ~ *arma togae* **C26.3**
Celibacy: ~ has no pleasures **J9.44**
Censure: No man can justly ~ or condemn another **B46.3**
Centre: ~ cannot hold **Y2.17**
Century: ~ of the common man **W1.1**
Certain: ~ because it is impossible **T6.1**
Certainties: If a man will begin with ~ **B1.1**
Certum: ~ *est quia impossibile* **T6.1**
Chains: everywhere he is in ~ **R19.1**
workers have nothing to lose but their ~ **M17.2**
Chance: man alone ain't got no bloody ~ **H19.2**
Change: ~ and decay in all around I see **L40.2**
ça ~ ~ **K21**
wind of ~ is blowing **M6.3**
Changè: *nous avons ~ tout cela* **M37.4.**
Changed: All ~, changed utterly **Y2.9**
we have ~ all that **M37.4**
Changes: more it ~ the more it is the same **K2.1**
Changeth: old order ~ **T4.9**
Chaos: thy dread Empire, ~ **P20.2**
Chapter: A ~ of accidents **C22.5**
Chariot: Time's winged ~ hurrying near **M15.5**
Charity: ~ shall cover the multitude of sins **B23.260**
have not ~ **B23.238**
now abideth faith, hope, ~ **B23.239**
Charley: ~'s aunt from Brazil **T10.1**
Charmed: I bear a ~ life **S15.176**
Chaste: My English text is ~ **G9.5**
Chastity: Give me ~ and continency **A27.1**
Chatte: *Quand je me joue à ma ~* **M38.3.**
Cheating: Gamesmanship or The Art of Winning Games Without Actually ~ **P22.1**
Cheek: bring a blush into the ~

Shall I compare thee to a
summer's ~ **S15**.253

Sufficient unto the ~ is the
evil **B23**.143

Sweet ~, so cool **H25**.6

To have and to hold from this
~ forward **P26**.10

Days: As for man, his ~ are as
grass **B23**.72

~ of our years are threescore
years and ten **B23**.71

~ of wine and roses **D21**.3

My salad ~ **S15**.6

Dazzle: mine eyes ~, she died
young **W12**.2

Dead: communication/Of the ~
E8.8

~ and... never called me
mother **W35**.1

God is ~ **N9**.1

great deal to be said/For being
~ **B19**.1

I would that I were ~ **T4**.23

Mistah Kurtz–he ~ **C38**.4

No longer mourn for me when
I am ~ **S15**.258

she has been ~ many times
P5.1

Something was ~ in each of us
W25.3

there he fell down ~ **B23**.37

they all ~ did lie **C32**.16

what the ~ had no speech for
E8.8

Deal: new ~ **R13**.1

Dean: Let the ~ and Canons lay
their heads together **S27**.6

Dear: thou art too ~ for my
possessing **S15**.260

Death: After the first ~ **T11**.5

All tragedies are finish'd by a
~ **B62**.18

any man's ~ diminishes *me*
D19.5

Be absolute for ~ **S15**.181

Be thou faithful unto ~
B23.264

Birth, and copulation, and ~
E8.25

~ after life **S36**.1

~ bandaged my eyes **B48**.22

~ be not proud **D19**.12

~ had undone so many **E8**.28

~ shall be no more **D19**.13

~, where is thy sting? **B23**.240

fear and danger of violent ~
H33.3

give me liberty or give me ~
H23.1

his name that sat on him was
~ **B23**.265

I should be glad of another ~
E8.14

In the midst of life we are in

~ **P26**.12

In the ranks of ~ you'll find
him **M40**.2

life half dead, a living ~
M34.35

Men fear ~ **B1**.3

nothing can be said to be
certain, except ~ and taxes
F18.3

one that had been studied in
his ~ **S15**.151

report of my ~ was an
exaggeration **T22**.2

there shall be no more ~
B23.270

though I walk through the
valley of the shadow of ~
B23.63

till ~ us do part **P26**.10

wages of sin is ~ **B23**.228

Webster was much possessed by
~ **E8**.33

Deaths: Cowards die many times
before their ~ **S15**.104

Decay: All humane things are
subject to ~ **D25**.8

Where wealth accumulates, and
men ~ **G18**.1

Deceive: When first we practise
to ~ **S9**.2

Deceivers: Men were ~ ever
S15.208

Deck: boy stood on the burning
~ **H18**.1

Declare: nothing to ~ except my
genius **W25**.21

Decline: writing the ~ and fall
of the city **G9**.4

Deed: right ~ for the wrong
reason **E8**.23

shines a good ~ in a naughty
world **S15**.197

Deep: I can call spirits from the
vasty ~ **S15**.79

Deeth: ~ is an ende of every
worldly sore **C21**.7

Defeat: After Alamein we never
had a ~ **C25**.18

Defect: Chief ~ of Henry King
B15.1

Defend: ~ the bad against the
worse **D5**.1

Delenda: ~ *est Carthago* **C13**.1

Delight: She was a phantom of
~ **W36**.20

we have a degree of ~ **B55**.1

Déluge: *Après nous le* ~
P19.1

Democracy: ~ and proper drains
B21.2

~ is the worst form of
Government **C25**.16

~ substitutes election by the
incompetent many **S16**.14

world must be made safe for ~
W31.1

Demonstrandum: *Quod erat* ~
E15.1

Den: snorted we in the Seven
Sleepers' ~ **D19**.10
ye have made it a ~ of thieves
B23.167

Denmark: Something is rotten in
the state of ~ **S15**.42

Deny: before the cock crow, thou
shalt ~ me thrice **B23**.175

Depart: I am ready to ~ **L3**.1

Depends: It all ~ what you
mean by **J7**.1

Depths: Out of the ~ have I
cried **B23**.76

Derangement: nice ~ of epitaphs
S19.3

Descensus: *Facilis* ~ *Averno* **V2**.6

Description: For her own
person,/It beggar'd all ~ **S15**.7

Desert: Stand in the ~ **S17**.14
Use every man after his ~
S15.55

Deserts: ~ of vast eternity
M15.5

Desire: ~ should so many years
outlive performance **S15**.85
few things to ~ **B1**.9
I will not choose what many
men ~ **S15**.188
it provokes the ~ but it takes
away the performance **S15**.161
Re-mould it nearer to the
Heart's ~ **F6**.8
Which of us has his ~ **T7**.3

Desires: ~ of the heart **A26**.1

Desolation: abomination of ~
B23.172

Despair: carrion comfort, ~
H37.1
Look on my works, ye Mighty,
and ~ **S17**.15
owner whereof was Giant ~
B53.5

Desperation: lives of quiet ~
T17.2

Despond: name of the slough was
~ **B53**.2

Destiny: ~ with Men for Pieces
plays **F6**.5

Destroy: not to ~ but to fulfil
B23.134
Those whom God wishes to ~
E16.1
Whom the gods wish to ~
C37.3

Destruction: ~ of millions of our
fellow-beings **H12**.1
Pride goeth before ~ **B23**.85

Detail: Our life is frittered away
by ~ **T17**.6

Deus: *homo proponit, sed* ~

disponit **T9**.2

Development: psychic ~ of the
individual **F20**.1

Devil: ~ can cite Scripture for
his purpose **S15**.186
~, having nothing else to do
B15.7
~ should have all the good
tunes **H30**.1
~'s walking parody **C23**.2

Diamond: ~ and safire bracelet
lasts forever **L32**.2

Diary: I never travel without my
~ **W25**.8

Dice: God does not play ~ **E6**.1

Dicebamus: ~ *hesterno die* **L19**.1

Dick: ~ the shepherd blows his
nail **S15**.145

Die: ~ but once to serve our
country! **A4**.2
~ is cast **C2**.3
He could not ~ **C27**.1
I shall have to ~ beyond my
means **W25**.22
If I should ~ **B43**.4
natural to ~ as to be born
B1.4
not that I'm afraid to ~ **A13**.3
Now more than ever seems it
rich to ~ **K5**.20
Their's but to do and ~ **T4**.4
those about to ~ salute you
S49.2
to ~, and go we know not
where **S15**.182
to-morrow we shall ~ **B23**.111
we ~ in earnest, that's no jest
R2.1

Died: Men have ~ from time to
time **S15**.24

Dies: Call no man happy until he
~ **S31**.1

Dieu: *Si* ~ *n'existait pas* **V6**.4

Difficult: ~ do you call it **J9**.33

Difficulties: Little local ~ **M6**.2

Digest: Read, mark, learn and
inwardly ~ **P26**.7

Directions: rode madly off in all
~ **L11**.1

Dis: ~ *aliter visum* **V2**.5

Disapprove: I ~ of what you say
V6.5

Disbelief: willing suspension of ~
C32.1

Discommendeth: He who ~
others **B46**.1

Discontent: winter of our ~
S15.237

Discretion: better part of valour
is ~ **S15**.81

Disease: strange ~ of modern life
A22.9
this long ~, my life **P20**.3

Diseases: Desperate ~ require

Facilis: ~ *descensus Averno* **V2.6**
Facts: ~ alone are wanted in life **D13.14**
~ are sacred **S7.1**
to his imagination for his ~ **S19.5**
Fair: Earth has not anything to show more ~ **W36.24**
~ is foul, and foul is ~ **S15.147**
~ stood the wind for France **D24.1**
None but the Brave deserves the ~ **D25.7**
So foul and ~ a day **S15.149**
Fairer: I can't say no ~ than that! **D13.12**
Fairies: that was the beginning of ~ **B6.1**
Fairy: little ~ somewhere that falls down dead **B6.2**
Faith: ~ is the substance of things hoped for **B23.256**
life of doubt diversified by ~ **B48.5**
now abideth ~, hope, charity **B23.239**
Faithful: Be thou ~ unto death **B23.264**
I have been ~ to thee **D21.2**
O come all ye ~ **O1.1**
Falcon: dapple-dawn-drawn ~ **H37.8**
Fall: Fain would I climb, yet fear I to ~ **R2.2**
He that is down, needs fear no ~ **B53.7**
we ~ to rise **B48.2**
Fallen: How are the mighty ~ **B23.43**
False: Thou canst not then be ~ **S15.40**
Falstaff: ~ sweats to death **S15.77**
Fame: ~ is the spur **M34.12**
Families: Accidents will occur in the best-regulated ~ **D13.11**
All happy ~ resemble one another **T20.1**
Famous: found myself ~ **B62.32**
Let us now praise ~ men **B23.126**
Fancy: Ever let the ~ roam **K5.6**
In the Spring a young man's ~ lightly turns **T4.20**
little of what you ~ **L27.1**
now the ~ passes by **H39.3**
Farce: Bring down the curtain, the ~ is over **R1.4**
first time as tragedy, the second as ~ **M17.5**
Farewell: ~, a long ~, to all my greatness! **S15.97**

~ the tranquil mind; ~ content! **S15.224**
Fashion: ~ of this world passeth away **B23.235**
Fat: Imprisoned in every ~ man **C37.4**
Ye shall eat the ~ of the land **B23.14**
Fate: could thou and I with ~ conspire **F6.8**
when ~ summons, Monarchs must obey **D25.8**
Father: child is ~ of the man **W36.13**
either my ~ or my mother **S42.5**
Full fathom five thy ~ lies **S15.272**
Honour thy ~ and thy mother **B23.22**
I must be about my ~'s business **B23.190**
Our ~ which art in heaven **B23.138**
when did you last see your ~ **Y1.1**
wise ~ that knows his own child **S15.187**
Fathers: He slept with his ~ **B23.45**
Fathom: Full ~ five thy father lies **S15.272**
Fault: ~, dear Brutus, is not in our stars **S15.102**
Faultless: Whoever thinks a ~ piece to see **P20.10**
Fay: ~ *ce que vouldras* **R1.2**
Fear: defence against the pure emotion of ~ **S45.1**
~ in a handful of dust **E8.27**
many things to ~ **B1.9**
only thing we have to ~ is ~ **R13.2**
perfect love casteth out ~ **B23.262**
There is no ~ in love **B23.262**
with ~ and trembling **B23.249**
Fears: Present ~/Are less than horrible imaginings **S15.150**
Feast: great ~ of languages **S15.144**
Feel: I see, not ~, how beautiful **C32.3**
Feet: three ~ long and two feet wide **W36.34**
Felde: faire ~ ful of folke **L6.2**
Fell: At her feet he bowed, he ~ **B23.37**
From morn/To noon he ~ **M34.2**
I do not love thee, Doctor ~ **B44.1**
It ~ to earth **L31.1**
Fellow-men: one that loves his ~

Funny: ~ peculiar, or ~ ha-ha? **H10**.1

Fury: beastely ~ and extreme violence **E11**.1
~ and the mire of human veins **Y2**.2

Fuse: force that through the green ~ drives the flower **T11**.4

Future: ~ shock **T19**.1
~ n. That period of time **B25**.5
I have seen the ~, and it works **S40**.1
You cannot fight against the ~ **G13**.1

Gaiety: eclipsed the ~ of nations **J9**.41

Gaiters: All is gas and ~ **D13**.20

Galère: *Que diable allait-il faire dans cette* ~ **M37**.3

Gallantry: What men call ~, and gods adultery **B62**.12

Gallia: ~ *est omnis divisa* **C2**.1

Galloped: I ~, Dirck ~ **B48**.11

Game: It's more than a ~. It's an institution **H43**.2
Play up! play up! and play the ~ **N6**.2
plenty of time to win this ~ **D23**.2

Gamesmanship: ~ or The Art of Winning Games Without Actually Cheating **P22**.1

Gamut: whole ~ of the emotions **P2**.3

Garde: *La* ~ *meurt* **C4**.1

Garden: Come into the ~, Maud **T4**.24
~ is a lovesome thing **B45**.1
God Almighty first planted a ~ **B1**.14
God the first ~ made **C47**.1
Our England is a ~ **K11**.9
We must tend our ~ **V6**.3

Gardens: Down by the salley ~ **Y2**.8
such ~ are not made **K11**.9

Garland: immortal ~ is to be run for **M34**.2

Gas: All is ~ and gaiters **D13**.20

Gate: Strait is the ~ **B23**.149

Gaul: ~ is divided into three parts **C2**.1

Gaza: Eyeless in ~ **M34**.33

Gazelle: I never nurs'd a dear ~ **M40**.1

Geist: *Ich bin der* ~ *der stets verneint* **G17**.1

Gem: Full many a ~ of purest ray serene **G22**.4

General: caviare to the ~ **S15**.54

Generals: I wish he would bite

some other of my ~ **G7**.1

Generations: No hungry ~ tread thee down **K5**.21

Genius: ~ does what it must **M27**.1
~ is one per cent inspiration **E2**.1
~ (which means transcendent capacity of taking trouble) **C10**.4
nothing to declare except my ~ **W25**.21
true ~ is a mind **J9**.39
What a ~ I had **S50**.16
When a true ~ appears **S50**.13

Gentle: Do not go ~ into that good night **T11**.1
His life was ~ **S15**.117

Gentleman: definition of a ~ **N7**.2
every Jack became a ~ **S15**.241
Who was then the ~ **B4**.1

Gentlemen: ~ always seem to remember blondes **L32**.1

German: ~ to my horse **C20**.1

Germans: Don't let's be beastly to the ~ **C46**.4

Ghost: There needs no ~ **S15**.44
Vex not his ~ **S15**.141

Giants: standing on the shoulders of ~ **N8**.1
There were ~ in the earth **B23**.11

Gifts: I fear the Greeks even when they bring ~ **V2**.4

Gild: To ~ refined gold **S15**.120

Girdle: I'll put a ~ round about the earth **S15**.201

Girl: There was a little ~ **L31**.7

Girls: ~ who wear glasses **P2**.1

Give: ~ and it shall be given **B23**.193
more blessed to ~ than to receive **B23**.225
We receive but what we ~ **C32**.5

Given: ask, and it shall be ~ you **B23**.147

Giver: God loveth a cheerful ~ **B23**.242

Giving: I am not in the ~ vein to-day **S15**.242

Glade: live alone in the bee-loud ~ **Y2**.12

Glass: ~ of blessings standing by **H25**.5
Life, like a dome of many-coloured ~ **S17**.3
now we see through a ~ darkly **B23**.239

Glasses: girls who wear ~ **P2**.1

Glisters: Nor all, that ~, gold **G22**.7

Global: image of a ~ village

of your ~ **S15**.166
Gold: Nor all, that glisters, ~
G22.7
To gild refined ~ **S15**.120
Golf: ~ may be played on
Sunday **L11**.2
Gone: All, all are ~, the old
familiar faces **L2**.3
~ with the wind **D21**.1
Good: Be ~, sweet maid **K10**.1
better to fight for the ~ **T4**.25
Evil, be thou my ~ **M34**.27
~ die first **W36**.2
~ is the beautiful **P16**.1
I can but trust that ~ shall
fall **T4**.12
it cannot come to ~ **S15**.34
Music, the greatest ~ **A4**.3
never had it so ~ **M6**.1
nothing either ~ or bad **S15**.50
only one ~, knowledge **S30**.1
tree of the knowledge of ~ and
evil **B23**.6
what ~ came of it at last?
S34.2
When I'm ~ I'm very very ~
W18.5
when she was ~/She was very,
very ~ **L31**.7
Goodbye: ~ to All That **G21**.2
Goodness: ~ had nothing to do
with it **W18**.3
~ in removing it from them
F4.2
Gormed: I'm ~ **D13**.12
Gott: *Ein' feste Burg ist unser ~*
L39. 2
Govern: No man is good enough
to ~ **L25**.1
right divine of kings to ~
wrong **P20**.1
Governed: nation is not ~ **B55**.4
with how little wisdom the
world is ~ **O10**.1
Government: All ~ is founded
on compromise and barter
B55.5
Conservative ~ is an organised
hypocrisy **D17**. 2
democracy is the worst form of
~ **C25**.16
~ is at best but an expedient
T17.1
~ is but a necessary evil **P1**.2
~ of the people, by the people
L25.3
one form of ~ rather than
another **J9**.19
people's ~ **W11**.1
Grace: There, but for the ~ of
God **B38**.1
Gramophone: puts a record on
the ~ **E8**.30
Grandeur: ~ that was Rome

P18.4
world is charged with the ~ of
God **H37**.3
Grape: peel me a ~ **W18**.1
Grapes: ~ of wrath **H40**.1
Grapeshot: A whiff of ~ **C10**.5
Grasp: man's reach should exceed
his ~ **B48**.1
Grass: All flesh is as ~ **B23**.258
All flesh is ~ **B23**.114
As for man, his days are as ~
B23.72
make two ears of corn, or two
blades of ~ to grow **S50**.4
snake lies hidden in the ~
V2.11
Grave: a-mouldering in the ~
B28.
Dig the ~ and let me lie
S44.3
~, where is thy victory?
B23.240
~'s a fine and private place
M15.6
paths of glory lead but to the
~ **G22**.3
Graves: Let's talk of ~, of
worms, and epitaphs **S15**.234
Great: even ~ men have their
poor relations **D13**.4
~ men are almost always bad
men **A2**.1
Some are born ~ **S15**.288
Greatest: I am the ~ **A11**.1
Greatness: Farewell! a long
farewell, to all my ~ **S15**.97
~ consists in bringing all
manner of mischief **F4**.2
some achieve ~ **S15**.288
Greece: dream'd that ~ might
still be free **B62**.20
glory that was ~ **P18**.4
isles of ~ **B62**.19
Greek: small Latin, and less ~
J13.2
Greeks: I fear the ~ even when
they bring gifts **V2**.4
When ~ joined ~ **L16**.1
Green: ~ grow the rashes O
B56.7
~ thought in a ~ shade **M15**.1
Greenwood: Under the ~ tree
S15.18
Grin: ending with the ~ **C12**.6
Grishkin: ~ is nice **E8**.34
Groan: men sit and hear each
other ~ **K5**.18
Ground: let us sit upon the ~
S15.235
Grow'd: I 'spect I ~ **S46**.1
Grundy: what will Mrs ~ zay?
M43.1
Gruntled: far from being ~
W33.2

C10.6

Increase: From fairest creatures we desire ~ **S15**.252

Index: marble ~ of a mind **W36**.18

Indian: Like the base ~, threw a pearl away **S15**.226
Lo! the poor ~ **P20**.17
only good ~ is a dead ~ **S18**.1

Indignatio: *saeva ~ ulterius cor lacerare nequit* **S50**.17

Indignation: fierce ~ can no longer tear his heart **S50**.17

Indignor: ~ *quandoque bonus* **H38**.2

Individual: liberty of the ~ must be thus far limited **M31**.5
psychic development of the ~ **F20**.1

Individualism: American system of rugged ~ **H36**.1

Individuals: all my love is towards ~ **S50**.7

Indulge: ~ no more may we **H7**.5

Industry: Captains of ~ **C10**.8

Inebriate: That cheer but not ~ **C48**.5

Inexactitude: some risk of terminological ~ **C25**.1

Infallible: We are none of us ~ **T14**.1

Infancy: Heaven lies about us in our ~ **W36**.15
Shin'd in my angel ~ **V1**.1

Infant: ~ crying in the night **T4**.12
~/Mewling and puking **S15**.20

Infected: All seems ~ **P20**.14

Infinity: ~ in the palm of your hand **B31**.1

Influence: How to Win Friends and ~ people **C11**.1

Ingratitude: ~, thou marble-hearted fiend **S15**.122
not so unkind/As man's ~ **S15**.23

Inherit: they shall ~ the earth **B23**.132

Inhumanity: Man's ~ to man **B56**.9

Injuries: adding insult to ~ **M39**.1

Ink: Every drop of ~ in my pen **W4**.1

Inn: Do you remember an ~ **B15**.10
For the world, I count it not an ~ **B46**.5
good tavern or ~ **J9**.24

Innisfree: go to ~ **Y2**.12

Innocent: one ~ suffer **B30**.2

Inns: you will lose your ~ **B15**.11

Inspiration: Genius is one per cent ~ **E2**.1

Institution: It's more than a game. It's an ~ **H43**.2

Insult: adding ~ to injuries **M39**.1

Integer: ~ *vitae* **H38**.7

Intellect: ~ of man is forced to choose **Y2**.4
Our meddling ~ **W36**.33

Intellectual: lords of ladies ~ **B62**.11

Intelligence: underestimating the ~ of the American people **M25**.2

Intensity: worst/Are full of passionate ~ **Y2**.17

Interfused: something far more deeply ~ **W36**.8

International: ~ will unite the human race **P23**.2

Internationale: *L'~/Sera le genre humain* **P23**.2

Interrupt: ~ a man with such a silly question **S42**.6

Intimacy: you should avoid any ~ **K13**.1

Intoxication: best of life is but ~ **B62**.16

Inventions: Our ~ are wont to be pretty toys **T17**.5

Ira: ~ *furor brevis est.* **H38**.3

Ireland: ~ is the old sow **J14**.1
Romantic ~'s dead and gone **Y2**.19

Iron: Earth stood hard as ~ **R16**.2
~ curtain has descended **C25**.15

Ishmael: Call me ~ **M23**.1

Island: Look, stranger, on this ~ **A26**.9
No man is an ~ **D19**.5

Isle: ~ is full of noises **S15**.274
Many a green ~ needs must be **S17**.9

Isles: ~ of Greece **B62**.19

Italian: ~ to women **C20**.1

Italy: ~ is a geographical expression **M29**.1

Itch: intolerable neural ~ **A26**.10

Jabberwock: Beware the ~ **C12**.18

Jack: every ~ became a gentleman **S15**.241

Jam: ~ tomorrow and ~ yesterday **C12**.25

James: ~ ~/Morrison Morrison **M33**.3

Jane: Me Tarzan, you ~ **B57**.1

Jardin: *Il faut cultiver notre* ~ **V6**.3

Jarndyce: ~ and ~ **D13**.2

~ of shreds and patches **S15**.66
our sovereign lord the ~ **R11**.1
Kingdom: horse! a horse! my ~
for a horse! **S15**.243
~ of God is within you
B23.200
~ of heaven is at hand
B23.127
My mind to me a ~ is **D30**.1
thine is the ~, and the power,
and the glory **B23**.138
Thy ~ come **B23**.138
Kings: right divine of ~ to
govern wrong **P20**.1
tell sad stories of the death of
~ **S15**.235
Kiss: break off this last lamenting
~ **D19**.7
come ~ me, sweet and twenty
S15.286
come let us ~ and part **D24**.2
~ me, Hardy **N5**.3
~ me Kate **S15**.269
make me immortal with a ~
M12.2
To part at last without a ~
M42.3
Kiss'd: I ~ thee ere I kill'd thee
S15.227
Kissing: when the ~ had to stop
B48.23
Kitchen: get out of the ~ **T21**.2
Knave: ~ of Hearts he stole
those tarts **C12**.13
Knell: Curfew tolls the ~ of
parting day **G22**.1
Knew: He builded better than he
~ **E12**.8
Knight: what can ail thee, ~ at
arms **K5**.9
Know: cold world shall not ~
S17.7
forgive them; for they ~ not
what they do **B23**.201
I ~ thee not, old man **S15**.88
I ~ what I like **B13**.4
we ~ not anything **T4**.12
Knowledge: all ~ to be my
province **B1**.17
for the ~ of a lifetime **W19**.2
~ enormous makes a God of
me **K5**.8
only one good, ~ **S30**.1
Science is organized ~ **S35**.1
search for ~ **R22**.1
tree of the ~ of good and evil
B23.6
Knyf: smylere with the ~ under
the cloke **C21**.6
Knyght: verray, parfit gentil ~
C21.2
Kubla Khan: In Xanadu did ~
C32.7
Kurtz: Mistah ~–he dead **C38**.4

Labour: profit hath a man of all
his ~ **B23**.93
Six days shalt thou ~ **B23**.21
Labourer: ~ is worthy of his
hire **B23**.194
Lacrimae: *Sunt ~ rerum* **V2**.3
Lad: many a lightfoot ~ **H39**.10
Ladders: I must lie down where
all the ~ start **Y2**.5
Lady: ~ doth protest too much
S15.62
Laity: All professions are
conspiracies against the ~ **S16**.6
Lamb: Behold the ~ of God
B23.206
Did he who made the ~ make
thee? **B31**.19
~ to the slaughter **B23**.116
Little ~ who made thee?
B31.20
Mary had a little ~ **H3**.1
to the shorn ~ **S42**.3
wolf also shall dwell with the
~ **B23**.108
Lamps: ~ are going out all over
Europe **G26**.1
Land: England's green and
pleasant ~ **B31**.14
~ flowing with milk and honey
B23.16
~ of Hope and Glory **B17**.1
~ of lost content **H39**.8
my own, my native ~ **S9**.1
out of the ~ of the living
B23.117
stranger in a strange ~ **B23**.15
There's a ~ that I heard of
H6.1
Ye shall eat the fat of the ~
B23.14
Lands: In ~ beyond the sea
W36.3
Language: cool web of ~ **G21**.1
decent obscurity of a learned ~
G9.5
~ is the dress of thought **J9**.40
with no ~ but a cry **T4**.12
Languages: great feast of ~
S15.144
Lards: ~ the lean earth **S15**.77
Large: ~ as life, and twice as
natural! **C12**.29
Lark: ~'s on the wing **B48**.20
Lasciate: ~ *ogni speranza voi
ch'entrate!* **D2**.2
Lass: Yon solitary Highland ~
W36.22
Last: ~ of the Mohicans **C40**.1
many that are first shall be ~
B23.166
Latin: small ~ and less Greek
J13.2
Laugh: I force myself to ~ at
everything **B10**.1

~ tends to corrupt **A2**.1
~ without responsibility **K11**.22
purpose for which ~ can be
rightfully exercised **M31**.3
They that have ~ to hurt
S15.261

Pow'r: wad some ~ the giftie gie
us **B56**.14

Practise: When first we ~ to
deceive! **S9**.2

Praise: Damn with faint ~ **P20**.4
I come to bury Caesar, not to
~ him **S15**.110
Let us now ~ famous men
B23.126
Of whom to be dispraised were
no small ~ **M34**.31
~ to the Holiest in the height
N7.1
they only want ~ **M21**.2

Prayers: Christopher Robin is
saying his ~ **M33**.4

Prayeth: He ~ best, who loveth
best **C32**.21
He ~ well, who loveth well
C32.20

Preaching: woman's ~ is like a
dog's walking **J9**.14

Precedency: ~ between a louse
and a flea **J9**.32

Prejudice: ~ runs in favour of
two **D13**.19

Presbyter: New ~ is but old
Priest writ large **M34**.43

Present: Absent in body, but ~
in spirit **B23**.233
if we lived in the ~ always
T17.8
un-birthday ~ **C12**.27
We want to live in the ~
F12.1
When the ~ has latched its
postern **H7**.1

President: When the ~ does it
N10.4

Presume: Dr Livingstone, I ~
S39.1

Presumption: you'll be amused by
its ~ **T18**.1

Price: All those men have their
~ **W5**.3
One man's wage increase is
another man's ~ increase
W30.4
~ of everything and the value
of nothing **W25**.14

Pricks: kick against the ~
B23.222

Pride: ~ goeth before destruction
B23.85
~ of Life that planned her
H7.2
~, pomp, and circumstance of
glorious war! **S15**.224

Priest: Will no one free me of
this turbulent ~? **H21**.1

Prime Minister: next ~ but three
B15.3

Primrose: ~ path of dalliance
S15.38

Prince: Else a great ~ in prison
lies **D19**.9
Good-night, sweet ~ **S15**.74

Principle: some strong ~ **M22**.1

Print: All the news that's fit to
~ **O3**.1

Printer: Time, tide, and a ~'s
press **F22**.1

Printing: Gunpowder, ~, and the
Protestant Religion **C10**.1

Prison: Else a great Prince in ~
lies **D19**.9
Home is the girl's ~ and the
woman's workhouse **S16**.16
Stone walls do not a ~ make
L35.1

Prisoners: Which ~ call the sky
W25.1

Prison-house: Shades of the ~
W36.15

Private: religion is allowed to
invade the sphere of ~ life
M22.2

Privileged: ~ and the People
D17.7

Prizes: The world continues to
offer glittering ~ **B27**.1

Probitas: ~ *laudatur et alget* **J16**.1

Problem: quite a three-pipe ~
D22.3

Procrastination: ~ is the thief of
time **Y3**.2

Procreate: ~ like trees, without
conjunction **B46**.4

Procul: ~, *o* ~ *este, profani* **V2**.7

Profani: *Procul, o procul este,* ~
V2.7

Professions: All ~ are
conspiracies against the laity
S16.6

Profit: ~ hath a man of all his
labour **B23**.93
what shall it ~ a man **B23**.183

Progression: Without Contraries is
no ~ **B31**.7

Propensities: excite my amorous
~ **J9**.1

Property: ~ is theft **P28**.1

Prophesy: your sons and your
daughters shall ~ **B23**.123

Prophet: I am a ~ new inspir'd
S15.231
~ is not without honour
B23.157

Prophets: Beware of false ~
B23.150

Proposes: man ~, but God
disposes **T9**.2

Propriété: *La ~ c'est le vol*
P28.1
Prose: Only connect the ~ and
the passion F15.3
speaking ~ without knowing it
M37.2
Prospect: every ~ pleases H15.1
noblest ~ which a Scotchman
ever sees J9.9
Prosper: Treason doth never ~
H8.1
Protest: lady doth ~ too much
S15.62
Protestant: Gunpowder, Printing,
and the ~ Religion C10.1
I am the ~ whore G27.1
Proud: Death be not ~ D19.12
Prove: Believing where we cannot
~ T4.10
Providence: I may assert Eternal
~ M34.16
Psychiatrist: Anybody who goes
to see a ~ G19.1
Public: as if I was a ~ meeting
V3.2
so ridiculous as the British ~
M1.9
Publish: ~ and be damned
W14.4
Publisher: Barabbas was a ~
C7.3
Pulse: feeling a woman's ~ S42.2
Pulses: proved upon our ~
K5.31
Pun: man who could make so
vile a ~ D10.1
Punctuality: ~ is the politeness of
kings L34.1
Punishment: let the ~ fit the
crime G11.14
Pure: Blessed are the ~ in heart
B23.132
Unto the ~ all things are ~
B23.255
Puritan: ~ hated bear-baiting
M1.4
Purse: Put money in thy ~
S15.216
Who steals my ~ steals trash
S15.222
Pursuit: indefatigable ~ of an
unattainable perfection S25.1
Pussy: What a beautiful ~ you
are L12.6

Que: ~ *sais-je?* M38.4
Queen: ~ of Hearts, she made
some tarts C12.13
Queer: All the world is ~ O8.1
Question: interrupt a man with
such a silly ~ S42.6
Others abide our ~ A22.10
To be, or not to be–that is
the ~ S15.57

what is the ~ S41.2
Questions: I have answered three
~ C12.4
Quick: ~ and the dead P26.4
Quiet: All ~ on the Western
Front R6.1
Anythin' for a ~ life D13.36
Quietness: Thou still unravish'd
bride of ~ K5.12
Quis: ~ *custodiet ipsos/Custodes?*
J16.3
Quit: ~ yourselves like men
B23.42

Race: most pernicious ~ of little
odious vermin S50.3
My ~ of glory M34.37
~ is not to the swift B23.98
Slow and steady wins the ~
L28.1
Rack: Leave not a ~ behind
S15.275
Radiance: white ~ of eternity
S17.3
Radical: I never dared to be ~
F21.4
~ is a man R13.3
Rag-and-bone: foul ~ shop of the
heart Y2.5
Rage: ~, ~, against the dying of
the light T11.1
Railway: Beautiful ~ Bridge of
the Silv'ry Tay! M2.1
Rain: droppeth as the gentle ~
from heaven S15.192
Hard ~'s A-Gonna Fall D31.3
~ it raineth every day S15.291
~ on the just and on the
unjust B23.136
Rainbow: ~ in the sky W36.13
Somewhere over the ~ H6.1
Raining: It was not ~ B11.1
Ranks: even the ~ of Tuscany
M1.7
Rapture: first fine careless ~
B48.10
Rara: ~ *avis in terris* J16.2
Rashes: Green grow the ~ O
B56.7
Rat: I smell a ~ R10.1
Rats: ~/They fought the dogs
B48.18
Rav'd: as I ~ and grew more
fierce H25.2
Raven: Quoth the ~ 'Nevermore.'
P18.3
Reach: man's ~ should exceed
his grasp B48.1
Reactionaries: ~ are paper tigers
M10.2
Read: man ought to ~ J9.10
~, mark, learn and inwardly
digest P26.7
Reading: ~ maketh a full man

B1.16

Reality: Human kind/Cannot bear very much ~ **E8.4**

Realms: Much have I travell'd in the ~ of gold **K5.23**

Reap: whatsoever a man soweth, that shall he also ~ **B23.246**

Reason: right deed for the wrong ~ **E8.23**

ruling passion conquers ~ still **P20.6**

Their's not to ~ why **T4.4**

Reasons: The heart has its ~ **P4.4**

two very cogent ~ **J9.31**

Receive: more blessed to give than to ~ **B23.225**

We ~ but what we give **C32.5**

Red: ~ Badge of Courage **C49.1**

Redeemer: I know that my ~ liveth **B23.55**

References: verify your ~ **R20.1**

Reform: Every ~ movement has a lunatic fringe **R14.2**

Refuge: God is our ~ and strength **B23.68**

Refute: 'I ~ it *thus.*' **J9.15**

Regiment: He led his ~ from behind **G11.1**

Monstrous ~ **K14.1**

Register: ~ of the crimes, follies, and misfortunes of mankind **G9.6**

Reigned: I have ~ with your loves **E9.2**

Relation: nobody like a ~ **T7.2**

Relations: even great men have their poor ~ **D13.4**

Personal ~ are the important thing **F15.2**

Relaxes: Damn braces. Bless ~ **B31.10**

Relief: For this ~ much thanks **S15.29**

Religion: no amusements in England but vice and ~ **S27.7**

One ~ is as true as another **B58.1**

~ is allowed to invade the sphere of private life **M22.2**

~ is an illusion **F20.2**

~ ... is the opium of the people **M17.4**

That is my ~ **S16.8**

There is only one ~ **S16.17**

Remarkable: there is nothing left ~ **S15.13**

Remedies: Desperate diseases require desperate ~ **F1.1**

Remember: I ~, I ~ **H35.2**

I ~ Adlestrop **T12.1**

We will ~ them **B26.1**

Remembrance: ~ of things past **S15.255**

Repay: I will ~, saith the Lord **B23.230**

Repelled: ~ by man **I2.2**

Repented: she strove, and much ~ **B62.13**

Repenteth: Joy shall be in heaven over one sinner that ~ **B23.197**

Report: ~ of my death was an exaggeration **T22.2**

Reporters: gallery in which the ~ sit **M1.1**

Republic: ~ is a government **B2.1**

Reputation: I have lost my ~ **S15.220**

spotless ~ **S15.230**

Respecter: God is no ~ of persons **B23.223**

Responsibility: Power without ~ **K11.22**

Rest: I shall shortly be with them that ~ **M34.37**

~ is silence **S15.74**

weary be at ~ **B23.51**

Reste: *J'y suis j'y* ~ **M5.1**

Resurrection: I am the ~ and the life **B23.216**

sure and certain hope of the ~ **P26.13**

Revels: Our ~ now are ended **S15.275**

Revenges: I will have such ~ **S15.126**

whirligig of time brings in his ~ **S15.290**

Reviewing: I never read a book before ~ it **S27.5**

Revolution: ~/Without general copulation **W13.1**

Reward: ~ of a thing well done **E12.3**

Rhythm: I got ~ **G8.1**

Rich: no sin, but to be ~ **S15.118**

Poor Little ~ Girl **C46.7**

~ are different from us **F7.2**

~ beyond the dreams of avarice **M39.2**

~ man in his castle **A10.2**

~ man to enter into the kingdom of God **B23.164**

sea-change/Into something ~ and strange **S15.272**

Riches: good name is rather to be chosen than great ~ **B23.87**

Infinite ~ in a little room **M12.5**

Riddle: ~ wrapped in a mystery **C25.3**

Ridiculous: One step above the sublime makes the ~ **P1.1**

only one step from the sublime to the ~ **N2.2**

Rift: little ~ within the lute **T4.8**

B31.1
way the ~ ends **E8**.13
we brought nothing into this ~
  B23.253
weight/Of all this unintelligible
  ~ **W36**.7
Whatever brute and blackguard
  made the ~ **H39**.12
wilderness of this ~ **B53**.1
~ is a comedy to those who
  think **W4**.2
~ is charged with the grandeur
  of God **H37**.3
~ is everything that is the case
  W32.1
~ is too much with us **W36**.30
~ must be made safe for
  democracy **W31**.1
~ nis but a thurghfare **C21**.7
~ was all before them **M34**.30
~ which seems/To lie before
  us **A22**.3
World-famous: ~ for fifteen
  minutes **W7**.1
Worldly-Wiseman: Mr ~ **B53**.3
Worlds: best of all possible ~
  C1.1
best of all possible ~ **V6**.1
So many ~ **T4**.14
Worm: invisible ~/That flies in
  the night **B31**.17
Worms: you have tasted two
  whole ~ **S37**.1
Worrying: What's the use of ~
  A23.1
Worse: Defend the bad against
  the ~ **D5**.1
Worst: it was the ~ of times
  D13.37
The ~ is not **S15**.130
~/Are full of passionate
  intensity **Y2**.17
Worth: If a thing is ~ doing
  C23.12
not ~ going to see **J9**.29
Whatever is ~ doing **C22**.2
~ makes the man **P20**.21
~ more than ever I yet was
  P9.3
Worthington: Don't put your
  daughter on the stage, Mrs ~
  C46.5
Worthy: I am not ~ that thou
  shouldest come under my roof
  B23.152
Would: He ~, wouldn't he? **R9**.1
Wrath: soft answer turneth away
  ~ **B23**.84
sun go down upon your ~
  B23.248
Wren: Sir Christopher ~ **B19**.3
Wrestle: intolerable ~/With words
  and meanings **E8**.7
Wrestling: I wretch lay ~ with

(my God!) my God **H37**.2
Wring: they will soon ~ their
  hands **W5**.1
Writ: New Presbyter is but old
  Priest ~ large **M34**.43
Writing: True ease in ~ **P20**.12
Wrong: Opinions, always in the
  ~ **D25**.5
Wrote: No man but a blockhead
  ever ~ **J9**.26
Wrought: What hath God ~
  B23.31

Xanadu: In ~ did Kubla Khan
  C32.7

Yarn: web of our life is of a
  mingled ~ **S15**.2
Yea: Let your ~ be ~ **B23**.257
Year: That time of ~ thou mayst
  in me behold **S15**.259
~ is dying in the night **T4**.15
Years: days of our ~ are
  threescore ~ and ten **B23**.71
~ to come seemed waste of
  breath **Y2**.11
Yes: Like an enormous ~ **L7**.2
~ I said – I will **J14**.7
Yesterday: thousand years in thy
  sight are but as ~ **B23**.70
We were saying ~ **L19**.1
Yesterdays: all our ~ **S15**.175
Yesteryear: where are the snows
  of ~ **V5**.1
Yo-ho-ho: ~ and a bottle of
  rum! **S44**.2
Yonghy-Bonghy-Bo: In the middle
  of the woods/Lived the ~
  L12.2
Yorick: Alas, poor ~ **S15**.70
Young: America is a country of
  ~ men **E12**.10
being ~ and foolish **Y2**.8
I have been ~ **B23**.67
I have been ~ **B32**.1
mine eyes dazzle: she died ~
  W12.2
Myself when ~ did eagerly
  frequent **F6**.3
Now as I was ~ and easy
  T11.2
what a very singularly deep ~
  man **G11**.17
Whom the gods love dies ~
  M24.1
Youth: Crabbed age and ~
  cannot live together **S15**.228
If only ~ knew **E14**.1
lying days of my ~ **Y2**.6
Remember now thy Creator in
  the days of thy ~ **B23**.100
sign of an ill-spent ~ **S35**.5
~ grows pale, and spectre-thin,
  and dies **K5**.19

Longman Group Limited,
Longman House, Burnt Mill, Harlow,
Essex CM20 2JE, England
and Associated Companies throughout the world.

© Longman Group Limited 1985

First published 1985

British Library Cataloguing in Publication Data

Popular quotations.
  1. Quotations, English
082   PN6081

ISBN 0-582-89286-4

Printed in Great Britain
by Spottiswoode Ballantyne Ltd., Colchester & London.